HOME-BASED BUSINESS IDEAS

FOR

- **FOR THE OVER 50'S**
- **THE LONG-TIME UNEMPLOYED**
- **HOME-BASED CARERS & PARENTS**

Judi Menzies
author of
How to get a Great Job – & Keep It!

Other Books by Judi Menzies

How to Get a Great Job - & Keep It!

Menzies, Judi
Home-Based Business Ideas SECOND EDITION (previously known as *Home-Based Businesses for the Over 50's*)

ISBN: 978-0-646-45213-5

ACKNOWLEDGEMENTS

The author would like to thank
the owners of the many home-based businesses who have so willingly
divulged the secrets of their success
to make this book possible.

CONTENTS

JVM Enterprises

INTRODUCTION

The original edition of this manual was written well before the corona virus hit the workplace. For decades, working from home had been just a dream for most people but gradually more venturous souls began realising that it could actually be done. Throughout the suburbs garages, sheds, granny flats and spare rooms were being transformed into offices and mini-showrooms, back gardens were turning into nurseries and home kitchens were becoming catering outlets. For the majority of people, however, home-based businesses remained a very distant goal.

When the pandemic arrived, it separated millions of employees from their jobs and children from their schools. The rules of quarantine and self-isolation were not totally without opportunity however, allowing those fortunate enough to be able to work online to experience a new way of life: working at home meant some measure of relaxation, parents found time to interact with their children and form closer ties, there was time for indulging in hobbies, interests and learning to enjoy exercise and the great outdoors.

Over the many weeks of social isolation, the pluses of working from a home base became attractively obvious. Many an employee whose 'office' was now the kitchen table or a desk and chair in the family room would think nothing of spending the morning in pyjamas while attending corporate meetings via Zoom or Skype. Soon many were dreading the day they'd be asked to return to the office full time.

Society became divided over the issue: there were those who actually longed to return to the stress-filled busy lives they had been denied for months but others wanted the new way to continue for ever.

Soon, however, it became obvious that post-pandemic, there may not be too many alternatives to consider as thousands of workers were not going to be able to go back to their jobs. Businesses had folded! Jobs had disappeared! Going back to the 9 – 5 grind would at least have meant an income. Was there no alternative way to make a living? People had mortgages, bills to pay! Where would they turn?

Nevertheless, the realisation started to filter into people's minds that there are other ways to earn a wage rather than being reliant on someone else to provide it. Why couldn't any capable person work and build a profit for themselves instead of some 'boss'? What was to stop anyone from establishing their own home-based business, have a 'work-from-home' lifestyle and become a business success in their own right?

Economists say working-from-home is predicted to be the preferred way of working into the future. Furthermore, there are more important issues that could potentially be solved by working for oneself.

For example, the accepted retirement age of the 21st century has not kept up with the rapidly increasing health and longevity of 22nd century people! For decades, workers have complained – rightly or wrongly – that an employer's interest in a worker's value generally starts to deteriorate as the latter approaches 'retirement age'. Instead of becoming more valuable to their firm as they get older and more experienced, the general consensus among workers appears to be that most feel less valued - sometimes even ignored - by the age of 50 or so.

This was the reason for the original version of this manual: to show the over-50's how simple it can be to set oneself up in a home-based business if they wished to keep working beyond retirement age, were retrenched or wanted to change careers. Yes, there are risks in setting up one's own business…but aren't there also risks in working for someone else? Wouldn't you rather be the one planning and having a say in what is going on, getting the right advice and directing the business on which you are dependent for your livelihood?

Today, working from home in your own business has the added purpose of giving you the opportunity to future-proof your employment. You would be the one at the wheel, making preparations, investing and re-investing, being vigilant and guarding your nest egg against pandemics and recessions.

So what could you do for a home-business? How should you start? In reality, wherever there are people, there is work to do. You just need to find out what needs to be done and how you can fulfil those requirements to a professional standard that people will appreciate.

Starting on page 239 of this book, you will find a useful 10-page Questionnaire that could help you find and hone a perfectly tailored home-based business:

How to Find the Right Home-Based Business for YOU!

Filling in the questionnaire will help you to gauge the type of business that should suit your specific capabilities: your financial and family situation, your strengths, weaknesses, home life, likes and dislikes. The questions have been designed by recruitment consultants of long-standing experience.

You will be asked to write the answers to each question openly, honestly and in private: no one but you need ever see your answers! The result will be a good representation of you in relation to what type of business would suit you, your experience, capabilities, goals and so forth. If you write your answers they will still be there intact when it comes time to measure yourself against each business opportunity you find.

One further point: in this book, you will notice that we have not focused on the plethora of mind-boggling technology-related opportunities that are now available for you to run from home on a simple laptop computer and phone. Living in a global world with few communication or trade barriers has opened enormous possibilities to practically everyone in this regard.

Admittedly, E-commerce in particular is bringing in millions of dollars to sellers whose ages range from children to seniors of advanced age. However, exciting as these job opportunities may seem on the surface, they are not without risk despite all the detailed courses and software available to support them. Such information, valuable as it could be, may not sit well in a manual such as this which is largely designed for those in search of steadier, more traditional money-earning pathways and free or inexpensive start-ups.

We hope you enjoy exploring this manual and that you will let us know how you go in finding your new home-based business!

Good Luck!

A

ABORIGINAL ARTS & CRAFTS

Aboriginal culture is of enormous interest to thousands of people, both in Australia and overseas, and lends itself to many avenues for the would-be entrepreneur. However, anyone contemplating a business in this area needs to understand that indigenous art is not 'artwork' in the traditionally accepted sense of the word as it can also represent the myths and symbols, sacred history, geography and even land titles of the Aboriginal people. Yes, incredibly beautiful though they may be, many of the paintings act as 'land rights certificates'! It is important that anyone planning to trade in these arts and crafts be mindful of the sensitivities and not infringe copyright. No work should be sold or exhibited without the permission of the artist or clan involved.

This said, there is still a diversity of opportunities left in which to involve yourself commercially in this rich culture. Assess your own interests, background and experience and take this into consideration in choosing the field best suited to you. Do you have a background in sales, wholesaling, e-commerce, art, design, writing, film making, history, clothing manufacture, food, teaching, music, languages, dance, tourism…or have you, as yet, had no real business exposure? Your answer could help narrow down your choices.

If your background is in *arts*, for example, you might decide to become a ***dealer in the paintings*** of one or more of the indigenous artists you admire. If you decide to do the buying yourself, it could involve quite a bit of travel, buying up work, maintaining your network of artists as well as establishing the market for selling the work. Do you wish to be involved in arranging exhibitions, selling to collectors, galleries, the tourist trade or to an overseas market?

You may prefer to obtain products such as modern hand painted or printed fabrics made at the Aboriginal missions, cultural centres or by clan groups then sell them by mail order or via the Internet. However, unless you source the products yourself, you will need to find a way of ensuring that they have actually been produced by the indigenous people themselves and that you have permission to sell the designs. Some carpet, napery and clothing manufacturers have, in the past, stolen sacred Aboriginal designs and flagrantly used them without permission, thus upsetting the lives of the originators to such an extent that some have actually given up their professions in disgust.

Are you interested in arranging tours? Why not bone up on Aboriginal culture and organise trips to places of cultural interest in Central and Northern Australia? You may end up becoming a specialist in such tours. Buses can be chartered and your potential clients are probably combing web sites and tour magazines right now for this very thing!

Are you a painter or fabric designer? If so, you might draw a whole exhibition or collection's worth of inspiration from a single trip to the incredible colours and landforms of Northern Australia and come up with your own individual landscapes, abstracts or print designs.

Have you an interest or background in photography, history, writing or film making?...and let's face it, *anyone* can make films these days! If so, a single trip to Arnhem Land photographing various aspects of the culture, lifestyle and landscape of these people for your books, articles and videos might set you on the road to a fantastic 'niche' *film or writing career*.

Your resulting information books and films could cover scores of subjects covering the lives, land and history of indigenous people: finding and preparing bush tucker, art techniques, crafts, myths, 'walk-abouts', healing methods, dance, singing, music and so forth. Again, permission should be obtained before embarking on any of these endeavours to ensure you are not transgressing any taboos or invading privacy in your productions.
(See under Mail Order, Information Products, Gallery Owner/Art Dealer, Desktop Publishing, Didgeridoos, Boomerangs, Tour Organiser)

ABOVE-GROUND POOL INSTALLATION, MAINTENANCE & REPAIR

Above-ground pools are as popular as ever - but what a pain it can be for new owners to have to erect them! If you are able to perform this service for home owners, you could conceivably build yourself a good little business. However, this job is for the physically fit individual who likes medium to heavy outdoor work.

Once your *system* for erecting these pools has been developed, the process is fairly straight-forward. In many instances, the ground may require more than simple levelling as clients often want their pools sunk partially into the ground. Therefore, you may need to hire or purchase the necessary excavation equipment if you wish to do the whole job yourself. Alternatively, you could decide to subcontract this part of the exercise to an excavator whenever necessary. Having a similar arrangement with a bricklayer and carpenter could also be useful, as clients often request enhancements such as brick or timber walls around the sides of the pool, a timber deck plus sails or even a pergola to protect it from the sun.

If your service includes pool **maintenance** or **repair**, you will need to learn to check and repair the various types of filters and heaters used as well.

Sale of *maintenance equipment, chemicals, pool inflatables* and *water games* could also represent potential extra income for you. It may be worth your while to carry an illustrated catalogue of your inflatables and water games to every job.

Good marketing will be essential. Your targets, apart from the various retail stores which stock above ground pools, might include individuals who wish to repair or relocate a pool...or simply re-erect one that has been stored away during the winter. Re-erecting a pool can often involve quite a lot of work. If it has been stored for a long time, it may require a fair bit of repair, and be cheaper for the owner to buy another pool. If you are requested to go ahead, charge by the hour as you may not be able to easily assess what you are in for until the pool is laid out and checked over.

ACTOR

This business can't be run *at* home but it can be run *from* home. And what an exciting business it could be if you have the *talent, patience* and *determination.* Don't waste your time or your life pursuing a career in this profession unless you have all three of these qualities.

If you are serious about acting, you would do well to get yourself on the books of a reputable casting agency. Most of the big agencies are well informed about the major facets of their industry and are generally the first stop for producers who are ready to start casting! If your face is on their books, you have a far better chance of being considered for a part in a production than if you simply apply on your own behalf.

However, be warned! Acting can be a volatile business! Even the most successful performers can find themselves receiving excellent income one minute and no work the next, so you will need to be prepared for the pendulum to swing.

- One popular career entry point for would-be actors is the *T.V. commercial.* Commercials require all types, ages, sizes and sexes and, generally, can prove much easier to break into than any other segment of the industry. One thing to watch out for is that, if you're serious about mainstream acting, appearing frequently in oft-run T.V. commercials *could* slow your progress somewhat! A face that becomes too closely associated with an advertised product risks losing its authenticity or credibilty when it comes to more serious character portrayal.

- Another entry point for your career might be to take on an unrelated job at one of the TV stations. If it's as an *on-set assistant,* lucky you! But it could be virtually anything going. Not only is one able to learn from watching the pros at work, you also get to know 'the people who matter' such as the directors and producers. It's a long shot but, ultimately, you *might* get a chance to perform! If *you're* there on the spot, ready, reliable and well-bonded with the team, who knows what could happen? Such experiences can prove to be very valuable on one's track record.

- Never acted in your life before? Don't know where to start? Try taking a short course or two in acting at the local TAFE or Uni. Not only will this give you the skills you need; it should introduce you to professionals who just might be able to help you if you turn out to be an outstanding talent.

- To help stabilise finances, actors often find that having *a second job* – or even another *home-based business*, whether related to acting or not – can be very helpful. However, in most areas of acting (other than perhaps live theatre), the hours can be erratic, so one needs to remain 'available' to work or rehearse day *or* evening. Therefore, if you do embark on a second business, it should be flexible enough to fit in with your acting career.

- Quite a few actors start up their own *acting school*. This can be run with minimal equipment or go 'high-tech' with lights, cameras, action! Again, because of the odd hours you may need to work as an actor, it might be helpful to have a stand-by actor-friend able to step in for you when you are unable to give lessons personally.

- Once you are firmly established as an actor, your growing network of fellow actors and entertainers might prompt you to start up a *TV and film agency*!
- If you can't quite get the start you were hoping for, you might consider producing *information films* and *audios*. This may sound a bit off-the-track for the type of life you had envisaged for yourself but, if you are well versed in some subject and would feel comfortable teaching it to others, you may be able to use your as yet unrecognised presentation skills to produce short training courses or travelogues and see how they go.
(See also: Information Products, Desktop Publishing)

ACUPUNCTURIST

This method of healing is said to have originated in China more than 2000 years ago. However, ancient as it is, it continues to hold its own even in the New Millennium. In fact, it is becoming more popular and respected every day in the Western world. It is used by many qualified doctors all over the world, as well as by naturopaths and others who have done special training in this field.

Many schools of Naturopathy offer courses in acupuncture and, although it takes a while to learn, it is not beyond any reasonably intelligent lay person to acquire the skills and become accredited.

In acupuncture, needles are generally used to stimulate the various points of the body where energy blockages are thought to occur. These needles can be manipulated manually or are attached to electrodes which do the manipulation.

How the needles effect a cure, whether they act like a TENS machine, releasing endorphins to block pain or whether they work in some other way has not really been proven. However, many patients swear by the effectiveness of the therapy and hold their acupuncturist in the highest regard.

If you are interested in this form of healing, read all you can about it then call a couple of schools of Naturopathy for further information.
(See Naturopathy)

ADVERTISING

Previous experience working in an established advertising agency would be beneficial before starting out on your own. You may be creative and highly talented but understanding the essentials of running a business and building a network of the right people is crucial.

If you are wondering how a lone home operator can possibly compete with the 'big names' of this industry, just remember that not *all* businesses have the *megabucks* to engage big names. Small businesses are often grateful to find a talented person who has low overheads, who can do a good job, yet is able to charge them reasonable rates!

A converted garage or bungalow can often make a great studio but, if you *must* use a room in your house, try to arrange *direct access* to it from the outdoors. Nothing looks less professional to a client than being asked to walk through a living room to reach the studio. Indeed, many councils will *insist* on separate work and living areas.

You may find a few restrictions when it comes to employing assistants in your home office. To get around this, you may need to outsource.

Remember, too, that *self-promotion* is vital if your business is to blossom in the backwaters of suburbia… but, after all, isn't promotion your forte?

AEROBICS INSTRUCTOR
(See Personal Fitness Coach)

AGED PERSON'S PERSONAL SUPPORT SERVICES
(See Personal Services for the Aged)

AGRICULTURE:
(For these home-based businesses, you should seek council permission and check on any certification you may require.)

- ***Fruit and Vegetables - Exotic***
  Even in suburbia, one can usually manage to grow some exclusive or *hard to obtain* fruits and vegetables. To find out just what is required by prospective customers (such as local food stores and specialty restaurants), ask them for their 'wish list' and if they would be willing to buy these goods from you if you could produce them.

  Some fruit and vegetables may require hot housing or special nurturing for growth but, for the most part, just the basic necessities of life like water, sun, nutrients and daily maintenance should suffice.

- ***Weatherproof Crops***
  With the cultivation of most crops, growers are at the mercy of the weather - and weather patterns are changing drastically these days. For a small producer to lose weeks or months of work to hail, drought or rain can be devastating!

  Yet, there are safe alternatives whereby you can grow your produce away from the extremes of wind and weather. For example, some crops, like ***mushrooms***, are easily grown in safe dark sheds.

  Others, like tomatoes, can be grown ***hydroponically***, in greenhouses. This latter method uses potting mix or water and other substances in solution, so the grower is dependent on neither the quality of the soil nor on the weather! Furthermore, the growing season for hydroponic crops is virtually 12 months of the year!

  Your local library, bookshop, garden centre and various internet sites should have heaps of information on out-of-the-weather methods of food cultivation.

As a full time business, this can be as big as your property, time and money will allow. As a home business, it could be ideal.
(See also Horticulture, Herbs & Herb gardens)

AIR CONDITIONING AND REFRIGERATION (INSTALLATION & REPAIR)

If you are not yet a qualified mechanic but feel this work is for you, there are courses available - some by correspondence - that should see you up and running in no time.

If you are already qualified, you might decide to offer your services directly under your own business name or subcontract yourself out to various manufacturers and local electrical retailers who may need a repair/installation person in your area.

While the majority of air conditioners sold require installation, there comes a time when all machines need repair! When warranties run out, the market is wide open for you!

Your marketing ability will be as much a key to your success as your mechanical ability. In your advertising, it may help to stress the generous length of your warranty and consider offering clients a little bonus at the end of an installation: a free timer, a magnetised calendar or a promotional mug with your name and phone number on it.
A magnetised business card would also be useful. Then, when customers need a serviceperson in the future, they'll know whom to call!.

ALEXANDER TECHNIQUE

This is a method of teaching people how to realign their body posture and to function as nature intended.

Poor posture is believed to affect our behaviour and emotion. For example, a tight neck and shoulders may exacerbate feelings of tension and stress whereas a balanced, easy posture is more likely to assist the body to feel relaxed and move freely.

Practitioners of the art are taught to visualise the vertebrae of the spine as one would visualise a pile of child's building blocks, balanced one on top of the other, with the head balanced on top. The idea is to keep this pile of blocks in perfect alignment at all times, whether standing, sitting or moving.

Lessons might be held at the teacher's home, a professional suite, a rented hall or even at the client's home or office. Generally, a session runs from 30 to 40 minutes and can consist of anything from a single visit to a course of 12 or more visits.

This technique lends itself to *individual* tuition but classes could work if they were structured with sufficient forethought.

AMUSEMENT MACHINES/ INFLATABLES/ ENTERTAINMENT

You'll need some up-front capital to purchase or lease much of this equipment... but what a choice you'll have! You might prefer to specialise in just one type of machine or ride, or combine a couple.

Here is just a handful of the many possibilities available to you. Some are coin-operated:

- Jumping castles
- Karaoke
- Dodgem cars
- Rock climbing walls
- Pinballs
- Chair-O-Plane
- Laughing clowns
- Spaceball
- Mini golf
- Circatron
- Inflatable slides
- Pony rides
- Merry-go-rounds
- Mobile farm
- Vintage fire engine rides
- Track & trackless trains
- Go karts
- Bucking Bull
- Fairy Floss Machines
- Dunking Machines

AMUSEMENT MACHINE MAINTENANCE & REPAIR

There are three potential ways to make money from coin-operated amusement machines: own 'em, hire 'em or fix 'em.

However, amusement machines are definitely *not* amusing when they break down! They represent the owner's hard earned dollars and may often be their only livelihood.

So, if you're electronically or mechanically minded - and like to feel indispensable - here's a job that could be just right for your interests and talents!

ANTIQUE DEALER

Beginners, *beware*! This market can be a con artist's dream and a new trader's nightmare! However, if you rely on knowledge and thorough research to guide you, you should have little to fear.

There are myriads of courses, books, videos, exhibitions, galleries, museums, internet sites, seminars and lectures that can help make you an expert in your chosen area in the shortest possible time.

This is a business that could be run from home in several ways. If you want only a small scale 'hobby' business, you might simply trade through newspaper classifieds, garage sales and auctions - and over the internet (but with *extreme caution,* especially when dealing with overseas sites! Take into account such things as the exchange rates, shipping rates, duty…not to mention the many rules and regulations that can differ from country to country.

If you are are a willing public speaker, you can run lectures and appraisals at various clubs and functions and this will give you quite a reputation in no time if done well. Perhaps you could also make a video or two on that period or those pieces in which you have the greatest expertise. These could be sold to libraries, antique stores or even from your own web site. A bit of PR makes people stand out from the crowd.

As a ***private vendor***, you may only be able to sell a few pieces at a time from your home. If you appear to be running an unauthorised retail business in an A-class residential neighbourhood, you could end up in trouble with the authorities. However, make application as much will depend on your zoning.

For the truly determined, there are a few ways around such restrictions. For example, if you were to buy or rent a suitable *shop with an attached residence* in which to live, you are more likely to create your home-based business legally! However, it would still require all the necessary permits, dealer's licence and so forth.

- ***IDEA***: In sourcing stock, don't discount those humble garage sales going on around you at the weekend or the piles of junk often awaiting collection on suburban nature strips. Many a valuable find has been made in these seemingly unlikely places by dealers who know their market and know what they're looking for. Some old pieces may just require a polish and paint; others may require a full repair job but you can pick up many items for absolutely nothing if you are quick, smart and know what you are looking for…but be sure there are no council restrictions in your area preventing you from doing this.

- *IDEA*: There is another potentially lucrative way of operating an antique business from home although its success will depend on your knowledge of the trade and traders - *and* your willingness to risk a fair bit of capital: that is, importing whole shipping container loads of antiques from overseas and unloading them to interested dealers here. *This is not a game for amateurs*. Your success will depend heavily on a trade network with access to the right connections.

Note: potential secondhand and antique dealers should check out zoning limitations in their area as well as fulfilling all licensing requirements before making their plans.

ANTIQUE FURNITURE RESTORATION
(See under Furniture Restoration)

ANTI-SLIP TREATMENT FOR FLOORS

This is a business which carries with it the satisfaction of knowing you are doing something positive to assist or protect others from injury.

Anti-slip treatments have been around for some time. As the name suggests, they are treatments that are applied to potentially slippery floor surfaces such as tiles, marble, granite and concrete. This is particularly helpful in areas frequented by the elderly or small children, as well as in hospitals, around swimming pools, on ramps, shopping malls, work places or wherever one finds that surfaces can become slippery underfoot.

You may be able to develop this type of business on your own (in accordance with all the health and safety rules and regulations). However, if you prefer to start off on a more secure footing with the encapsulated knowledge, training and backing afforded by a going concern, it may be worth the initial outlay to obtain a licence from a reputable company. Some licences require no ongoing fees or royalties.We cannot make any recommendations about any particular company or franchise here. It will be up to you to check out and investigate all possibilities.

APARTMENT GARDENS

Today most countries are liberally sprinkled with retirement villages many of which have small balcony gardens but these are not always easy for their elderly owners to maintain. While the foliage and flowers may give great joy to the occupants of the apartments, the cleaning, maintenance and stocking of these mini gardens with plants and flowers that suit the varying directions and aspects of the units can require the expert knowledge of an experienced gardener. Is that you?

If you are interested in this type of gardening, it may be worth speaking to the managers of various retirement homes to see if their residents already have their apartment gardens maintained. If not and they are willing to allow you a trial period as gardener, you may have found yourself a lucrative job as well as an opportunity to give a great deal of pleasure to elderly residents who will be able to enjoy their own little gardens of beauty and colour every day.

Such a venture could take a great deal of creativity and planning: the right van equipped with tools, trolleys, ways of transporting soil and possibly water up to apartments, lightweight pots and plant stands and all the other requirements of an apartment gardener

APARTMENT HOUSE

There's no need to live in your income-earning apartment house yourself…but if you do, it may offer you quite a few tax advantages. If you expect to receive a good return and keep your tenants satisfied, you need to maintain your complex well. Rooms that are attractively decorated and have clean, spotless facilities are much easier to let than accommodation that is dingy, obviously unloved and poorly decorated.

Decorating does not have to mean big expenditure; it just means 'good taste'. Much of your furnishing materials might come from garage sales but they can still be washed and ironed. Drapes can be given small touches like swags and tie-backs that appeal to the romantic streak in your would-be tenants. Doors and cupboards can be given a fresh up with modern, well shaped handles. Spotless bathrooms and toilets and a welcoming entrance are a given and gardens, too, should be kept in good order. However, while most decorating and maintenance costs are tax-deductible, you may elect to do the on-going maintenance yourself. If not, simply outsource these services to experts and…collect the rent!

There is something else you should plan to collect, too: the capital improvement when you sell your complex 10 or 20 years down the track. If your apartment house is well situated, well built and reasonably maintenance-free, you might find it provides you with quite an easy income.

AQUARIUM MAINTENANCE

There is the story of a young man who dreamed of becoming a millionaire…but he could not even get a job! One day, with his mother's bucket, mop, cloths and a lot of determination, he started an aquarium cleaning business…and attained his financial dream in just a few short years!

Here is a business for someone with practically no start-up capital. With basic tools (and some preparatory self-training on the maintenance and handling of fish), you might find yourself following in that young man's footsteps!

Homes and pet shops are not the only places you will find aquariums. Offices, clubs, restaurants (particularly Asian restaurants) are also potential clients. Don't be backward about presenting yourself at such places. Explain to the owner or manager what you are about and how *well* you do your job. Leave them one of your brochures. If you haven't heard from them after a month or so, pop back in again and remind them of your service, leaving another brochure. This time, tell them about your newest 'special' deal: it might be a '10% discount for new clients' or 'a *free* clean for every six sessions paid for in advance'!

However, if you promise these types of promos, you'll be obliged to *fulfil your obligation*. For this reason, be sure that aquariums are your scene before making too many promises to customers about the future!

AQUARIUM MANUFACTURE

Aquariums are a peep-hole into another world. They can help bring beauty, peace and tranquillity into any home or commercial property. Enhance their ability to produce magic in a mundane world by adding a few shapes and styles that are a little different from the norm: cylindrical shapes, large spheres, columns, modern squares or doughnut shapes.

Whether you manufacture for sale direct to the public or sell through retail outlets and wholesalers, outstanding customer service should be at the top of your priority list to ensure your business stands out from that of your competitors'.

Could you offer clients an information booklet with each tank, showing instructions on the set up or the types of fish suitable for that particular tank? Or maybe a list of the *aquarium maintenance services* around your city or suburb?

Perhaps you will become *an agent* for some maintenance company and thus get a cut from each job contracted! Could you work 'in sync' with a member of your family, with one member running the *'aquarium maintenance'* business while you look after the *manufacturing*?

If zoning, time and space permit, you may also decide to sell *accessories*: sand, rocks, stones, weeds, fish foods and ornaments - even the *fish* if you have the resources to look after them!

Think hard about your business name. Choose a magical name (perhaps something like *'Underwater World' or 'King Neptune's Farm'* rather than just a basic *J. J. Smith Aquariums*.)

AROMATHERAPY OILS

Aromatherapy oils can be bought in bulk, then poured into small, elegant, individual containers topped by ornate stoppers and bearing beautiful labels. You may decide to commission a glass blower or potter to make your containers and stoppers for you.

A desktop computer could be used to print exotic coloured labels for your bottles or jars and also tiny information booklets about the oils they contain. As well, you will need to come up with creative ways to market your products. Research the beauty habits of the ancients or the health benefits of those plants from which your oils are extracted. Weave this information into your designs, themes and stories.

If you sell your oils in *individual bottles*, tie the little information booklets around the bottle neck with coloured ribbon or silk tassels. *Boxed sets* might carry a more comprehensive, illustrated booklet covering each of the oils in the set. These booklets and the dressing up of your product in this way should add a lot of *perceived value* from the customer's point of view.

AROMATHERAPY PRACTITIONER

Aromatherapy is what is known as an holistic method of healing. Its practitioners believe it assists in improving the *overall* condition of the body rather than just dealing with one specific ailment at a time. The beautifully scented oils that are used are derived from various plants and are thought to possess healing properties. Some of the oils are inhaled; others are massaged into the skin.

Aromatherapy can be an excellent work-at-home business. However, your clients need to understand that you are *not* advocating this therapy as *an alternative to medical assistance for serious problems*.

And a further word of warning: just because you are working at home in a nice, seemingly safe little salon does not mean you can afford to dispense with insurance cover. For example, some people may be allergic to some of the oils you use or they could trip over the cat going down the front steps. Yes, insurance can be expensive, particularly for a small business just starting up…but it can become even more expensive when things go wrong if you don't have cover!

As well as working at your home salon, you may decide to go mobile - or offer your massage service to a *specialist shop* that sells aromatherapy oils. You will need to have acquired the appropriate training in massage and fully understand the properties of the oils before you start but short courses are widely available in most towns and cities.

Keeping your work environment quiet, clean and peaceful, free of clutter and loud noises and using fresh, good quality towels and sheets is so important.

A small and attractive cabinet with polished glass shelves could display your oils and burners. However, if you wish to sell them from home, you will need to obtain council permission.

ART AND CRAFT

Don't let anyone tell you that you can't make money in art and craft if you are truly talented! The key to financial success in this field is to find a 'niche market' for what you do best…or *adapt* what you do to an already popular market!

Turning one's hobby or artistic talent into a commercial venture presents you with an almost endless stream of possibilities. However, you can narrow it down somewhat to fit your business capabilities and financial circumstances. Unlike the artist-in-the-garret, willing to live on air and water in order to produce 'art from the heart', the artist-entrepreneur needs to be willing to forfeit a few ideals and determine just what it is that *the market* wants.

Question: how does one gauge just what it is that the market wants? Answer: by observation and research!

Look around you! Do you live in or near a tourist area? Are you surrounded by famous landmarks? Do people come from miles away to view the dolphins in the bay, the wildflowers in the nearby fields? Are there koalas in the gum trees at the local park? Are there historical sites just up the road? Is your area famed for its snow-covered mountains, its trams or shopping strips, its mineral springs or famous churches? Try painting some of your area's ***famous local features and landmarks*** and see how they sell.

What if there are no landmarks? What if you live in a new estate full of babies and children? Then, would **child** or **baby portraiture** be a more viable business for you? Or **general portraiture** covering all types of subjects?

Similarly, if you live next to an air force base, how about opening a home-gallery specialising in paintings of **vintage planes** or fighter aircraft? Or **wildlife** if you live near a wildlife park? Or famous **lighthouses** if you live near a lighthouse?

Yes, this is *very commercial thinking* and the 'true artist' would probably look down on you for selling your soul for money! But there's far less chance of you going hungry or your children going barefoot if you start to think commercially!

Much will depend on your talents and interests, of course, but the point is that, if you want to make a business of art or craft, your work needs to be *what your clients want*.

- *Paintings (landscapes, seascapes - local focus):*
  Is your studio capable of being turned into a **display gallery** at weekends? In the right sort of locale, particularly in a touristy area, small private galleries can often do quite well if they are marketed aggressively and stocked with paintings of the surrounding places of interest. You could also take samples of your work - and a good photo folio - to all the local galleries, shops and tea rooms around your area to see if they will stock your work on consignment. While visitors and travellers like to buy a visual memento of their travels, don't underestimate the locals. They, too, may take pride in buying paintings of their area.

  Local landscapes, landmarks and seascapes can often be sold at local art exhibitions if they are of a good standard. Find out from the local council what exhibitions are on in your area and enter as many pieces as you can. But there's no need to stay local! Enter some of the hundreds of painting competitions that are held in every state around the country. You don't have to accompany your work when competitions are far afield as there are *art couriers* who will transport your paintings for you anywhere, interstate or even internationally. Many art magazines (such as *Australian Artist*) offer a monthly listing of many upcoming competitions.
  Never display repeats of the same painting in the same gallery, display or exhibition. Some artists who paint from photos have done this to their detriment, not realising until too late just how much it tends to devalue their work.

- *Still Life*
  Good quality *Still Life* often sells well at art exhibitions. As mentioned above, there are plenty of art couriers who will transport your paintings to these competitions; you do not have to take them yourself. Your paintings do not

have to win a prize to sell, either. Work that has not even received a mention from the judges is consistently sold to members of the public.

Consider arranging your *own exhibitions* from time to time. If you do not have enough work to justify renting gallery space, join up with a few other artists and craftspeople willing to share the cost of the exhibition with you. (But be sure the work of these artists is of a quality similar to - or better than - your own work!)

If you win a prize in a competition, capitalise on your good fortune by advertising yourself as a *'prize-winning artist'* in your brochures and flyers. Inform the local press, too: they may write an editorial.

In addition to all this, you may decide to run **art classes** in conjunction with your painting career. Teaching has helped many artists to land on their feet financially.

- *Portraits:*
  If you're a good portrait painter and can capture a likeness so well that you are willing to offer clients a *guarantee of satisfaction*, you may find yourself making a mint from your own home studio.

  Warning! Don't get caught up sketching on-the-spot portraits at fetes and markets for paltry sums…unless you're doing it for sheer pleasure. If you want to make *big* money – (and a talented artist *can* do well in a portraiture business) - you'll need to work professionally in a studio. A converted garage or a good sized room at home is perfectly acceptable. (Some well known portrait artists have even used their lounge rooms, complete with velvet drapes, carpet and all!)

  All you need to get started, apart from the studio and the necessary materials and equipment, are clients! So advertise! Put an occasional display ad or classified in the weekend newspaper, distribute flyers to shops and, when you can afford it, place a permanent ad in the Yellow Pages. (If you are a registered business, you should be given a free listing.)

  However, do appraise your work with honesty: unless you're talented, don't waste your time or your money!

- *Portraits of Pets*
  Once again, *incredibly lucrative* if you are really gifted in this area *and* know how to market.

All the above information (*see Portraits*) applies to Pet Portraiture...
although in this case, an *external* studio is absolutely essential! A converted
garage would be ideal. On rainy days, after a number of long-haired dogs
have visited you, you will be *so* glad your studio is outside!

Pets are not as easy to paint as people unless they are very well behaved.
Cats, particularly, are hard to keep still when they are in unfamiliar territory.
It is often necessary to supplement your sketches with photos and colour
notes if your models are frisky. You can work from all this material later
when they have gone home.

Generally, clients do not mind waiting a few weeks for their portraits. If a
painting is commissioned as a special gift for some occasion but cannot be
completed by the deadline, the gift giver may be quite happy to settle for a
Gift Voucher instead. The recipient of the voucher can then come to your
studio at a later date, and have the portrait painted at leisure.

- *Paintings on Velvet*
Many people love paintings of animals such as dogs, cats and horses, painted
on velvet. The technique is not much different to painting on canvas or any
other fabric but because of the stark contrast of the paint against the dark
velvet background, the portrait can appear quite outstanding.

 If you decide to paint animals on velvet, it is suggested that you firstly
produce a sample or two of your work to hang on the wall of your studio and
also on the walls of the local veterinary surgery.

Landscapes and other scenes painted on velvet do not seem to be as valued
by the public as animal paintings, possibly because of the many imports
available. One tends to equate scenes on velvet with home decor, whereas
animals have far more exclusivity and are taken more seriously.

- *Abstract and modern painting*
Don't waste your time on abstracts...unless you are *very* talented...or
just *love* painting. If you do have the talent, a gallery may be interested in
representing you or, if you know how to market yourself, hire a gallery and
hold exhibitions either on your own or with a group of other artists.

- *Decoupage*
Decoupage is a beautiful and popular art and can be applied to most furniture
and home decorator items. Small pieces such as trays, place mats etc. are best
for the beginner.

You can do this work from a home studio such as a converted garage but it is most important that you have a completely *dust-free area* for drying the highly lacquered pieces.

Marketing ideas: gift shops, decorator shops, markets and fairs. Hold an occasional exhibition and share the costs with other exhibitors. You might also consider supplementing your income through ***teaching*** this art either in person or through videos and books.

- ***Hand-painted & Decorated Items***
  Many items can have their perceived value increased through the addition of hand painting. ***Furniture***, for example, can go from ho-hum to exquisite when painted with ***folk art designs*** or ***exotic designs and motifs***.

  Even plain ***toy chests*** can be spiced up with wonderful, imaginative designs like wild animals or nursery motifs...or turned into a work of utter sophistication with a coat of red or black lacquer, decorated with a few Chinese characters and a touch of gold plus unusual hardware or gold tassels. A plain desk, table, chair - or even the walls and floors! - can be transformed into 'must have' decorator items with paint and a little talent.

- ***Babies' and children's furniture*** can take on a whole new atmosphere when painted. So, too, can walls decorated with murals and nursery characters. *(See below: Murals & Trompe l'oeil)*

  The value of even the smallest, most insignificant items can usually be increased by beautiful decoration. ***Combs and hairbrushes***, for example, are only as dull as you allow them to be. When a talented craftsperson adds paint and creativity to such mundane items, they can be transformed into collectors' items!

- ***Murals & Trompe l'oeil***
  A mural is a magic carpet that can whisk you to any place you care to go. It can spirit you to a jungle hideaway, an autumn forest or a pristine beach. In reality, your window might look onto a ramshackle building or an inner city block of flats...but you can mask that with a simple curtain and paint a fantasy instead!

  For the ultimate in wall décor, a trompe l'oeil decoration is a must. What is trompe l'oeil? It translates from French as 'fool the eye' and refers to a mural that is so real, you'd believe the scene actually exists. You may think that you are looking through the kitchen to a door that it is partly open...and there, on

the doorstep is a cat sitting in the sun... but go a little closer and you'll see
that the whole scene is just a clever paint job!

In the dining room, bedroom, family room or by the pool, the imagination can
take flight if the mural artist is clever enough. In children's rooms, a mural
can be truly inspiring with anything from nursery characters to aliens!

Murals and trompe l'oeils can fetch a great deal of money for the artist but
they must be done well. If you have an ability to paint on a large scale (albeit
in rather uncomfortable positions sometimes!), you could build up a great
little business for yourself providing you market it well.

- ***Silk Painting***
  Silk painting is easy to learn and easy to do - yet it can produce the most
  stunning results: ***scarves***, ***wall hangings, dress lengths, wraps*** and other
  items that shimmer with the colours of a butterfly's wings.

  You *can* go to a lot of trouble preparing your own dyes or weighing up the
  powders like an ancient alchemist...but why bother when there are so many
  beautiful, ready-to-use dyes on the market that will work for you like magic?
  It is best to take a short course on silk painting to find out the methods you
  prefer.

  Generally, a piece of silk is stretched across a frame, the sketch or design is
  placed underneath and traced with 'gutta' (a thick, gooey water repellent).
  Coloured dye is then dropped into each segment of the design with a damp
  wad of cotton wool or brush and immediately spreads out to the gutta
  barriers. Where two or more colours meet and run into each other, the result
  can be fabulous.

  You will need to make sure you use the best, bright, colourfast dyes. Ensure
  that all the gutta is removed after heat setting and rinse the finished articles
  well until the colour (even the so-called *colourfast* colour that has been
  set!) stops bleeding out. The silk is best heat-set by sending it to be done
  professionally. However, if you are serious about the art, you could buy
  a special stainless steel steamer for this purpose but these can be quite
  expensive.

  Organise to have someone sew and edge your garments for you or do the job
  yourself. While silk items can be machine-hemmed, a hand-rolled edge can
  make an exquisite finish, especially if silk thread is used. Sometimes senior
  school children like to take on small edging jobs at home but only relinquish
  your silk garments to their care if you can be sure the fabric will be kept
  perfectly clean and oil free.

Many galleries carry a range of painted silk items. So do many tourist outlets, gift shops, fashion and accessory shops.

- **Screen Printing**

  Technology has taken over much screen printing work but many people still prefer to work manually. *Screen printed fabrics, curtains, blinds, quilts, cushion covers, dress lengths, T-shirts* and other clothes are always in demand.

  For a 'crafty' couple, where one is a screen printer and the other a dressmaker, a very profitable home business could be created in manufacturing *exclusive beachwear, evening wear, sleepwear, manchester* or *home decorator items*.

  When it comes to screen printing and manufacturing from a home base, you will need an appropriate workroom. A converted garage or bungalow, preferably detached from the house, would suffice and should be totally dedicated to your work and to displaying your creations. Offering clients a choice from a few garments hanging on a rack in the living room is just not on! Of course, you will have to gain permission from the local council for any such venture.

  Your designs will need to be something out of the ordinary if you are to compete in today's market but the clothes themselves should not be too way out. One-size or looser type garments like *beach and evening coats, wraps, summer muumuus, tops and shifts* are best as they appeal to a wide market. They are also easiest to handle if you are planning to sell them by mail order. Returns are less likely with *one size fits all*.

- **Clip Art**

  If you draw well, you might like to consider producing a book of clip art with a CD tucked in the back. You will need to be fairly prolific and produce work in many categories and for various occasions such as the four seasons, travel, people, animals and so forth.

- **Copper Craft**

  One of the most beautiful wall murals I have ever seen was made of burnished copper. It was around 6 feet by 3 feet, set into the wall, and the subject was a Roman battlefield, complete with chariots. The statement made by this incredible piece of work was truly amazing.

  However, not all copper murals need to be of such a gigantic size. The process itself is really quite simple: the illustration or design is copied onto a sheet of copper, special tools are then used to stretch, beat or raise various areas to make the piece 3D. This is done on the back or front of the piece so occasionally the sheet will need to be turned. The hollows can then be filled from the rear with melted wax and, when set, the whole thing is attached to a backing board and framed.

You can teach yourself the basics of copper craft with a simple copper foiling set from a children's toy shop or craft shop. Usually these sets contain all you will need for the piece, including the copper.

ART OR CRAFT CLASSES

Art and craft can generally be taught anywhere: at home, in a hired room in a hall, in a recreational centre...even in the backyard! However, some crafts are messier than others or require lots of equipment, so these things must be taken into consideration before deciding on a venue.

Wherever you decide to have your studio, ensure it has good cross ventilation, good light and water as well as sufficient easels, chairs, tables and any other materials you think you will need. Simple easels can be made in the home workshop or purchased quite cheaply through the classifieds or at garage sales.

For the most part, students should bring their own art materials while you supply the equipment such as tables, chairs, easels, still life items and so forth. If you are teaching painting, a collection of empty cans for turps or water is always handy. A list of student requirements can be issued on enrolment.

It can be beneficial to run a variety of classes: beginners, advanced, day, evening, weekend and children of various age groups. Make it a rule that all your students - adults and children alike - clean up their mess before leaving the studio, otherwise you will spend hours needlessly cleaning up after them!

Hold exhibitions of your students' best work - and your own, of course - and invite students' relatives and friends to the showing as well. Students love these get-togethers and may even want to purchase one of their teacher's works!

ART AND CRAFT SUPPLIES (MAIL ORDER)

You don't necessarily need a shop to sell your art and craft supplies: they can often be sold quite profitably by mail order. This way, you don't have the big overheads of a retail store and can more comfortably compete in the market by offering sizeable discounts and specials. However, in calculating discounts for mail order customers, take into consideration the postage and handling costs that would be unnecessary if they were to buy retail.

Art and craft books and videos are also extremely popular among artists and students.

As a mail order business, you may not even need to stock certain items to be able to sell them: for example, some expensive equipment like opaque projectors, pottery wheels and kilns can often be 'drop shipped' to your client. This is where your networking skills come in: you must build up a network of reliable suppliers. *(See Drop Shipping)*

ARTIFICIAL & DRIED FLOWER ARRANGEMENTS

These arrangements are not the fad they were way back in the sixties! However, there is still a need for really up-market arrangements. Prepare a folio of beautiful illustrations showcasing your work and take it around to decorator shops, retail stores and florists' shops. It would be best to make an appointment first.

You might also consider leasing some of your arrangements to offices, theatres, hotels, motels and reception centres to decorate their foyers or interiors.

ART METAL WORK

How nice it is to be living in the New Millennium with all its cool technology. It can make living and working so much easier!

Home-based metal workers, for example, can now produce so many wonderful items in their backyard with the help of the simplest machinery. They don't even need heat to bend and scroll many of their materials any more! Many metals can be twisted and bent like chewing gum!

Simple welding and other skills can be easily learned through attending short courses at your local TAFE or recreation centre or via private tuition.
Once you know how to turn plain metal into beautifully wrought balustrades, gates, fences, furniture and sculpture, you will have learned how to turn plain metal into money legally!

ASTROLOGER

Today, astrologers have gone hi-tech and seem to be everywhere: on the radio, the TV, in the newspaper, in magazines, at the end of the phone line and on the Internet…which suggests that society feels a definite need for their services.

If you are clued-up in this area, you might like to consider a few other ways of providing your service apart from the normal person-to-person consultation. For example, writing a book or making a video on the subject and self-publishing it might even lead the way to a weekly newspaper column or an interview on radio!

A really comprehensive and outstanding Home Page on the internet crammed with unusual information about your subject plus on-line horoscopes might bring your site more hits than a comet in the asteroid belt!

Many courses are available in this subject if you are new to the subject: several are offered by correspondence, which would allow aspiring astrologers to continue working in their day jobs while studying and preparing for the future in their spare time.

AUDIO TAPE & CD PRODUCTION

If past experience has led you to acquire specialised knowledge about a particular subject, perhaps you could write an engrossing script suitable for an audio tape or CD. Rehearse, record a dummy run, then play it back, making any changes necessary. Keep practising your presentation until you feel you have done your best. Get some feedback from your relatives and friends before placing it on the market.

Having completed and succeeded with the sale of the first audio production, it is a lot easier to make a second…and a third…and so on!

If you are unable to read aloud smoothly and fluently, perhaps you could hire a professional to read the manuscript for you. Information tapes don't necessarily have to be of the same standard as music tapes but they should at least be produced in a soundproof environment. Background traffic noise, barking dogs or children playing in the next room will kill your production!

There are thousands of subjects that would be of use and interest to the public: health, adventure, philosophy, business, how-to and so on. You may doubt whether you, personally, have anything of interest to teach others but, if you thought about it hard enough, you may discover you know a great deal about things that others would like to learn about. If not, you could simply be a *producer*, inviting experts and interesting people to impart their knowledge solo or in interview fashion..

Producing and selling information tapes or CD's is not difficult and can be extremely lucrative. If you need more information on this subject, please contact our office. Covers for your CD's and cassettes can be produced on a home computer and colour printer for a truly professional look.

AUTO MAINTENANCE AND RESTORATION

The auto body repair business could be run as a **mobile service**, with much of your work being done 'on site' at a client's premises. Alternatively, provide a complete **'pick-up-and-delivery** service' for clients, doing the work at your home. In this case, you will need a partner (your spouse perhaps?) to assist in driving one of the cars when necessary.

For a vehicle restoration business to be set up at home, you would need at least a large, well equipped double or triple garage.

Here is just a small list of services you may be able to offer from your home-based business:
* *auto detailing*
* *scuffed bumpers*
* *windshield repair*
* *small dents and hail damage repair*
* *paint chip repair and touch ups*
* *full respray*
* *interior repair including torn, burnt or stained upholstery*
* *an oil change service*
* *brake repair*
* *window tinting*
* *gold plating of accessories*
* *odour removal*
* *upholstery repair*
* *carpet repair*

You may prefer to offer several services - or specialise in only one. Either way, as a home-based business, you will be able to charge lower prices thanks to low overheads.
While quality work and reliable service is expected in this game, the true entrepreneur will realise the enormous value of good marketing and constant networking. Forge links with car dealers, panel beating and detailing firms, motoring organisations, car importers...in fact, anyone with whom you feel you

may be able to do business.

Think laterally. Could you come up with some *unusual* service like '***vacation maintenance for your car***'? Your advertising might read: '*Holidaying abroad? Give your car a vacation, too! We will service it, protect it, polish it, pamper it so that it looks and rides like new when you return*!'

Such a service may entail you meeting clients at the airport carpark when they leave on vacation and taking away their car to your home workshop. When they return, their 'like new' car could be back at the airport waiting for them - shiny, spotless and superbly tuned.

AUTO INSPECTION SERVICE – MOBILE

If you know cars inside out, you may be able to provide a mobile car inspection service for potential buyers of either new or second hand cars. Help out the less knowledgeable hundreds who are forever getting ripped off buying cars through private sales or car yards.

Advertising could be by way of leaflet, the classifieds and appropriate magazines and newsletters. As well, maintain good signage on both your car and your house.

AVIATION

Pilots! You don't even need your own plane! Lease one instead! Now all you need is good marketing ability, a pilot's licence - and a good safety record! There's a variety of services you could run. Here is a handful of suggestions:

- *joy flights*
- *private flying lessons*
- *business flights*
- *scenic adventures*
- *'Air taxi' service*
- *cultural tours*
- *aerial photography*
- *local tours*

AVIARIES

(See Bird Breeding)

B

*Important: Always check to see what regulations apply when making babies'
and children's items. You may be required to observe certain specifications in
manufacture, even to the type of paint used. Do check these things out <u>thoroughly</u>
before you start any projects.*

BABY MERCHANDISE

The area of baby merchandise can offer great money-making opportunities. True,
you'll have lots of competition...but there are enough little customers arriving in
the world every day to keep creative entrepreneurs on their toes.

Home-manufactured baby goods lend themselves to being marketed in many
ways, depending on their classification. Some might be sold direct from home,
through retail outlets, by word of mouth, others through classified or display ads in
newspapers and magazines, at weekend markets or through the internet.

Maintaining a permanent stall at a *busy* weekend market can often be as lucrative as
running a small shop in a local shopping centre: you don't have the big overheads
eating away at your takings but you do have the volume of shoppers. Customers
soon get to know the regular stall-holders at the markets and are often happy to
place orders or recomment you to their friends.

As far as manufacturing ***baby furniture*** is concerned, you will need to check on any
special specifications and regulations. You'll also need to find out from your local
council if the type of equipment you are intending to use in your home workshop is
acceptable environmentally. In some areas, there are restrictions on noise and even
limits on the horsepower of machinery. You may also need to reassure council that
you do not expect a tangle of clients' cars outside your premises at any one time.

- **BABY FURNITURE – NEW**
  If your workspace is small, specialise in making just one or two lines...
  e.g. bassinettes or toy boxes. You may be able to flat-pack some items for
  self-assembly by customers or simply *flat store* the components, making up
  articles yourself as orders come in.

  There are countless goods that can be made in a home work shed: changing
  tables, cots and basinettes, swing bassinettes, wooden toys, rocking horses,
  rocking chairs, high chairs, toy boxes and hundreds of other items.
  ***(Once again, certain items may require you to abide by a set of standards,
  so check on regulations.)***

- **BABY FURNITURE - USED**
Second-hand baby furniture and toys, although sometimes less profitable than new furniture, can be bought and sold at garage sales, local markets, fetes, through the classifieds, your own web site, at auctions, even through letter box drops.

Sometimes, excellent items can be found on the nature strips of various suburbs before junk collection days but check your area has no restrictions on your collecting them. Also, you'll need quite a bit of storage if you plan to renovate and store bulky items.

Some parents like *unpainted* furniture for babies and toddlers; others prefer paint and decoration. Restore pre-loved goods in a variety of ways and you will be amazed how good they can look! They often scrub up like new!

- **DECORATING READY-MADE BABY FURNITURE**
If you do not wish to build babies' furniture, but enjoy adding value through beautiful decoration like painting and decoupage, you could buy *raw* furniture wholesale or have items made to order for you. Then, all you have to do is the fun part: prepare the ready-made furniture, paint and decorate!

- **BABY PHOTOGRAPHY**
If you're a photographer, you're in luck! There are so many options available to you as a 'home' operator. Photographing babies can be one of the more satisfying. Browse through relevant photography books: those baby photos by Anne Geddes will knock your socks off! - and get lots of ideas for your business by turning to the entry under *Photography* in this book.
Note: some mothers can be nervous about photographers using flash lighting around babies, so try to take your photos in natural light wherever possible.

- **BABY PORTRAITURE - IN OIL, WATERCOLOUR OR PASTEL**
Artists who have a talent for children's portraiture can often make big money if they specialise in this field. Basic sketches of babies can even be done while the latter are asleep! However, once children are a few months old, it's best to include photographs in your reference material because your small, restless models may move around too much to enable you to capture their likeness successfully and they tire of sitting.

Keep your compositions simple, centred on the subject. Baby portraits can be particularly stunning when complemented by plain dark backgrounds and a simple quilt or floor rug. Develop your own technique and stick to it so that clients get to know your style!

- **BABYWEAR, SEWN & KNITTED**

  If you can knit, sew or crochet baby clothes quickly and expertly, you should be able to build a very nice little home business. There are so many items you could make for babies: *shawls, bonnets, booties and jackets, matinee jackets, pillow covers and quilts, embroidered baby towels, bibs*…the list is almost endless.

  Think about creative ways of gift packaging matching items (eg a towel and washer set, a pillow cover and quilt or a matching bonnet and booties). Package them attractively and attach a glossy, up-market label.

  The children's wear buyers at department stores are possible targets for your marketing push as are local babywear shops: some may be willing to accept your work on consignment.

  However, if giving away half of your profits to retailers is *not* the way for you, there are plenty of other avenues for selling babywear! For example, it is surprising how much merchandise that a weekend stall can sell at a very busy market… and, by selling direct to the public, *you* get to keep most of the profits. While manning the stall, you can continue to knit and finish off garments between customers.

  A market should be chosen with care, not because it's local or easy to reach. Even if you have to drive for an extra hour to reach a really popular locale, you'll probably find that, at the end of the day, it was worth the extra trouble.

  Don't forget the opportunities offered by the Internet, too. A well presented web page laid out with your various baby garments and gift sets could really catch on.

- **NURSERY MURALS**

  You don't need to be able to draw particularly well to become a painter of nursery murals. You just need a flair for decoration and colour. Simply *project* an image of the proposed mural onto the nursery wall, *trace* it carefully, *paint* it with flair…and voila! A masterpiece! Beware of copying other people's illustrations, however, as you could be infringing copyright!

  When decorating, some parents prefer to use *odourless* paints in their children's rooms. Others may want *washable* paint on which their children can draw…or even *magnetic* paint for holding magnetic characters!

Take time to investigate the properties of the various paints and other decorative materials that are on the market so you can discuss the options freely and knowledgeably with your clients.

- **NURSERY MOBILES:**
  Some mobiles can be truly spectacular! Look at the various materials available and think up unusual, spectacular ideas of your own...for example, *themes from nursery stories*. If you are adept with a fret saw, you could make and paint nursery characters out of wood: Old King Cole, Peter Pan, The Old Lady Who Lived in a Shoe and so forth...or have fairies flying around the room.

  Take photos of your completed mobiles and use them to make a presentation folio of your work. This, plus a couple of completed mobiles, could be shown to retailers such as toy shops: they might accept some of your goods on consignment. As well, try selling from a stall at a weekend market.

  Perhaps you and a few like-minded, crafty colleagues could share a web site showcasing baby goods *and* sell your mobiles from there.
  (See also under Garage Sales)

BABY SITTING
(See under Child Care)

B&B ESTABLISHMENT

Running a B&B is the equivalent of having a continuous stream of house guests to your home... except that these guests will be *paying* for your hospitality! If you are the sociable, friendly type that one needs to be to run an establishment like this, you'll be amazed at the wide variety of travellers, interstate and international, that you could have staying with you.

No matter how people-oriented you are, you will need to retain a place in your home that is off-limits to anyone but *you and your family*. A private sitting area (even a parents' retreat off the main bedroom), will give you a place to unwind, relax...and come out again smiling! Separate bathroom facilities, too, are essential.

The location of your B & B could be anywhere travellers like to go - rural, seaside, mountains...even the suburbs, providing zoning regulations permit.

There are quite a few rules and regulations to observe: how much of your home you can let out to guests, whether you have adequate safety measures in place, whether you have acceptable food preparation areas, bathroom facilities, insurance, permits and so forth. Check out every aspect.

Keep clients coming back year after year by offering them comfortable, top quality beds, quiet and spotless rooms and good homely food.

If your B&B can supply only one guest room, don't let this deter you. There are seven days in a week: if you ask only $100 a night for that one room, it could ideally bring in $700 a week in the high season.

On the other hand, if you have a large, well-located establishment of *several* spare rooms, and you have the determination to work the business professionally - even to international standard - you could make excellent money.

Another plus with a B & B is that you should be able to live off the business: food, electricity, gas, rates, cleaning, laundry, gardening, furniture, motor vehicles and more are all business expenses.

Think about ways you could make your service truly outstanding. For example, if you happen to live in a geographically or historically interesting area, you may be able to offer guests *day tours* of the locale as a bonus.

Don't forget to provide for younger guests, too. You may not have the luxury of a pool or a tennis court, but it doesn't take much to put in a swing, see-saw, trampoline and some comfortable outdoor furniture on the patio. Many of these items can be purchased in quite good condition from garage sales.

Offer a variety of games like totem tennis, darts, basketball, shuttlecock, quoits and even electronic games if you have the space and equipment. Do you have a spare shed that could be converted into a recreation room for table tennis, cards, chess and other indoor games? The more comforts and attractions that you can offer guests, the more memorable will be their stay - and the more likely they'll be to return!
(See under Motel: also under Room/Flat Letting in Your Home)

BADGE MANUFACTURING

Who needs badges? Well, just for starters: schools, businesses, clubs, churches, hospitals, industry, party givers…you name it! They're required for a multitude of reasons from promotional purposes and fund raising events, right down to identifying staff or team members.

Button badges particularly, can be very easy for a home business worker. They can be made with a simple little machine in next to no time, either on the kitchen table or at the school fete! This inexpensive equipment is often advertised in business opportunities magazines as well as the Yellow Pages.

Some makers of button badges set themselves up at weekend markets and fairs. However, you don't have to produce solely *name badges.* Get creative and produce *a list of incredibly wise or funny phrases* for sale: list the choices on a cardboard stand from which clients can choose! Or make up *slogans or phrases relating to local areas* for the tourist market.

There is a good demand for professional and corporate badges that are:
• enamelled   • embroidered   • engraved.   However, these require more complex equipment and knowledge.

There is also the tourist trade to consider. In fact, metal badges could be used to decorate many souvenirs such as *collectable teaspoons*.

If you have a computer and good colour printer, you might also be able to make *greeting cards* which incorporate button badges. Badges containing large coloured numbers representing various ages could be placed on birthday cards while funny sayings could be on the badges decorating humorous cards.

BAG MAKING

To make handbags as a living, you will need expertise in both manufacture and marketing. But this is not to say you can't succeed if you have the necessary push and talent...and can come up with creative and unusual ideas!

Leather is often a first choice for those wanting to make handbags but there are so many leather accessories coming in from overseas that it is almost impossible to compete unless you are producing goods that are very *up-market* and unusual.

If you are selling leather bags at markets, give a demo. This draws interest like nothing else can! People love to watch skiving, stamping and so forth ...but whether they will actually *buy* your pieces will depend on your sales ability.

To make serious money as a home-based manufacturer, you need to target *the upper echelons of the fashion market!* Consider *beautifully beaded* and *woven ribbon evening bags* made in exotic fabrics like velvet, satin and silk. Or bags heavily appliqued or embroidered. They could be marketed (and sold on consignment, perhaps) through many smaller fashion and accessory outlets.

Another way to sell bags is through the ***party plan*** method. Parties can be organised at the homes of friends and acquaintances where bags are modelled, passed around and, hopefully, sold! Of course, you would be expected to give your hosts a special deal or even a freebie for their trouble!

Another potentially profitable area of bag making is ***adventure travel gear***. Although there is a lot of competition with these lines, there could still be room for your product if it is a good one as the market is so large.

One of the main problems doing this heavier work at home could be the restrictions on machinery and also on assistance permitted. However, not all councils have the same rules and regulations. You might be lucky, so make the necessary enquiries.

A few of the products you could consider making are: ***back packs, travel packs, hydration packs, wet packs, sports packs, ski and surfboard packs, wheeled backpacks*** and so forth.

Think about selling by ***direct mail*** (you'll need a mailing list and illustrated brochure) and consider having your own illustrated ***web page***.

BALLOONS

- ***Greeting Delivery Service:***
  High volume advertising, great marketing and creative ideas are the keys to building up a balloon greeting delivery service.

  Having balloons delivered by assistants in fancy dress can help make the occasion memorable for the recipient: will they be delivered by a *Gorilla*? *A fairy with hairy legs (The Hairy Fairy?) An oversized Belly dancer? A Vampire? A Stripper?* But check on regulations first!

  When you turn up at the recipient's front door, make the act a real spot of fun and you'll have everyone talking about it for weeks!

- ***Balloon Wrapped Gifts:***
  Real fun is a 'Balloon wrapped' gift! This service encloses small gifts or even money inside a see-through, inflated balloon. They are generally hand-delivered but you could arrange to fulfil orders through party shops and gift outlets as well as selling direct.

  If you'd like a ready-made business in Balloon Wrap, look through the ads in the Yellow Pages, various business opportunity magazines or speak to balloon manufacturers direct.

- ***Gift Basket Balloons:***
  One exquisite idea is a multicoloured balloon attached to a mini basket containing a gift. The balloon itself would be a helium filled 'greeting balloon', usually bearing an appropriate message such as: 'Happy Birthday', 'I Love You', 'Get Well Soon', "Happy Valentine's Day'.

- However, your balloon repertoire could be a lot more creative than this if you think about it! You could have balloons made-to-order to look like old world ***'Montgolfier' hot air balloons*** with the little passenger basket below bearing the present. This would be the ultimate wondrous gift!

- ***Balloon bouquets,*** with or without a gift, can make a beautiful presentation for those celebrating birthdays, Valentine's day (especially with heart-shaped chocolates included!), engagements, graduation, the birth of a baby and many other special occasions.
  (See also Talking Ribbons; this may be a good adjunct to your business.)

BASKET MAKING

There are so many woven imports these days, it is unlikely that this craft would be worth pursuing unless as part of a *related* business. For example, as part of a ***Gift Basket/Balloon*** business *(see above)*.

You could also manufacture ***specially shaped baskets 'to order'*** as containers for the corporate, promotional or homewares market. This may be worth investigating.

BATTERY RECONDITIONING

Would you enjoy reconditioning secondhand batteries for a few cents…and selling them again for dollars? Reconditioning kits are often advertised in the business and opportunity magazines. One long-time company is selling their kits in two sizes: a 'start up' kit for beginners and a 'commercial' kit for those who want to add this service to a full-blown automotive concern.

Your market could be local service stations, spare parts outlets and similar as well as the everyday motorist,

A home garage or work shed should make a fine place to work but you could also offer a ***mobile service*** for customers who cannot get to you (…because they have a flat battery!)

If you already own an auto outlet of any type, battery reconditioning might prove to be quite a profitable arm to your business.
(See also under Car Battery Reconditioning)

BEADS – HANDMADE

Beads can be made from wood, plastic, metal, glass, agates that are tumbled and drilled - and many other natural materials, including clay (if you have access to a kiln). There are many short courses on this craft being introduced now.

You could even use Das, Fimo or any other good, fast-drying clay if you wish. Some of these clays dry naturally; others need to be placed in the oven to harden, so read the instructions carefully. The final result is hard enough to be painted, decorated, varnished and then threaded.

You could also decorate your beads according to certain 'themes' such as wildlife, birds, national flowers, astrological signs, runes, flags, shipping symbols, Chinese characters and so forth. Even an endangered species theme may sell well in certain quarters.

Talk to specialist gift shops, jewellers, craft and crystal shops about your highly original creations. You might try selling by mail order, direct mail, an illustrated web page, at markets or by the party plan method.

Consider, too, how easy it would be to make up some of these wonderful beads into jewellery items such as bracelets and necklets. Much dress jewellery these days has dispensed with difficult-to-do-up clasps and merely strings the beads and other components onto elastic.
(See Jewellery, Crystals)

BEAD SUPPLIES

Make them yourself, buy them wholesale - or both! Beads are really *in* and many people are cashing in on their popularity. Most bead companies tend to have a point of display like a small shop where they not only sell all types of beads from wood to crystal, they also run craft *classes in beading*. Many maintain a mail order service as well. *(See also under Beads-Handmade)*

If you do not wish to run craft classes, you could quite easily run your business by *mail order from home*. You would require illustrated brochures, a few unusual lines and some good advertising. A web page could be considered.

Devise slightly different ways of selling such as offering clients a varied sample of your wares to choose from.

Unfortunately, one of the biggest costs will be advertising as you really need to obtain *display advertising* in the glossy craft magazines to compete with the high fliers in this business.

BEAUTY CONSULTANT

You may need to do an accredited course or apprenticeship before entering the area of your choice in this industry. However, there are also quite a few jobs you can do without formal qualifications providing you have some experience. You will need to make enquiries related to your area of interest.

Much beauty consultancy work can be done from a home base, but don't overlook the possibility of becoming a *visiting* consultant to local hairdressing and beauty salons on a *part-time or casual* basis.

If you prefer to work *totally* from home, be sure your salon is as comfortable and modern as possible so your clients will enjoy their experience and look forward to coming back to see you again and again.

There are many basic treatments that can be offered depending on your knowledge and qualification. Decide on the area that interests you most. Are you adept in performing facials, waxing, peels, brow shaping and tinting? There are several top **brow shapers** who specialise in just this one area alone and some are making a mint! Or do you prefer make-up, manicures, massage?

Perhaps you would like to run short courses and seminars: '*skin care for the mature woman*', '*for the elderly*', '*for men*', '*for the traveller*', '*for the bride to be*', '*for teens*'...or you may enjoy doing a bit of everything. The list of possibilities open to you is almost endless.

If you are not yet qualified or experienced in any area that you would like to learn about, take a reputable course in the subject (part-time, if necessary), to add to your repertoire of services.

Marketing will be a most important part of your business. Are **wedding and party planners** aware of your service if you are a **make-up artist**? Introduce yourself to cosmetic firms, chemists and large department stores who give beauty demos and consultations. Speak to the make-up departments of major **TV and film studios, theatrical groups and modelling agencies**. Leave them your brochure, CV and business card.

Advertise to the public at large by flier, poster, through the classifieds and the wedding-related sections of the media! See if you can bag an editorial or two in local papers about the pleasure you bring to people. Or try writing a feature article or two about your work and send it to a major magazine!

BEE KEEPING (APIARIST)

Before starting an apiary on your property, your plans will need to be checked out and approved by the local council. This may not be so easy in the suburbs...but, on the other hand, suburban apiaries do exist. In a rural area, you will probably be encouraged.

When your business is up and running, you may feel it's time to consider introducing a few related products which could be anything from natural foodstuffs to health and beauty products made with the alleged wonder of wonder products, Royal Jelly!

If you are creative, have determination and energy - as well as the right kind of zoning - bee keeping has every likelihood of bringing you good financial rewards.

BERRY FARM

Strawberries, blueberries, raspberries...if your property is large enough and in the right area with the appropriate zoning, a berry farm could be quite a money magnet if run with some marketing creativity. Even a hobby or weekend farm could provide you with an opportunity to establish yourself on a small scale.

There are many spin-off products which you could manufacture and sell, on site, not only to the berry lovers who come a'picking – and a'paying to get in - but commercially as well. Jams, bottled berries and other berry products might wind up being your prime business.

Visit the various berry farms in your state and see how they operate. Do they sell just one type of berry: if so, why? Talk to fellow pickers to ascertain if they like what they see and what other features they would like.

Ask questions of the operators and bring home a few sample products to try plus an armful of literature. Do they sell recipe books, booklets that explain the health benefits of berries, videos?

Then sit down and figure out how you could do better!

BICYCLE REPAIRS

Buy up used bikes and scooters from garage sales (there are dozens available every weekend!) or roam the suburbs at junk collection time: you will find literally scores of bicycles lying on the nature strips ready to supply you with spare parts like seats and tyres, even if the bikes themselves are irrepairable. However, ensure your council has no restrictions against your collecting these items.

You may be able to clean and repair the better pre-loved bikes then try *reselling them at a profit*. Always offer customers a guarantee.

Your *repair service* could be advertised in the local classifieds, by flyer, on local posters and from an appropriately sized notice on your property. (Check with council as to the size of notice permitted). Local shops which you patronise might place brochures in their window. Supermarkets have community noticeboards: use them, too...with permission, of course. Another excellent place to advertise would be in school newsletters. They are read by the parents of hundreds of little bike riders and usually charge only a fraction of the normal advertising fee.

You should find that determined advertising, plus word-of-mouth promotion, will bring you a ready supply of used machines and customers.

BIRD BREEDING

If you breed doves, pigeons, parrots or other noisy birds at home, you may need a large property so that your aviaries can be placed well away from neighbours. Many people find that living next to a cage of cooing doves can be as annoying as living next door to barking dogs, particularly at night.

Pigeon breeding can be quite lucrative, especially if your birds are trained as racers but once again, serious breeding is best undertaken in rural or semi-rural areas.

Exhibit your best birds in shows and exhibitions whenever possible. If you can get that magic title *'prize winner'* after your name, it could make a big difference to your image and your success.

One of the cheapest forms of advertising will be through bird breeders' and fanciers' newsletters. Advertise, too, in specialist magazines, even those for the entertainment industry. For example, magicians are just one group that have an interest in well-trained pegeons and doves. So too are businesses, government bodies and charities that are likely to require flocks of doves for openings and commemorative events.

Pet stores might be willing to supply you with a list of bird fanciers' names for a price - or even for a supply of birds for their shop!

Exotic birds can bring importers quite large incomes and could involve you in travel to some of the most exciting places on earth. Imagine taking a trip to the Amazon each year for 'business purposes'! Lucky you!

Maintaining your own special-interest web site might give you lots of scope to show off your feathered money-makers, as well as providing free information and help to the many bird fanciers out there.
(See also under Pets)

BIRDCAGE COVERS
(See Sewing)

BIRDCAGES
(See Metalwork and Woodwork)

BLIND & SHUTTER CLEANING

For the beginner, a franchise is often the easiest way to go for this truly underrated business! Franchises are advertised in the Yellow Pages as well as various 'business opportunities' magazines.

Clients can range from private homes to large multi-storied (and multi-windowed!) businesses and factories.

It's important to build up a name for reliability and good service right from the start. Advertise anywhere and everywhere: by letterbox drop, the local classifieds, school newsletters, even a notice on the gate of your house and on the side of your van.

Always place a sandwich board outside the premises you are working on for all to see!

BOOKKEEPING

If you are already conversant with bookkeeping and bookkeeping software, you may decide to set up a small bookkeeping business in your home office...or go mobile.

Despite the plethora of bookkeeping software available to the public these days, most people like this job about as much as they enjoy scrubbing floors or mowing their lawns! It takes time away from fun, family and relaxation. If you can show them how giving this obnoxioius chore to you can improve their lifestyle, you should be welcomed with open arms by a queue of clients! However, to make your own job a little easier and to avoid facing too many shoeboxes full of accounts, you may like to train clients in just the basics of accounting software in order to save you time and save themselves money.

Like the thought of ultimately becoming a home-based bookkeeper but have no experience and no idea where to start at this stage of your life? Some taxation specialists provide basic short courses to number-literate novices like you and will then offer the better graduates work in the preparation of tax returns.*(See our info pages)*. This is a great way to gain tuition and experience; however, there is a cost for these courses.

BOOMERANG MAKER OR DEALER

There is quite a market for boomerangs of many types and sizes, although true collectors of such artefacts obviously want the authentic items actually produced by Aboriginees. However, everyday tourists are rarely so particular and seem ready to buy all forms and sizes from tie pins to superb working examples of aerodynamics.

If you trade in working model boomerangs, it would be helpful to include instructions plus a little background on their place in Aboriginal culture. However, not all boomerangs are meant to return to sender! Some are simply used for throwing to kill or maim the animal being hunted. Others are used for warfare. So, if you are producing boomerangs for the tourist or overseas market, state on the pack whether yours is a returning boomerang so as to avoid disappointment.

Beware of selling mass produced articles decorated with Aboriginal designs, however; as such designs belong to the indigenous people themselves.

If you are able to throw a boomerang well, you might be able to produce a short instructional video to go with the product you are selling.
(See also Woodworking, Didgeridoo)

BOTTLED SHIPS

One of the most fascinating hobbies could also become a fascinating business: bottling ships! Build and erect these amazing maritime structures in a bottle whose neck in only wide enough for a cork! Mast to keel, the height of the ship is about the height of the bottle on its side. 'How did it get in there?' the viewer wonders! Yet, the art is not so difficult to learn and there are many books on the subject.

You might make models of *famous ships* or even winners of the *great yacht races* like the America's Cup and sell them to collectors and yachting enthusiasts. One needs to be very precise when engineering the craft in its collapsed form.

IDEA: Tool kits for bottled ships: Could you make up and package tool kits, instructions and model components for would-be bottled ship makers, selling them by mail order? It could represent a nice little sideline to the business above.

BUILDER'S CLEAN UP SERVICE

After the builders, the roofers and tilers, the cabinet makers and electricians have left the building site, who is to clean up all the mess? You, of course. In fact, you will not only be gathering a substantial fee for the clean up; you might also gather up the more useful left over lumber, wiring, hardware, tiles and anything else they've left and sell or use it in some secondary business.

BUYER'S ADVOCATE SERVICE

Here's one for the born bargainer! Negotiate the very best prices possible on goods and services for your clients by accumulating volume orders for goods, then haggling in style on your clients' behalf. Remember, you'll be buying and selling from home, on the phone and the web, so *you* won't have the huge overheads that can cripple the big stores!

C

CALLIGRAPHY

Your services as a calligrapher are most likely to be required for invitations and other formal correspondence, certificates and greeting cards. You may also be asked to perform your beautiful handwriting for book titles and to accent the work of graphic artists and photographers, so investigate all such markets.

Some craft markets which sell beautifully illustrated greeting cards now have a calligrapher at the ready to write the recipient's name on the card in style! These can be very popular with customers.

CANDLE MAKING

Candles are quite easy to make once you know how. Buy or borrow a comprehensive book on the craft if you have never attempted the craft before and try out a few different types and styles of candles to see if you enjoy it. *Note: extreme caution must be taken when handling the hot wax.*

In business, time is money! Many candle makers go overboard with sculptured and moulded figurines and other unusual shapes but, if you're in candle-making for the money, keep your products simple! Just go for beautiful blends of colours, scents and various sizes.

You'll need a place to work that has good ventilation: an outdoor laundry or garage could be ideal.

Sell your gorgeous, rainbow-like creations at weekend craft markets and fetes. They could be wrapped in cellophane and grouped together for effect so that they present a dazzling display of delectable colours and sizes on your table or counter.

You may be able to make up *boxed sets of scented candles* tied with lovely satin or silk ribbons and containing booklets outlining the properties of the scents they contain. Meditation or relaxation candles can be quite popular as gifts.

CANINE MERCHANDISE & SERVICES
(See under Dog Merchandise)

CARPENTER

There is so much that a creative carpenter can make and one of those is money! But there are other, not so readily obvious areas for your work, too.

Perhaps you could come up with a line of domestic *saunas*. Or you might build *pool decks* that fit around above-ground pools. Could you develop something like a simply made *Fijian Burre* or Indonesian style *summer house* for suburban backyards? Or an ourdoor, collapsible bar for the barbie? Or a roll-around kitchen bar cupboard with hideaway, *retractable seats*? Or a *dining table* that rolls over to become a *guest bed*? Or even outdoor stairs! Yes, this is the newest thing on the block for outdoor living: rough-sawn timber steps in modules. They are about a metre wide and can be used for accessing above-ground pools, ledges and rockeries, garden paths and so forth. So easy but so handy!

Note: these suggestions are only to get you thinking. They are not necessarily being advocated as things into which you should invest time or money. But this is the type of brainstorming that someone with your capabilities should be doing whenever possible.

Whatever you do, remember that one can achieve economies of scale by coming up with just one line of unusual but finely built articles. By marketing them over time, in the right place and in the right way, you could build up quite a name for yourself. *(See also Children's Furniture, Babies' Furniture, Furniture)*

CARPET CLEANING

Few people actually like cleaning and vacuuming but being paid excellent dollars per hour makes it far more tolerable.

The easy way in is to obtain a reputable franchise with full training and marketing assistance, plus customers. On the other hand, if dollars are tight or you simply prefer to stand on your own two feet from the start, you may prefer to set up your own cleaning service.

Either way, make a booking or two with some franchised cleaners and ask them to clean your own carpets. You will then be able to see the way they work, how you are treated and what your reaction is to the final result. Find out, by chatting to them, as much as you can about what they like and don't like about their job and their franchise.

Before you even think of starting up a business of this sort, discuss your plans with key professionals such as your accountant and bank manager and research every nook and cranny of the business.

CARTOONIST

You don't need to be a brilliant artist to become a cartoonist: You simply need a brilliant sense of humour that you can translate into drawings. Nor do you need to wait to be asked to produce work; simply draw up the cartoon and send it in with a covering letter to one of the hundreds of publishers who use them.

To find out which publishers are accepting cartoons, take a look in the current year's *Australian Writer's Marketplace* put out by Bookman Directories (there may be a copy in your local library) or look in the various writers' newsletters.

CAT BREEDING

Breeding cats can bring tremendous enjoyment. There is nothing more entertaining than a house full of kittens or more endearing than a mother cat feeding and looking after her babies! However, depending on the extent of your commercial aspirations, it can also be quite hectic.

To do well financially in breeding pedigreed cats, particularly the exotic varieties such as Siamese, Burmese, Persian and so forth, you need to be part of the show circuit producing champions! This can mean hard work, especially at the weekends, with quite a bit of networking and even occasional interstate travel to shows.

However, you may be quite content to breed everyday, ordinary cats...is there such a thing as an ordinary cat?...simply for the love of it and bring in a bit of welcome pin money on the side.

Parting with your little adoptees can be difficult but it should not be long before the next litter comes along.

CAT PRODUCTS
(See under Pet Products, Pet Accessories, Pet Portraits)

CATERING

A catering business could be as small or large an enterprise as you can envisage. However, the bigger it is, the more it will require from the operators in terms of experience, finance, talent, energy, staff, equipment and marketing ability.

On the other hand, small scale catering can offer many opportunities for the home operator. Even beginners working from their own domestic kitchens can find certain catering ventures highly rewarding providing they remain within the bounds of their expertise. preparing the types of food with which they are familiar and in quantities they are able to manage.

There are many regulations covering the handling and preparation of food for public consumption and all necessary requirements should be fulfilled before going into business. These may vary from state to state.

What types of food could you prepare in that kitchen of yours? Well, this will depend not only on your ability but the size of your kitchen. While some clever little French restaurant you know may produce the most incredible dishes from the teeniest kitchen you've ever seen, remember that they have somewhere to put their dishes when they have prepared them: on the customers' tables out in the restaurant!

A home-based caterer, on the other hand, must have room in the home kitchen to not only prepare food but store it as well. You will need to take into account the preparation and storage space you will have available, the equipment you will need, the transportation you can offer, refrigerated vans and so forth.

But there are so many types of foods you could offer that generally, you will be able to find a way around most apparent hurdles. Perhaps you will be content to concentrate on producing *quiches and flans* for local cafes and restaurants. Maybe you will cater for *Finger Food* parties. You might even decide to offer *Spit Roasts*, *baked potatoes and salads*, taking the spit to the venue and doing the cooking on the spot!

A simple alternative might be a *barbeque party*. If there is no barbeque set-up at the venue, you could transport your own. Then it's just a matter of doing what you do at home most Sundays anyway, only on a larger scale: cook the meat and potatoes, and serve out the salad.

You really need to decide whether you want to transport only the ready prepared food and serve it...or do the cooking on the spot. Also determine if you want to provide food only or will you provide the plates, dishes, cutlery, napkins and decor as well?

It is also possible to procure *ready-made food in bulk* such as sweet & sour, beef stroganoff, pasta and so forth then simply reheat the food on site and serve it out individually with the appropriate side dishes such as rice, potatoes or salad. Great care must be exercised in reheating bulk foods, however, and you will also need to have absolute faith in the food handling methods of your bulk provider.

Consider some of the following catering ideas:

- spit roast
- barbeques (the steak-out!)
- finger food parties
- cocktail parties
- private dinner parties
- birthday parties
- stuffed potatoes
- seminars & conferences
- corporate catering
- buffets
- Xmas parties
- break-up parties
- boardroom lunches
- small weddings
- product launches
- club functions

- business breakfasts
- Italian cuisine (pasta parties)
- film crew catering
- cheese 'n fruit platters
- budget catering
- quiches & flans
- Hawaian luaus
- seafood platters
- children's parties
- morning & afternoon teas

There is plenty of training available, day or evening, if you feel you need it. You will be able to choose from short TAFE and Rec. Centre courses, private cooking schools to accredited training programmes for serious caterers.

Get all the information you can, talk to your local council about permits and requirements, to chefs, caterers and catering schools...and to those professionals in your life whom you feel will be able to advise you on the pitfalls. You need to get your system and your business plan worked out before going into action.
(See also Children's Parties, Party Planner and Events Organiser for more)

CEILING AND WALL CLEANING

Here's a fairly new business that is said to be taking off world-wide: cleaning ceilings and walls in both domestic and commercial premises. The ceilings might be painted, vinyl covered, industrial acoustic tiles or even decorated with ornate plaster. Your job will be to render them free of grease, smoke residue, fungus and bacteria.

One group offering licenses and full training in this treatment facility also promises licensees that there will be 'no ongoing fees or royalties'. However, you may prefer to develop your own cleaning methods or simply buy advice and training.

It may be possible to tie in a business of this nature with other domestic or corporate cleaning services, such as carpet cleaning. This way you can take advantage of the benefits of synergy.

CERAMICS

This can be a great home business if you have the studio and necessary equipment. Even a kiln is not strictly necessary as firing can usually be outsourced.

Producing nothing but pots is unlikely to get you far in a home pottery business. There are just too many imports of these everyday items to compete. It is *creative design* and 'niche' products that are more likely to save the day. Think about producing items for the ***tourist industry***, ***personalised items*** for children, ***promotional*** products for local businesses and so forth.

If you have a bent for sculpture, you might consider producing a few decorated hand-built items: again, consider finding niches in the market. For example, if you live in a tourist area, you might devise products that reflect *local attractions*. Maybe the local lighthouse, the wildlife, the local pub, nearby goldfields, bathing boxes or something else around your area that is famous and draws tourists. Such ideas could present excellent markets for your work.

As an artist/sculptor, you may be horrified by these suggestions of crass commerciality, but you'll feel a lot better about it if the money starts rolling in.

And don't overlook the opportunity of making a few extra dollars on the side from teaching your craft to others. Ceramics is quite popular in most communities. *(See under Art & Craft)*

CHALKBOARD SIGNS

Beautifully designed blackboards - some of them quite ornate - are designed for pubs, restaurants, cafes, delis, fish and chip shops and other food outlets to show information that changes frequently.

These boards usually have a permanent or semi-permanent border (often of fruit, vegetables, sea creatures, arabesques or other designs) and an ornate header, with a blank area left for chalking up the changing information. As the more intricate borders can be expensive to redesign or repair, they are sometimes painted in acrylic. (Check your client's preferences.)

To make these boards, you won't need a great deal of start-up capital but you will need persistence in marketing them. You'll also need to transport them, so a car or 'ute may be required!

Take photos of your finished jobs for your folio and have these with you when you go out looking for work. If you are a beginner and have not yet worked on an assignment, you may need to make a few sample boards at home and photograph them for the folio, as most potential clients will want to see some examples.

CHANDELIER CLEANER
(See Lighting Maintenance)

CHEMICAL MANUFACTURING

Many soaps, detergents, polishes, disinfectants and other household and industrial chemicals can be made at home in your garage and sold for good profit, particularly if you can negotiate high volume commercial and industrial sales.

You might start up a manufacturing business yourself if you have the knowledge - or perhaps you will prefer to buy the necessary training. (Check through some of the home business magazines.)

Start-up costs can be surprisingly low on many high-margin products. Of course, you may prefer to do the planet a favour and produce an organic (chemical free) version of the recognised products. This could be your niche in a sometimes sensitive market.

Check to ensure you have all the necessary knowledge, permits, licences and insurance you need for producing these products at home.

CHILD CARE

Child care offers many options, such as:

- *Nanny*: day care (full or part time) at the client's home or yours.

- *Babysitter* : by the hour, the day or the evening.

- *Children's Taxi*: Transport children from home to school and back each day, take them to various after school activities, to visit relatives...even to the airport! Perhaps you could have the back seat fitted out with DVD players to keep your charges quiet during the journey.

  There are many times that working or ill parents cannot accompany their children and need a safe, reputable and well recognised 'taxi service'. You will need to obtain all licenses and permits, personal checks and insurances required.

- *Day Carer:* If you have a child of your own, why not offer to look after a limited number of other pre-schoolers in your home during school hours? After all, if you have to look after one, you may as well look another 3, 4 or so!

  Of course, there are certain regulations that will have to be met and permits obtained but, if you can fulfil these requirements, caring for other people's children might be a nice source of income for a stay-at-home Mum...and could be great fun for your own child!

- *After-School Carer*: One of the most difficult problems for working parents with school aged children is how to cope with those difficult hours between the finish of school and the time the parents get home from work.

  If you were to collect children from school - or opt for older children who can come to your home on their own - you would save a lot of headaches for the parents...and quite a few dollars for yourself!

  Generally, after school, children need afternoon tea, homework supervision, a period of supervised play and, in some cases, may require dinner if parents come home late.

- *Childcare agency*: In this business, you will be employing others to perform the above childcare services. It can involve a lot of preparation, reference checking, on-going organization and interpersonal skills but it can also be very rewarding.

  It is possible to purchase information packages covering this business that will tell you many of the basics from set-up to running costs, the pitfalls and ways around them. *(Check in the business opportunities magazines and the Yellow Pages.)*

  You may decide to work for an existing agency for a while before starting up on your own in order to accumulate first-hand, on-the-job knowledge.

  Find out all you can before even thinking of starting up, check on any professional prerequisites. insurance requirements etc from the relelvant professionals.

CHILDREN'S ACTIVITY CENTRE - WEEKENDS/HOLIDAYS/PARTIES.

Children's activity centres entertain our very important little citizens at weekends, during holidays, birthdays and so forth. You might simply provide the venue plus the fun and games facilities such as slides, jumping castles, monkey bars and so forth, leaving the supervisory responsibilities to their families. Check out zoning, permits, insurance requirements and so forth before going too far with your plans.

Or you could provide the supervision as well. In this case, children might be dropped off and left with you to enjoy a couple of hours of fun and various crafts while parents shop or work or you might even run parties and other events.
(See also Children's Party Planner) .

CHILDREN'S ART & CRAFT CLASSES

If you have a background in one of the arts or crafts, you may like to consider holding weekend/holiday/after-school art classes or craft groups. A large garage or airy backyard bungalow could make a studio.

If you prefer not to use your own home, you may prefer to rent a hall (the local church hall or recreation centre) by the hour. Holding potentially 'messy' classes like art and craft in a place other than your own studio can be problematic, however, when it comes to cleaning up and transporting art materials back and forth.

If you decide to run these activities in your home, be sure to get permission plus any certification and insurance necessary
(See Children's Party Planner & Organiser)

CHILDREN'S AUDIO CASSETTES

Do you read well? Could you read bedtime stories to children via audio cassettes? These could then be attractively packaged and sold either in sets or singly by mail order or through display ads in local papers and school newsletters.

There are many such tapes around however, so you would need to produce only the best in order to compete in the marketplace.

CHILDREN'S CLOTHING - NEW & SECOND-HAND

- *New:* There are so many excellent business possibilities in this area that we suggest you look in this book under the following headings:
  Sewing, Babies' Merchandise, Children's Merchandise, Screen Printing as well as Arts and Crafts.

- ***Second hand clothing*** can be obtained fairly cheaply from garage sales and op-shops. However, in most of these establishments, garments are rarely ironed or well presented. If you take the time and trouble to value add and repair, wash and iron the clothes, sew on occasional appliqués, frills, buttons or lace where needed, it could make quite a difference to your bottom line.

  If you do not want to sell from home, you could maintain a well laid out stall at a busy weekend market or sell through occasional garage sales.
  (See Garage Sales)

CHILDREN'S FABRIC BOOKS AND WALL-HANGINGS

Activity books and wall hangings made of fabric, such as felt or hand painted cotton, are loved by small children. However, most of these things are fairly labour intensive and would only suit someone wanting a small 'hobby' business.

- Making *fabric books* in a plain, natural fabric like cotton or felt can be very simple. Just fold several equal strips of fabric in half to make the pages, sew along the 'spine' with strong thread, trim right around all raw edges with pinking shears...and you have a 'fabric book'. Place in a cellophane pack.

- Felt 'alphabet' hangings with little pockets for each letter of the alphabet are always popular. Place a felt animal whose name starts with the relevant letter in each initialled pocket.

- Illustrations could be painted in fabric paint or drawn with fabric pens on cotton pages. Always place a piece of waterproof material in the fold of each of the pages when painting to avoid having the paint seep through to the page behind it. Remove this protection when paint is dry, then iron the illustrations thoroughly to heat-set them.

- *Wall hangings* can be *screen printed* if you expect to produce at high volume. Hand painting is suitable for the hobbyist. Finish off the edges, fold the completed panel over at top and bottom to make rod pockets, slip a dowel through each and tie an attractive hanging cord to either end of the top dowel. Finish with tassels if you wish.

- Stunning wall hangings can be made of hand-painted silk if you are talented in this area.
  (See Silk Painting)

- *Fuzzy felt sets*: The background board can be made of felt, glued to a heavy cardboard. Cut out stencils of small animals, birds, numbers, alphabets or any other shapes in coloured felt. These will 'stick' on the background felt so the child can arrange and rearrange them at will to make various 'scenes'.

CHILDREN'S FURNITURE MANUFACTURE

A great business for the woodworker or welder! Consider these few items for a start:

*• general nursery furniture • toy chests • imaginative 'adventure' beds
(that suggest cars, trains, rockets and boats) • functional furniture like
chairs and tables, desks • toys • cubby houses • see-saws • billy carts*

• hobby horses   • pull-along toys   • dolls' houses and mini furniture
• rope ladders & other climbing equipment!

There is no end to the products, both simple and complex, that you could produce and sell. Use off-cuts for games, blocks and rope ladders.

Wooden rocking horses are a perennial favourite with children. Finish them beautifully with flowing mane, tail and eyelashes. Paint face, eyes and coat attractively and don't forget a superb saddle and some shiny stirrups! You may be making heirlooms that could stay in families for centuries. (Maybe you'd better sign your work discreetly!)

If welding is part of your repertoire, you may be able to make a host of other items at home. For example, a whole business could spring up from manufacturing just one item such as *monkey bars, swings* or other *climbing equipment*.

Where do you sell these items? Through various retail outlets, toy stores, weekend markets, your illustrated web page, via letterbox drops, through the classifieds, the Trading Post and *school newsletters*. If you are an organised, conscientious worker, you could make excellent money in this field. If time and space are at a premium, specialise in just one or two items.

CHILDREN'S PARTY PLANNER AND ORGANISER

If you're a parent, you hardly need to be told that big money can be made in organising 'themed' parties for children.

An organiser can provide entertainment only - or go the whole distance with everything from catering, cake, games, dress-up costumes (if required), balloons, even invitations!

Perhaps you could negotiate to hire and transform a spare room in a toy store. It is hard to think of anything more synergistic than toys and parties! Several toy and games shops have rooms set aside for parties. Originally, these may have been nothing more than mere store or junk rooms…yet they have been magically transformed into fairy grottos, 'salons' for make-up and hair parties and so on.

If you understand what children want and enjoy, you might simply go *mobile* as a visiting fairy, clown or any other character that kids love. Clowns and fairies can hold groups of littlies spellbound for hours.

Whether you wish to provide catering as well is up to you …but why not? If there are two of you in the business, one could be the entertainer (the fairy?) and the other, the caterer. With such a combination, the money could conceivably roll in without any magic whatsoever!

Of course, whatever gig you decide on needs to be well rehearsed until you are word-perfect. You'll also need the necessary insurance and permits for whatever you are doing, plus a van or car. If you plan on providing food, further permits will be required.

To organise children's parties successfully, it helps to be genuinely fond of children. These little people can sense when you like them…or if you think they're little brats!

Food is nowhere as important to children as it is to adults…except for the cake! What they love most is to be surprised and entertained. Captivate their interest by a chain of ever-changing, interesting activities, jokes and stories.

The types of parties you could offer are limited only by your imagination. Some suggestions are:

- *Fairy parties* with a Fairy Queen who tells the stories and weaves the magic spells

- *Witches and wizards* with a wizard or witch magician able to mesmerise the crowd with a barrage of incredible magic tricks.

- *Treasure hunt party* with maps, pre-hidden clues and treasure

- *Pool parties*: King Neptune (the party organiser) could tell jokes and fishy stories, arrange water games and do tricks for the invitees who are dressed up as mermaids or mermen. Blow-up sea creatures swim in the pool, submerged prizes need to be retrieved from the bottom of the pool and there are even lycra fishtails for all to wear!
  (Caution: only for older children who can swim! Even then they should be monitored continuously by competent adults!)

- *Craft-making parties* such as plaster moulding, face-painting, box and balloon decorating.

- *Animal nursery* - if you have the necessary permits to keep and transport the animals for this purpose, what a wonderful birthday you could provide!

- *Pony rides:* what about a party with a Western theme?

- *Clown parties*: the clown is not only the party organiser but is also a clever, non-stop entertainer who arranges unusual games, tells funny stories, can do magic tricks that go terribly wrong and endears himself (or herself) to all.

- *Jumping castles* or other hired amusement equipment. *(see under Amusement Machines/Inflatables)*.

- *Make-up* or *hair styling* parties with make-up, body paint, wings and other accessories.

- *Space Invaders parties* (with hired flying saucer rides and bubble machines)

- *Picnic* or *barbeque parties,* run on an appropriate theme. For example: a *cowboy* and/or *cowgirl party* authenticated by wagon and pony rides! If the party is in a place where fire safety, zoning and full surveillance of participants can be organised, a 'campfire' barbeque or sausage sizzle might be possible!

Parties for children can also be run by professional organisers at many other venues such as zoos, theme parks, skating rinks, rock climbing centres, parks or flagged beaches: anyone for *a volleyball party*? It's all a matter of your creativity, a well-practised gig offered in absolute safety...and activities suited to the age and interests of the children.

Although invitees may be charged 'per head', be sure the Birthday Boy or Girl gets the fun for *FREE*!

CHILDREN'S PERSONALISED BOOKS

There can be big money here in producing and marketing these books. Consider:

- *A franchise:* If you're not sure how to start off a business of this type on your own or you doubt your storytelling and bookbinding ability, it is possible to buy a franchise where everything is provided for you. However, be warned: you will need a fair bit of both start-up capital *and* working capital. The franchise itself can cost several thousand dollars...plus you will need to buy ongoing supplies such as the ready-made book covers and other materials *plus* pay for advertising.

  As far as the manufacture of these books is concerned, computers make the process very easy. The software generally consists of pre-written and beautifully illustrated stories into which you insert the name of the individual child...and occasionally, the names of relatives and pets as well.

  You then print out the story, bind the pages in a specially made hard cover (following a most ingenious and simple binding method), trim and voila! Your book is ready!

This method gives you a professional, well-bound book printed in minutes. Many of the pre-written stories available are about famous characters, including several of Disney's best known. Aren't they copyright? Yes, but the franchiser owns and bestows the reprint rights!

As with any franchise, you should check your choice of company very thoroughly before handing over your hard-earned money. The names of franchisers can usually be found in the pages of the various 'business opportunities' magazines and on the internet.

- *D.I.Y.* This is not the easiest exercise to do on your own - *unless* you possess writing, illustration and bookbinding skills...*and* lots of time.

  You may know how to *write and illustrate* a personalised book on your computer - *and* even print it out via your own printer - but how will you bind it professionally without it costing you a leg and an arm? Remember, each single copy of the book must bear the name of a different child and thus must be printed *individually*.

  Until you discover a method of doing this efficiently and economically, you may well prefer to go the route of the well-rehearsed franchise, despite the expense.

CHIMNEY SWEEP - DOMESTIC OR COMMERCIAL

This is one of those essential services that nobody seems to *want* to do - but those who do can make good money, particularly if they market themselves creatively and churn out a torrent of brochures and ads in the right quarters.

The techniques are not difficult to learn - but you will need to be in good physical shape to enable you to cope with the volume of chimneys you will need to sweep to make an income.

Don't want to do the work yourself? Then perhaps you could start a chimney sweep 'agency' and let others do the hard work for you! But be prepared! There could be occasions when one of your sweeps gets sick or does not turn up. Then, guess who will be sweeping the chimney?

Give your business cards to Real Estate Agents, fireplace manufacturers, domestic and commercial cleaning agencies and other likely outlets. Drop your pamphlets in the letterboxes of every house that has a chimney; put ads in the classifieds, in 'antiques and old wares' magazines...and try to get an editorial in a few of the local papers.

CHINA PAINTING

China painting is a beautiful art but unfortunately you will gain more satisfaction than income if you approach it only as a hobby.

If you want to make china painting a business, you will need to find a 'niche market' or a market specific to your area of interest.

- You may be able to devise an *'Australiana' theme* (of national wildflowers, fauna, landscapes and so forth) for sale to souvenir and gift shops or tourist outlets.

- Why not do a bit of research into your *local heroes* and *local scenes*? As examples, if you lived in Broome, you might design pearl fishing scenes to paint on china... or gold mining scenes if you lived near the goldfields. *Ned Kelly* might be a possibility for Glen Rowan - or coral reefs and underwater scenes for tourist areas along the Queensland coast. Brainstorm creatively, then plan well ahead for seasonal and commemorative occasions.

- *Nursery rhyme and fairy story* illustrations could be another 'niche' market...but be careful not to infringe copyright!

- *Personalised plates* might be a great little business, too. For children, ready-to-sell plates, mugs and dishes could carry some of the more popular names while unusual names could be ordered.

- Businesses, too, could place their orders for *promotional* mugs and plates carrying their logo and a greeting.

Advertising could be by way of brochure, newsletters, the classifieds, display ads in special interest magazines and other likely publications. Try selling your work at markets, craft fairs, gift shops, souvenir shops and let clients know that you take orders.

You may decide to hold an occasional exhibition of your work in conjunction with other artists such as painters, ceramicists, glass artists and others who would share the costs of exhibition space.

CHOCOLATES AND CONFECTIONERY

Can you make money producing sweets from your home-sweet-home? You betcha! If they taste good, are packaged attractively and marketed professionally, how will your competitors stand a chance?

Alternatively, you can buy ready made *bulk* sweets & chocolates to package under ***your own irresistibly attractive label*** and place them in jars, boxes, baskets, bottles or wrap them.

- *Personalised chocolate bars*
  Franchises are available for printing personalised chocolate and candy bar wrappers. (Look for information in the pages of the various home business magazines)

  Generally, a *franchise* has you buy the glossy, pre-printed wrappers by mail order ready to personalise with your computer or you can make your own personalised or 'themed' and wrapped chocolate bars.

The dollars in this business are more likely to come from printing personalised wrappers for ***corporate clients***, clubs and large group functions. However, you might also sell your personalised bars to specialty shops, at your weekend stall at a market or by mail order from your web page.

Take orders for birthdays, Christmas, New Year, weddings (white chocolate?), engagements, bucks' nights and so forth.

Making sweets for the commercial market is not as easy as making chocolate crackles for the school fete. Check that you have all certification or licences needed to cover the production of these foodstuffs at home.

CLEANING SERVICE - DOMESTIC OR CORPORATE

Don't turn your nose up at this one! If you want to become a multi-millionaire, the service industry is just waiting to make you into one!

If domestic or commercial cleaning is a new world to you, it would be wise to gather first-hand experience by getting a job with an accredited agency for a short period just to see how it all works. Go out on your own only when you have acquired the know-how, spoken to others in the business and understand the traps and pitfalls.

After establishing your own business, you may decide to gradually introduce *other* related services to assist your busy clients: ironing, dry cleaning, blind cleaning, carpet cleaning, ceiling and wall cleaning, lawn maintenance, dog clipping and other services that can be indispensable to them!

If you are an agent for any of these extra services, you will get a fee each time they do a job for your clients, so the money starts to really add up!

It's important to start off small - but it shouldn't take too long before you're walking tall! There is no end to what a smart, dependable person can make in a service industry these days.

CLEAN-UP SERVICE

Would you like to help clean-up after such disasters and emergencies as accidents, fires, floods, storms, wind damage etc? Working with insurance companies, emergency services, police, fire, estate agents in this way can be hard work at times and the things you may have to do could be very unpleasant but, if you are a person who gets joy out of helping others in dire need and making their lives livable again, this job could be very satisfying for you.

CLOCK PRODUCTION

It is possible to buy basic clock mechanisms quite cheaply, create or design *specialty clock faces* and put them together in no time! Here are a few ideas:

- *For art lovers:* maybe a wooden art palette with two brushes for hands and a squirt of different coloured paint in place of the numbers.

- *For racing enthusiasts:* Bet your bottom dollar on a green flock clock face that looks like a 'race track'. Trim it with a tiny white wooden rail around the perimeter. Affix small lightweight horses to each of the clock hands and see which one wins!

- *For children:* how about painting your clock face to look like nursery scenes or well known children's stories? But beware of infringing copyright! Alternatively, your illustration could be scanned into the computer, then printed out to size and *pasted* onto the clock face. You might illustrate a scene showing Cinderella running down the palace staircase, closely followed by Prince Charming. Her glass slipper lies discarded on a stair while the *clock on the palace wall* shows the time...

- *For cat, dog or bird lovers:* a different breed of cat, dog or bird might illustrate each hour.

- *For fishermen:* a different species of fish for each hour of the day. Think up some creative ideas of your own.

You might like to try 'test marketing' your specialty clocks through special interest clubs and groups, newsletters, special interest magazines, weekend markets, gift shops, home decorating shops and other outlets as well as from your own internet page. If the test market goes well, you might be on a winner!

CLOTHING – PRELOVED

Second hand clothing can be bought cheaply at garage sales and op shops so you should have no trouble in piling up stock. Sometimes, just a good wash and iron, a bit of mending and an appliqué here and there can make these clothes look almost new.

To make money out of preloved garments from a home base, you may need to do the actual repair and preparation at home but sell the goods at a weekend market stall. Dress your stall elegantly, display and accessorise garments as if you were in Fifth Avenue and hopefully, you'll find the extra effort pays off.

(If you want to be more adventurous in the 'pre-loved' arena, see Bridal or Evening Clothes Hire in this book.)

COACHING (EDUCATIONAL)

Knowing your subject is one thing but being able to break it down to understandable increments and having the ability to explain it at a level the student can follow is another. If you have such a gift, coaching could earn you quite a good income!

- *Coaching Tertiary Subjects:*
  Try to obtain permission to place your advertisements on *every* noticeboard, in every building in your local University or TAFE college. This represents *target* advertising - and it's usually free! Also, try placing ads in the local classifieds and newsletters.

  Your clients could be tutored on an hourly basis in their own homes, your home or even on campus if you can find a quiet area of the Uni or college.

- *Secondary Subjects:*
  Coaching is sometimes carried out in the teacher's home, sometimes in the student's. Advertise your services in school newsletters, local newspaper classifieds, community noticeboards and through letterbox drops.

- *Preschool Subjects:*
  If you love being with teeny tots and have had some teaching or pre-school experience, help prepare littlies with their reading or math skills in small

groups or individually. Be sure you have all insurance and permits necessary if you are teaching in your own home.

COACHING *(professional, special interest or hobby)*

If you have a qualification or experience in any field, you can usually find people who would like to learn about it. Art, music, singing, writing, literacy, craft, languages, fly fishing, sailing, cooking…no matter what!… help others understand the subject and rake in the dollars at the same time.

Here are just a handful of subjects for which people may require coaching:

- Acting for stage & screen
- Aerobics - high impact, low impact, over 50's etc
- Art: *drawing, watercolour, pastel, oil, acrylic, pen & wash, pencil, mixed media and so forth. Will you teach landscape, seascape, abstract, wildlife art, portraiture (children, pets, traditional, glamour), a combination of styles? Maybe you'll teach painting on velvet or silk, collage, art history, arrange gallery tours!*
- Astrology
- Audio Production
- Basketball
- Beauty therapy
- Blind making
- Bookbinding
- Bookkeeping
- Boat building
- Bowling
- Business subjects
- Cake decorating
- Carpentry - for adults, teens or especially for children!
- Cartooning
- Ceramics
- China painting
- Climbing
- Computer graphics
- Computers
- Computer applications
- Cooking:
  Cordon Bleu, Asian and other ethnic styles, Pritikin, Low Fat/Low Salt, Fast and Easy, bread making
- Crafts *(See under Art and Craft)*:
  drawing, decoupage, screen printing, weaving, leatherwork, upholstery,

picture framing, leadlighting, glass blowing, carving, jewellery making,
woodworking, sculpture, gift-making, knitting, crochet, embroidery, T-shirt
painting and printing

- Dancing:
ballet, classical, modern, jazz, Spanish, belly, Greek, Hula, Scottish, Irish,
Indian and other folk dancing, ballroom, Line Dancing, Square Dancing,
tap, rap
(Make it fun with special *themed* evenings where your students dress in the
appropriate costumes, contribute a national dish for the 'feasting' afterwards
and dance in competitions for which you give prizes.)
- Digital Photography
- Doll Making *(See under listing)*
- Dramatic Art/Speech Training
- Dressmaking and/or Tailoring
- Driving
- English:
preschool, primary, secondary, remedial, advanced or tertiary, journalism
- Feldenkrais
- Finance
- Furniture making:
upholstery, re-upholstery, furniture finishing, repair
- Gardening
- Greeting Cards
- Home Decorating
- Herbalist
- Knitting:
hand or machine
- Languages
- Massage
- Martial arts:
kung fu, karate, tae kwon do, judo, jujitsu, aikido
- Mathematics
- Meditation
- Millinery
- Motivational subjects
- Music:
guitar, piano, organ, violin, trumpet, sax, drums etc
- Naturopathy
- Nutrition
- NLP (Neuro Linguistic Programming)
- Organic Gardening Skills
- Parenting Skills
- Personal Trainer / Physical Fitness
- Philosophy
- Personal Wellbeing

- Photography:
  general or specialist: babies, children, wildlife, life, landscape, glamour
- Picture Framing
- Poetry
- Public Speaking
- Quilt Making
- Reading Skills:
  various age groups
- Reflexology
- Riding
- School subjects
  primary, secondary
- Selling
- Sewing:
  general, tailoring, machine & overlocking, embroidery, quilting, finishing, pattern making and a host of affiliated skills
- Shiatsu
- Silk painting
- Singing
- Skating (ice)
- Skating (rollerblade)
- Skiing (water or snow)
- Speech training
- Stained glass
- Surfboarding
- Sweet making
- Swimming
- Tai Chi
- Tailoring
- Tennis
- Toy Making
- Typing
- University-level subjects
- Video/camcorder
- Volleyball
- Water skiing
- Weaving
- Weight loss
- Wind surfing
- Woodworking skills:
  children, teens, adults
- Writing:
  children, teens, feature writing, Romance, fiction, autobiography, editing, biography, writing for radio, screen, TV and stage, crime, humour, history, school magazines, business, letter-writing, journal writing.

Whew! What a list! Are you able to teach any of these subjects?

Depending on your subject, you may find it best to offer only private tuition at first until you build up sufficient students, then start classes if you feel it is warranted.

Teaching can represent a good sideline when you are starting off a home business as it gives you quite a bit of flexibility: you can arrange lessons at times that suit a second part-time or casual job as well as gaining the extra income.
(For a different slant on coaching, look under Information Products)

COIN OPERATED MACHINES (AMUSEMENT & VENDING)

You won't need your own arcade for these machines! Just negotiate with shop owners and proprietors in high-traffic, commercial areas to place your machines in strategic positions on their premises, remembering that, to make these machines make money, position is everything!

Consider sporting and entertainment venues, hotels, cafeterias, delis, cinemas, milk bars, hamburger outlets, pizza parlours, shopping malls, tertiary institutes, railway and bus stations. *Your* part in all this, once the machines are in position, is the maintenance once or twice a week, and *unloading the money*!

What could you sell? Here are some ideas:

• Sweets	• Sandwiches
• Nuts	• Toys
• Children's rides	• Videos
• Jukebox music	• Driving & other games
• Shooting games	• Soccer tables
• Air hockey	• Pinball games

(See also under Amusement Machines & Vending Machines)

COIN OPERATED WASHING/DRYING MACHINES

- *Washing machines and dryers:* Lease your machines and dryers to body corporates, motels, laundrettes and so forth. You will need to provide maintenance.

- *Laundromat:* How can a commercial laundromat be classed as a home-based business? Well, it can't...unless you have a shop and residence combined! Such a set-up may work out quite well for you if you want a job where you do not have to be on duty all the time or you have another home-based business to look after as well. A simple *'ring bell for service'* sign might free you from the shop for much of the time and allow you to get on with other duties in the residence.

Value-add to your business by offering other essential services as well such as an ironing or mending service. These services can generally be out-sourced to local workers from whom you extract a fee.

Machines can be bought or leased. If council will permit, put in a coin operated machine for tea, coffee and cold drinks as well!
(See Amusement Machines, Food Vending Machines)

COINS

Collecting and trading coins and medals can be a fascinating and fun-filled hobby... but you need to have a fair bit of expertise behind you before risking your capital in a business of this type.

Trading can take place in many ways: with other collectors: through the classifieds, the internet, through numismatic clubs and magazines, relevant newsletters, the Trading Post, garage sales, coin shops, antique stores, at exhibitions.

If you trade through internet auctions, be cautious. You need to understand the culture and learn the methods available of ensuring that what you are buying is indeed what you *think* you are buying.

COLLECTIBLES/MEMORABILIA

This can be absorbing as a hobby and financially rewarding as a business, especially if your interest is in rare or unique items.

'Collections' can be made up of virtually anything, from coins to teapots, netsukes to Barbie dolls, old records to teddy bears...but to make money from them, you need to be well informed, always on the prowl and extremely organised!

Become a *specialist* in what you're looking for. Know the where, what, why, when and how of every aspect of your passion! Keep a data base of auction and sales results of items that interest you, learn about their previous owners, absorb anecdotes and historical facts. If you do this, you will not only be well ahead of your competitors in this fascinating road to riches, you will be less likely to have the wool pulled over your eyes by some charlatan.

Collectibles and memorabilia can pop up anywhere: charity shops, antique shops, friends' attics, bazaars, local markets, jumble sales… even on nature strips..but ensure there are no council laws against your collecting these 'finds' in your area. You need to be ever vigilant. When it comes to bargaining for that prime piece you've been searching for over the past 20 years, you will need to keep a poker face!

Whether you start up a shop, kiosk, stall or simply trade from home, nothing will take the place of *networking*! When you can afford it, take a stand at your local antique fair! Keep in touch with other collectors, too, via special interest newsgroups, bulletin boards and chat rooms.

Consider some of the following for a start:

stamps	medals	coins
paintings	first edition books	fountain pens
watches	Barbie dolls	Disney figures
old magazines	teapots	Beatlemania
famous autographs	old wind-up toys	ancient cameras
old clocks	pioneer items	unusual shells
rocks & fossils	Toby jugs	old medical equipment
ancient jars/bottles	teddy bears	old dental equipment

(See also under Antiques)

COMPANION/CARER FOR THE ELDERLY

You may be surprised to learn how many elderly people sit looking at the four walls of their room day after day, unable to go out by themselves because they are disabled in some way...or are simply too frail to cope alone with traffic and crowds. However, many residents of Nursing Homes and others are able to manage outings to relatives, a movie or shopping if they are accompanied by a carer.

If your client is wheelchair bound, a 'maxi-taxi' can ferry both you and your client to your destination and back; the wheelchair is simply rolled up a portable ramp into the cab.

Assisting elderly people can be very rewarding. There are many levels of care that one can offer, depending on one's experience and qualifications. If you are an ex-nurse, for example, your options will be far greater than someone who is without any qualifications whatsoever.

You will find many opportunities, too, for full-time or live-in companions - a good job for a retired widow/widower who does not relish living alone.

While volunteer carers are in desperately short supply throughout the community -

and probably always will be - there are many thousands of financially well-off older people who are happy to pay good money to have a carer take them out for the day.

Some excellent agencies have arisen from arranging companionship and outings for the elderly: your's could be one! However, it would be wise to join an agency at first, to learn the ropes.

Do NOT, under any circumstances, take on the role of carer or companion without the appropriate insurance, not even for day care. If you are not with an agency and can't afford to arrange insurance for yourself and your clients, then don't take on this job!

COMPUTER-RELATED SERVICES

If you ever wanted to know what it feels like to be a hero, ***Computer Servicing*** could do it for you! Whatever the problem or need, if you can fix it, your frazzled clients are likely to welcome you with open arms!

There are many home-based opportunities for the computer-savvy, both in the domestic and commercial arenas. Many may necessitate being on-site; others can be run totally from your home.

Here is just a handful that may get you thinking:
- Manufacturing and assembly
- Repairs and maintenance
- Networking
- Installation
- Software creation
- Upgrades
- Data organization
- Training: software
- Training: hardware
- Web page creation

(See also Computer graphics, Desktop publishing, Writing)

CONCRETE CLEANER

If you have the tools, all you need is the patience - and the ability to market your business. When advertising, think outside the square! As they say: 'don't sell the *method*, sell the *benefit!*'

Nobody wants to know about your equipment or how good it is. They just want their job done well. Tell them how good their paths, drives and patios will look when you have completed the task, how fresh their houses will appear.

Appeal to home owners and sellers as well as commercial premises. Leave your card and brochure with all local Real Estate agents as well. And, when you're on the job, make certain you have that ever-important sandwich board outside advertising what you do.

CONCRETING

For a talented concreter, this is one of those perfect home businesses that could earn you heaps if you build up a good reputation. Work on small *residential* jobs to large *commercial* sites. or *specialise* in a certain line like pools, concrete tanks, standardised steps, pontoons and jetties. You have a world of choices open to you!

Many 'concrete beautification' products and impressions of slate and other materials are becoming exceedingly popular, particularly for the residential market. You might like to think about impressions and spray-ons as an adjunct to your business.

Another business that is going well is slip-free surface treatment for public places like pools, hospitals, shopping centres and so forth. This could fit in well with your finished product.

CONSULTING

Consulting is the retiree's dream and the retrenched executive's saviour. So be sure to keep your old networks alive! *Consulting* can cover a multitude of services and subjects and can often provide those who really know their subject with extremely high remuneration. There are always people wanting to learn from 'experts' so get ready to pass on your knowledge and expertise!

Organisations are outsourcing many of their specialist services these days in order to cut departmental costs: accounting and bookkeeping services, recruitment, PR, time management consultants...the list is endless! Whatever you can do well should be capable of being turned into a service.

You will need a self-contained office, preferably with its own entrance. If you cannot arrange this where you live, you may prefer to search out a local serviced office to rent on an 'as needed' hourly basis for special clients.

CONVENIENCE STORE

A convenience store is far from convenient for you when it it not integrated with your house. If you want a store of this nature, make sure it has a comfortable attached residence in which you are happy to live. Family members can then take turns in manning the shop or lying down to have a snooze, as hours can be long.

Many entrepreneurs take on run-down businesses of this nature, improve them, then sell them at their peak. Excellent profits can often be made this way.

COOKING CLASSES

If you know how to cook, you can probably teach others. However, if space is at a premium in your kitchen or you prefer not to teach cooking in your own home, there is a much easier way to pass on your knowledge. Furthermore, it is a way that may bring you fame and fortune as well: through producing your own cooking classes on video and DVD! Today's cameras and computers have made producing one's own films a cinch and the sales of info videos in increasing at an incredible rate.
(Turn to Information Products, Desktop Publishing, Video Production, Catering.)

CORRESPONDENCE SCHOOL

If you are or have been a teacher or trainer in an art, craft or business subject and have a network of teacher friends, you may be able to team up and organise a private correspondence school offering subjects in which each of you is qualified.

If doing this on your own, perhaps you will devise a 'niche' course that can be marketed to special interest groups through their magazines and newsletters.

COSMETICS MANUFACTURE

There is a plethora of people making and bottling beauty cremes and potions for sale at their kitchen tables all over the countryside! However, to compete, these cosmetics must yield results! They must also be well packaged, beautifully labelled and well marketed.

It is best to start off small with just one or two effective products containing 'natural' ingredients - and build up a name selling these. Stress the fact that they are 'natural' in your advertising, highlighting their benefits over more traditional products.

Research all you can about skin care, then use that knowledge in your manufacturing and marketing! Lecture on beauty and skin care at charity lunches and clubs. Write a beauty book. Make a promotional film. *Make* yourself an expert!

COURIER

You'll need a van, a driver's licence, a great sense of direction...and some customers! And you'd be wise to accumulate some smart marketing knowledge before even thinking of starting up because you'll have plenty of competition!

Advertise, network, get editorials, do your PR stints everywhere it counts. You'll be constantly working against the clock but this is a business where time really counts. In your advertising, emphasise your *timeliness* and *reliability*.

If you just want to work locally, you may be able to tie your service in with another courier whose service is more widespread.

CROCHET
(See Knitted Goods)

CROSS STITCH SUPPLIES & INSTRUCTION

Do you love cross stitch? Are you able to dream up some unusual and outstanding cross stitch designs? Could you write a booklet of instruction to go with your patterns and designs? Is your ability such that you could run classes on cross stitch? If you can do any of these things, you have a potential business!

Advertise in the classifieds, in craft magazines or newsletters and by brochure in craft and embroidery shops. Selling these supplies by mail order and direct mail is fairly straight forward but you do need to advertise in the right places.

CRUISE CONSULTANT

These days, travellers have become a little less willing to travel by plane, with the result that cruise ships are having a field day.

However, security is not the only benefit on people's minds. Being able to pull into port in a foreign country and not have to pack or unpack is a boon. It means that the moment you arrive, you can start exploring without wasting a minute.

You might prefer to arrange cruises in a very small way simply by organising groups of travellers for available tours and accept a commission - or a free trip if you're lucky - or arrange your own.
(See under Tour Organiser, Travel Guide)

CRYSTALS

The New Age has given birth to many a fascinating crystal shop, offering jewellery, accessories, crystals in their natural state or polished, as well as fashioned into ornaments or sculptures.

When selling crystals, there are many ways you can add to your stock. Make up little packets or exquisite bags of various crystals, tie with ribbon, then add a tiny information booklet about that stone's alleged health and mystical properties.

Dream up mail order promotions with crystal packs, maybe even generalised monthly horoscopes, for birthdays using the appropriate birthday stones and colours. Arrange seminars at local libraries or give talks at club meetings and lunches, educating the audience on the mysterious properties of your stones - while displaying your wares for sale, of course.

Some proprietors make much of their own jewellery while waiting for customers, whether at home or manning a market stall. People love to watch such demonstrations. Much jewellery is strung with elastic these days, so coping with difficult hardware like clasps is not really necessary. It is quite simple to string combinations of prepared stones to make bracelets and necklaces.

Rummage around at garage sales each weekend for second hand jewellery. Some of the beads and tokens from this preloved junk can often be used to enhance your jewellery.

CUBBY HOUSES FOR CHILDREN
(See Children's Furniture and Carpentry)

CURTAINS & DRAPES

You'll have a lot of competition from the big stores…but as you are working from home, you will not have their mighty overheads! If you are a fast worker, organised and able to make some of those painfully expensive accessories like pelmets and jabots reasonably cheaply, go for it!

You may be able to organise others to do piecework for you if the workload becomes too great or you are faced with jobs that are beyond your expertise. Of course, this can cut your margin to shreds but it also means you can take on a far greater volume of work to make up for it. Such a set-up requires very good organsation, however.

Let the world know you are there through advertising widely in newspapers, letterbox drops, a notice on your house wall, your business card and notices in all local shops you frequent and so forth.

You might also think about writing an illustrated book – something along the lines of *'Beautify Your Home With Drapes And Curtains'*. Give free talks and lectures showing slides of your work to interested women's groups and luncheons.

You might take your folio around to decorator stores, too, but these places will want a huge slice of your profit if they commission you to do any work for them!

D

DECKCHAIR HIRE

It's all the rage in Europe on the beaches and in the parks; so why not here as well? All that's needed is a quantity of good quality deck chairs, a receipt book…and *you*!

You will also need council permission to set up your hire business but once that's negotiated, it should be all plain sailing. To be sure that customers don't run off with the chairs when they've finished using them, they should be charged a deposit large enough to cover the cost of replacing them at wholesale price.

After a few weeks, when you've shown that you can maintain a much-appreciated and well run service, you may be able to talk the council into allowing you to sell a few useful products like 'sunsafe' items (sun hats, beach mats, towels, thong sandals and even sun glasses) from your stand. If there is no food outlet or food van around the area, you may even be permitted to sell cold drinks, ice creams or watermelon pieces as well! If you don't ask, you'll never know!

DESKTOP PUBLISHING

There is so much business out there for a determined, energetic person with DTP capabilities…but you need to let people know you're there! Continuous advertising, marketing and networking are vitally important to your success.

There are quite a few courses available on DTP, some by correspondence, but one needs to be very careful to choose from only the most reputable.

Here are few opportunities that you may like to investigate:

- *Corporate and club newsletters*: your target would be special interest groups, large businesses and clubs and you would offer to produce their monthly or quarterly newsletter for them. Be prepared for quite a bit of hard work, however, as not all the information will be handed to you on a plate. Much of it you will have to ask for or research and follow up yourself as club members are often unused to the deadlines associated with publishing..

- *Produce your own newsletter* if you have a particular passion or talent and are able to write about it.

  You may be able to buy a *mailing list* of people who could be interested in the subject. Send each a brochure about your coming publication, outlining the proposed contents and assuring potential readers that each edition will be thoroughly researched.

   Your ads need to convince likely clients of the enjoyment and knowledge they will derive from your publication.

  Perhaps you could offer subscribers a *bonus* related to the subject as an incentive to join up for the whole year. Of course, if you do this, you will need to be sure that you can fulfil your promises and produce an *entire 12 months' worth* of information.

- *Writing – Feature Articles*
  What are readers interested in? How can you find out? Read the newspapers and magazines, listen to radio, watch TV and learn about the topics of the day. Absorb

the facts, then research them further and provide a few as yet unknown facts and figures.

Nothing sells like the words of an expert so, if you can get a few interviews with people who are recognised for really knowing their subject, you should soon be on the road to success!

Don't bother writing personal opinion pieces unless you love getting rejection letters! Publishers only want to hear what *'experts'* say or believe!

It is a good idea to send a *query letter* to the editor of your target magazine or newspaper *before* sending in your manuscript. Then, if you get a green light, do a final draft for good measure, double check it - then send it off.

If your submission is rejected, re-read your article and see if you can make any improvements. Then market it to the *next* likely publisher!

Most writers get rejected from time to time, and it is not necessarily because their submission wasn't well written. It may be that the publishers had recently published a similar article or have something like it already in the system.

- ### *Writing - Children's Stories*
  To get a feel for the type of writing children enjoy, read the most popular children's books on the market. Your local library should be able to help you out with a list. If you intend to write for a particular age, focus on books written for that age group.

  Again, you would do well to become a member of some Writers Clubs (e.g. Federation of Australian Writers). The annual subscription fee is usually very low when compared with the invaluable information you receive each quarter from their newsletters. Many major publishers list their current requirements in such newsletters, telling you whether they are accepting new material or not, what they are looking for and how to go about submitting your manuscript to them.

  Another possible avenue for children's writing could be the school magazines. Send for an upcoming subject list.

  Important:
  send your manuscript only after you have sent a query letter…or at least spoken to the editor. Unsolicited manuscripts generally end up on the 'slush pile' and can sit there for months or even years!

- *Writing - Fiction*
  Want money *and* satisfaction? Then write *non-fiction*. However, if you're happy with *satisfaction only*, go ahead and indulge yourself in fiction!

  Few fiction writers make it to the top…but that's not to say that you won't be one of the lucky ones! Maybe you'll be another Jeffrey Archer or Barbara Cartland! However, no matter how confident you are of your ability, don't give up your day job…not yet, anyway!

  As suggested under Feature Writing (above), it benefits most would-be writers to join a reputable Writers' Club. Be guided by their advice and the publishers' requirements that are found in their newsletters.

  These newsletters also list up-coming writing competitions which you may decide to enter. It sure will help sales if you can say on the dust jacket of your new book that you're a 'prize-winning author'!

- *Writing – Plays for TV, Radio, Stage and Screen*
  If you have a talent for writing plays for TV, radio and screen, you should be able to write your own ticket! There are never enough good writers of this genre.

  However, if you can write superb comedy, lucky you! You may as well go buy the yacht and mansion right now!
  (For more information on this subject, go to the main entry under Writing.)

- *Writing 'How-To' Books for Mail Order*
  Many writers prefer not to have to deal with publishers. With desk top publishing software so freely available and easy to use, many people are writing and publishing their own books.

  If you have special knowledge of a particular subject, or you know an expert or two willing to divulge a few 'secrets', perhaps you could produce an information or *'how-to'* book for mail order. The book could be produced in many forms: a) you could take it along to a printer and have it 'perfect bound', b) make it up yourself in a loose leaf 3-ring binder, c) have it spring-bound or present it in any other way you wish. You could even make an audio book by *recording* it into your computer, then making a CD!

  If you judge the 'how-to' market correctly and write what it is clamouring for, you could do very well! Sports people, adventurers, artists and crafts people, finance and business executives all have interesting and potentially saleable information to impart.

Of course, you only publish information about which you are 100% certain and quote only recognised experts! The crux of your success will be the quality and efficacy of your *information*.

Go to see a solicitor if you're in any doubt that readers may misunderstand or misconstrue the information in your book.
(Find out more under Information Products)

DIDGERIDOO MANUFACTURER/TRADER

The didgeridoo is a wonderfully-sounding Aboriginal musical instrument, and is sought by collectors, artefacts dealers, galleries, museums, souvenir hunters and tourists both in Australia and overseas.

There is quite an art to making didgeridoos but, if you have a good musical ear and can find an expert didgeridoo maker to teach you this craft, you are bound to find it most absorbing.

If you prefer to be a reseller only, finding a reliable source of instruments and ensuring dependable delivery will be crucial. While certain markets will accept only authentic didgeridoos, there is still plenty of scope for commercially made instruments in the tourist and souvenir markets.

There is also a small market among musicians and quite a few have added the haunting sounds of the didgeridoo to their arrangements.

DIRECT MAIL

Direct mail is becoming more popular every day. It is a method of promoting your business directly to a target market. However, where simple Mail Order advertises to the mass market and must then wait for interested customers to respond, Direct Mail actively searches out and finds likely customers. This is often done through obtaining mailing lists and names of people who have already professed interest in similar deals or bought similar products.

Your target market could also include people who have bought from you before. New customers might be found in special interest clubs and classes or be workers in a particular industry relating to your product.

If you are new to Direct Mail and have no idea how to locate an appropriate group, contacting a reputable list broker and renting a list of *relevant* names can often be a more sure-footed way to go. Before you do this, however, ask yourself whether the

Yellow Pages might reveal the list you are looking for – for free. (If your product is for schools, for example, a full list is right there beside your telephone!)

Catalogues or literature are sent directly to potential clients in various ways: via mail, telemarketing, e-mail or even handed to participants at special interest exhibitions (*after* obtaining permission, of course. For example, if you had a product specifically for dogs, you might distribute your literature at dog shows and to veterinarians. Even letterbox drops could conceivably work as Direct Mail in certain instances - for example, where all the recipients have something in common that could benefit from your product.
(See also under Mail Order and Mailing Lists)

DIRECTORS' CHAIRS – PERSONALISED

Want something a little out of the ordinary for the star-struck? How about buying up some plain directors' deck chairs and *personalising* them as they do in Hollywood? On the back of the chair, you could screen print in large, white block letters the recipient's name...followed by the magic word *Director* or *Star*.

These chairs would be a great gift for the budding actor, singer, musician – in fact for entertainers and dreamers of all types.They would also be the most sought-after chair at the weekend barbeque!
(See Screen Printing)

DISPLAY STANDS FOR ART EXHIBITIONS

This could be a good home business for a carpenter or welder. Wood or metal stands are bought or hired largely by artists, photographers and galleries for their showings.

While there are many types of stands available, one popular, easily made and easily transportable type has a frame made from square or tubular steel. The fill, which holds the paintings or other exhibits, can be anything from perforated hardboard to canvas-covered board. Exhibition display stands are usually double-sided so that exhibits can be hung on both sides.

Dismantled stands can be stored in the home garage. A van will be necessary if you decide to offer a pick-up and delivery service.

Your service could be advertised in art magazines, at tertiary institutes, in art and craft societies' newsletters, on posters and pamphlets in art and framing shops and to private art schools, galleries and photographic studios.

You may be permitted to place a small poster or pile of leaflets around any exhibitions for which you're supplying stands. If the convenors do not want this, they may at least mention your business on the back of their catalogue if you request this.

DOG/CAT BREEDING

To make any worthwhile money in dog or cat breeding, you would need to deal in top lines and be fully au fait with what you are doing. Run professionally, this could represent a nice little part-time or sideline business.

Another possibility might be to breed and train *guard dogs* if you are able to do the training yourself and then, sell the trained animals as a going concern.

However, check on council regulations regarding the number of dogs you can maintain on your property at any one time. Many areas have strict rules about this.

DOGHOUSE MANUFACTURE

This could be an excellent, flexible 'at-home business' for a handyman or carpenter. Doghouses could be made to customer specification while you run a line or two of your own design. Samples of stock items could be displayed around the entry to your work shed for clients to see. A folio of sketches or photos could display others you have built. Larger doghouses might be constructed 'on site' at the client's property.

Your work could be advertised under *made-to-order* or *pets' accessories* in the classifieds and in dog magazines and newsletters. You would also be wise to distribute flyers far and wide: to dog clubs, training schools, veterinarians, pet shops and dog shows. A few samples of your work might be offered to the pet shops on a 'sale or return' basis.

Use your imagination in designing your dog houses: will they have windows and porches, be quaint or modern, look like beach houses or ranch houses? Your success will depend on Fido's satisfaction

DOG MINDING/PRIVATE KENNEL

As we have mentioned previously, there is often a limit to the number of dogs permitted on any one property at a time.

However, looking after just two dogs at a time might be sufficient to help the finances or fit in with the running of another home-based business.

Dogs don't need your attention all the time. They only need to be walked, fed, played with a little, groomed and their quarters kept clean.

Once your private minding service gets a good name, you will probably find holidaying dog owners will prefer your caring service in a private home to a kennel, even if you do cost a little more!

You will need to work out the costs involved and negotiate prices with suppliers of dog food and other necessities. Some clients insist on special diets for their little darlings and all this must be factored into your quote.

DOG LIFE-JACKET MANUFACTURE

There are thousands of dogs who love to hop aboard their masters' and mistresses' boats at weekends and holidays…but, unfortunately, accidents do happen.

Certainly if there is a boating accident when there are children aboard, the first priority will be the children, not the dog. However, if the dog-passenger is wearing a simple, buoyant but comfortable life vest, it's life might also be saved.

If you can develop a simple, super-comfortable canine life jacket, it could become a hit with boat-loving dog owners all over the world! If it does, you should be able to buy yourself that yacht you've always dreamed about…and a seafaring dog to enjoy it with!

DOG PEDIGREE CERTIFICATES
(See under Personalised Products)

DOG PRODUCTS
(See under Pet Products)

DOG TRAINING

Are you a 'dog whisperer' at heart? There are some people who have 'a gift' for training animals! If you're one of them, you might make a good living teaching poor helpless dog owners...i.e. those people who are actually owned by their dogs!...to regain their freedom and self-respect!

Visit your unruly canine students at their homes - or train them in yours if you prefer. Maybe you could arrange to give lessons in the park when the weather is fine.

Depending on where you live, you may only be permitted a certain number of dogs on your property at one time - so check with the local council.

DOG WALKING/FEEDING FOR ABSENT OWNERS

This little hobby business can bring you extra dollars while keeping you in tiptop physical condition, especially if you enjoy walking and love animals.

Unfortunately, there's a limit to how often you can walk in a day and how much time there is to do it! For this reason, don't count on this job to make you big money.

You might decide to complement an 'at-home' business with dog walking as a *sideline*. If you are involved in sitting down a lot in an at-home job, walking dogs two or three times a day could give you all the exercise – and extra pocket money - you need.

DOG WASH AND GROOM (MOBILE)

This is a business that has really taken off in recent years. You might be able to start it up yourself 'from scratch' if you have been in the business before or have had a lot of experience with grooming animals. However, if you are a newbie, an easier way might be to buy a franchise. A *reputable franchise* not only gives you 'know-how' but can generally furnish you with clients as well.

If you prefer to fully *create your own dogwash* service but have never had any experience in this area, it may be wise to at least get yourself a job with one of the well established mobile dog washes for a short while to familiarise yourself with how things work - and don't work! - in that arena.

A van and equipment can be quite expensive so try to procure a second hand outfit: the dogs will never know! You will also need a mobile phone...and a warm coat, too! It can be cold and draughty in some of those vans in the winter, especially when a recently bathed mutt shakes his wet coat all over you!

DOG WEAR

You may find this hard to believe but some clever entrepreneurs are making *obscene* incomes from selling dogs' clothes and accessories! This could be big, big business for you, too, if you have a sense of canine style, can sew well…and know how to market!

What items could you manufacture? Coats, rain coats, hats, shoes - and accessories such as collars and leads. The more up-market, unusual and attractive your products, the quicker you could be a millionaire!

For sales, you might use the classifieds, display ads in appropriate canine and other magazines, dog club newsletters, letterbox drops, pet shops, school newsletters, gift shops as well as weekend markets and from a stand at dog shows.

Cyberspace is full of dogs! So, a top class, illustrated web page that is well maintained, well promoted and handled with flair, could be the ultimate sales route. If you find you can't manage all the work on your own, you can always outsource! Other people love to work at home, too, and will be happy to sew or do deliveries for you.
(See also under Pet Products & Dogs' Life Jacket Manufacture)

DOLL MAKING

Turn dolls into dollars! The doll business is no longer 'kids' stuff'. In fact, it could explode into a multi-million dollar business for the serious entrepreneur.

Expect a bonus, too, of tax-free travel to the many seminars and trade shows around the country and around the world if you go into this field in a big way.

Porcelain doll manufacture can be a big money-spinner yet the art is fairly easy to come by. There are numerous doll-making workshops in the suburbs which can be attended day or evening. If you love to work with your hands, enjoy sewing, attending sewing circles and trade and doll shows, this craft could be as satisfying emotionally as it could be rewarding financially.

Whether you want a part time, low key business selling from home or a huge involvement with big returns in the professional arena, you could tailor a doll making business to suit your requirements - providing you have the will, marketing knowledge and talent for the craft.

There are many 'niche' markets and spin-off products for dolls. As in every endeavour, however, it is the creative, determined and highly entrepreneurial person who is likely to reap the advantages.

Perhaps you could come up with some unusual line of dolls. For example, could you make emu egg-sized heads of historical figures such as prime ministers, presidents and so forth then attach them to small, authentically dressed bodies? Actually, I wouldn't mind buying one of those myself! They could become collectors' items one day!
(See Dolls' Clothes, below)

DOLLS' CLOTHES

Would you like to make and sell beautifully styled dolls' clothes for fetes, craft markets, gift and toy outlets...or make special orders for **valuable antique dolls**? This latter job could entail your starting a collection of old laces and fabrics as well as more modern fabrics and accessories. You might also offer a repair service.

Alternatively, you might simply dress **ready-made dolls** for resale. The basic dolls could be purchased wholesale and then dressed in a variety of outfits made by you: fairy, baby, ballet, ethnic and bridal etc. You might create **unusual lines** for various niche markets. Some could be packaged **with a story book** or a sound cassette.

The good thing about *dressing dolls* as a home business is that you can proceed carefully, producing and testing various styles in short runs. If one outfit proves a poor seller, you can then change it, using the same dolls, but at very little cost.

To gain ideas, you will need to attend as many dolls' shows, craft and sewing exhibitions and craft markets as possible, checking out just what is being produced or what trend is gaining popularity.

Become an avid reader of doll and craft magazines from all over the world to flood yourself with ideas.

DOLLS' HOSPITAL

This could be a good business to run in conjunction with a doll making business. You may be asked to repair china, plastic, porcelain, fabric or even mechanised dolls from various periods. Some parts are likely to be hard to get so maintain a collection of pre-loved and broken dolls for your supply. You may need to repair dolls clothes as well so it would be wise to learn basic sewing and how to do invisible mending.

Dolls are not always 'children's playthings'; they could be part of a very valuable collection. Some antique dolls and certain teddy bears can command hundreds of dollars!

Gain exposure to doll collectors and doll makers by advertising in various, up-market doll making magazines, antique collectors' magazines and school newsletters…and remember the potential inherent in networking!

DOLLS' HOUSE FURNITURE

A lot of dolls' furniture is imported from Asian countries now and can be quite cheap to buy, so expect a lot of competition. One good market, however, is child-high kitchen and laundry 'furniture' that is for the personal use of the child in a play house: wooden stoves, fridges, iron and ironing board, sink etc. Or you may prefer to fashion miniature furniture in great detail.

Research the market and test it thoroughly before going too far. Assess *what* is wanted, by *whom* and *where*. Fairy and toy shops or your own weekend market stall might be a good start.
(See Woodworking, Children's Toys)

DOONA COVERS AND PILLOWS
(See under Sewing, Quilts and Screen Printing)

DRAFTING

This is not the sort of job to make you a millionaire overnight but it may help to earn you a few extra dollars part time. It could provide very useful experience for architecture and engineering students. Clients might be found anywhere: from people wanting to build extensions, outside offices, garages and pergolas to architects needing outside drafting services.

DRESSMAKING

If you think this is a business without much potential, you're wrong! Dressmaking can be as small or as large as you want it to be! In fact, many dressmakers are now franchising! Much will depend on your skill, your creativity, your business 'nous' and your willingness to extend yourself and think outside the square!

A few decades ago, dressmakers would never have believed that sewing could bring them a *six figure income*…yet, these days, there are many opportunities easily achievable for the astute home-business entrepreneur who can sew.
(For a fuller report, see under Sewing)

DRIED FLOWER ARRANGEMENTS

Once dried flower arrangements were all the rage but these days, one needs to come up with something rather special to become a success in this business.

That said, there are still openings in this field, such as dried floral arrangements for business premises and reception centres, theatres, exhibitions and seminars, hotels and so forth.

However, only those energetic, entrepreneurial marketers who are well-networked and switched-on are likely to get sufficient assignments to stay afloat.

DRIED FLOWERS AND HERB SACHETS

For these beautiful fragrance sachets, you don't even have to grow your own herbs! If you prefer, just buy the dried herbs and flowers in bulk, divide them up and place portions into individual packs. Attractive labels can be produced very simply on a home computer. Also on the home computer you could make illustrated paper envelopes for perfume sachets for slipping into one's purse or drawer.

Beautiful and unusually shaped glass or plastic containers, made to order, should help to popularise these products, particularly if you were to produce tiny booklets (again on the computer) explaining the origin and uses of the herbs or flowers they contain. These little booklets could be tied around the necks of the bottles with ribbon or silk cord.

Merchandise might be sold from home, from a market stall, by mail order, through gift and decorator shops, health food shops, naturopaths…or even from your own informative web site.
(See also under the various headings: Herbs, Gifts, Horticulture and Aromatherapy for other ideas.)

E

EASTER EGGS

You might give out Easter eggs on only one day of the year but what a day of high-volume gift-giving that is! And, as an adjunct to *related* business, the manufacture of Easter eggs could prove a very worthwhile enterprise indeed.

If you do not want to make **chocolate** or **sugar eggs,** natural eggs can be carefully blown, dried, then treated and decorated. *(This is described elsewhere in the book under Egg Shell Décor)* Many basic craft books give instructions on this art.

Here are a few ideas for decorating hen, duck, turkey, goose and ostrich eggs. They might be:
- painted or coloured with dyes (or crepe paper dyes)
- etched
- leaf decorated
- gilded
- decorated with batik
- decorated with decoupage or stickers
- made into little vases
- made into candles

(See entries under Egg Shell Décor, Candle making)

E-COMMERCE

Welcome to e-commerce, the biggest trading centre on Planet Earth! Do you have a business in The Mall of all Malls? Not only does the internet offer almost endless trading opportunities 24/7, it can provide just about any Business2Business services or information you could wish for as well.

Without moving a step outside your door, you have trading, wholesaling, importing, exporting, auctions, education, publishing, market research, programming, live seminars and more right at your fingertips. If you're not yet using this way of doing business, you're making it nice and easy for your e-commerce-savvy competitors to round up all the customers for themselves. *(See under Information Products)*

However, because e-commerce is a relatively new area, there is quite a bit for beginners to learn if they are to successfully manage their business without getting stung.. Ease of showcasing products, offering information about them and on-line ordering is fine but, when it comes to actually having clients *pay* on-line, you may still find some resistance. Only time, better security and more experience will convince the buying public that on-line is the only way to go..

You may find it simpler to establish your business in the real world first, then *add* e-commerce facilities as an ***additional*** way of doing business later on. It is indispensable when it comes to B2B transactions.

There are scores of potentially lucrative paths in e-commerce other than sales such as date collection & information, importing and exporting, education, publishing and so on and these will multiply exponentially as time moves:on.The ***setting up*** of web sites, even ***teaching clients*** how to set them up for themselves, is now a more easily negotiated learning curve than it was just a couple of years ago. The internet is so full of video help these days that there is little we can no longer do:and much of it is offered freely!

A web site you should find helpful: AUSe.NET (The Australian Electronic Business Network)...*www.dcita.gov.au/bits*

EGG SHELL DÉCOR

You've seen them in the glossy magazines, in history and art books, behind bullet-proof glass in museums and galleries: simple hen, ostrich and emu eggs that are now collectors' items. They have been transformed into jewel boxes, trophies and art works through the addition of exquisite decoration. Some have been enhanced through painting, decoupage, satin linings, ornate holders in gold or silver, the lavish application of pearls, gold and lace! The famous Faberge eggs can fetch a fortune!

Like most people, you have probably wondered at the fragile beauty and artistry of these precious pieces. Yet...this wonderful craft which has been going for centuries is still popular today and could become quite a business for the artistically inclined. Could that be you?
(See also under Easter Eggs)

ELECTRICIAN - DOMESTIC, COMMERCIAL OR INDUSTRIAL

If you're a qualified electrician, why give the *boss* your hard-earned dollars? You could be your *own* boss if you worked in your own business, which means you could keep all the profits for yourself.

Most tradespeople have the potential to achieve success in their own businesses these days if they are skilled in their trade and understand how to *market* their business. .

Your **business name** is also important: something 'catchy' and memorable that will stay in people's minds longer than 'Ernie's Electrics'!

Important, too, is **image**. Some tradespeople fail to realise the brownie points they can accumulate when they appear at jobs in a clean car and outfit, *on time*! Even such niceties as taking one's shoes off at the front door of a domestic residence and cleaning up the mess after a job can put you so far ahead of your competitors, you'll never know you had any!

Networking is indispensable in your self-owned business: relationships do not stop at the doors of house owners but need to extend to builders, architects, Real Estate agents, fellow electricians, retailers, air conditioning manufacturers, white goods resellers and so forth. See them, visit them, talk with them. Figure out how you might be able to help them. Place **permanent** ads in your local papers, if possible, and one in the Yellow Pages!

This is a work-from-home business that could make you a fortune if you run it professionally.

EMBROIDERY - CLOTHES, TABLE ACCESSORIES, GIFTS

Embroidered and beaded tops, bags, sweaters, evening dresses and jackets can bring big dollars if you aim for *the high end* of the fashion market with your needlework skills. Make up portfolios of your work (desktop-published in colour if possible) to give to various up-market fashion boutiques. This will facilitate choosing items and placing orders. An illustrated web page, too, might evolve from producing such a portfolio.

Another possibility is to use your skills to embroider logos and symbols on various **promotional products** or as **gift sets** for sale. This would have to be machine embroidery to make it viable. Your gift sets could target 'niche' markets such as tennis, golf, karate, basketball, swimming, cycling, bowling, baby, wedding and so forth. They may consist of nothing more than an embroidered hand towel, sweat bands and a sunshade or incorporate all manner of small and useful related products.

Sell your embroidered sets at weekend markets and through related retail and sporting outlets. They could also be sold from a web page, by mail order or direct to members of special interest and sporting clubs.
(See under Gifts, Cross Stitch Supplies & Instruction, Personalised Products)

EMBROIDERY KITS

Longstitch kits with canvas, needles, wools, designs and a glossy, self-published book of instructions could be offered to craftspeople through direct mail or even from just a small ad in the classifieds. If you find the business taking off, you might think about a display ad in one of the major glossy craft magazines.

When interested enquirers ring in response to your ads, offer to send them an illustrated brochure of your designs. (You can simply use an answering machine to take the names and addresses of enquirers if you do not wish to monitor the phone.)

EMPLOYMENT AND RECRUITMENT AGENCY

This business could cover permanent or temporary employment...or both. Satisfying the staffing needs of an organization involves bringing together employers and candidates and matching them rather as one does couples in a dating service! Human beings are very complex creatures and it requires quite a bit of experience to understand the underlying needs and wants of both parties to make a good match.

If you have had experience in the human resources profession, you will know this business can be set up and run extremely successfully - and profitably - from a home base. However, access to nearby serviced offices (hired on an hourly basis) might be helpful for interviewing certain clients.

But how do you get a business like this up and running if you have had *no* experience whatsoever?

Ideally, you can learn the ropes by working for a while in an established recruitment agency, do a course at a TAFE college...or join forces with an experienced recruiter. However, finding a qualified HR person willing to team up with you will be a lot easier if you have some meaningful *start-up capital*!

Starting up on your own can be risky unless you are well known in the industry. If you're starting from scratch, start *small*, perhaps placing temps or 'office and secretarial' staff, until you get the feel of the business.

You will need quite a bit of professional advice in the planning phase and certainly more professional help starting up but...expect big rewards when the 'establishment' phase is over!
(See also Resume Preparation, Consulting)

ENGRAVING

There are many uses for engraving, from trophies to name bars, but not all will be equally viable in a home-based business.

For many people, engraving will be no more than a useful add-on to an existing business such as that of a trophy maker, jeweller or producer of certain types of promotional products. For a few, it can mean full-time work. It can be a craft in its own right and is capable of adorning many different materials.

Today, engraving with laser is an easy and popular way for both artistic and commercial applications. Even franchises are available for laser engraving as a home business. The equipment is simple, sits on a desk top, takes up little room, can hook up to a computer and engraves a wide variety of materials.

Here is a handful of the many possibilities you could contemplate as an engraver:

- personalised products
- garden markers
- trophy engraving
- wood carving
- glass etching
- name plaques
- corporate awards & promotions
- auto detailing
- memorial plaques
- personalised jewellery

ENVELOPE STUFFING

Some envelope stuffing businesses make grandiose promises but, to make the sort of money they say is possible, you would have to work like an over-zealous beaver.

However, this work could suit people tied to the home, such as parents of small children, the partially disabled or carers who cannot leave their dependents.

Shop around, though, and find out what each organisation expects of you. In some instances, you will be required to pay a hefty 'registration fee' before you sign up with them.

ERRAND SERVICE
(see Gofer Service)

ESCORT SERVICE FOR THE AGED

There are escort services – and, well, there are 'escort services'! Unless you know the business well and are willing to take some very big risks, escorting strangers and loners can be very dangerous work! It may bring big dollars but considering the many other businesses from which you can make good money, why take the chance?

On the other hand, with the huge increase of **older people** in the community, there is a growing need for **reputable escorts** and **carers to accompany aged** members of our society, day and evening. Many of these elderly people may be physically able to get around but are nervous about going out by themselves, particularly at night, to restaurants, opera or theatres.

As a recognised **security escort for the aged**, you could organise special evenings for older clients (working through churches, hostels, nursing homes and senior citizens' groups) and even organise group bus or car outings. (Be sure you have the permits, licences and insurance necessary!)

Businesses such as these would need you to maintain an impeccable reputation and have the backing of police, government, some religious authority or charitable organization.

If you are interested, discuss the possibilities with various welfare, church and geriatric organisations as well as your local small business bureau.

EXCAVATOR

If you own a mini bobcat or any excavation equipment, you should be able to build yourself a business working for builders, landscapers, pool builders and so forth. This type of equipment is not cheap but it can be bought second-hand from a number of dealers.

Once you own a good piece of equipment and can handle it well, the rest is mostly a matter of good, solid marketing of your service and networking among the people who matter.

In this type of business, it never hurts to have several strings to your bow. If you are a bobcat driver, for example, learn a few other allied skills as well. Remember that equipment can always be leased but knowledge cannot. By becoming multi-skilled yourself in an area such as this, you may be surprised at the opportunities that present themselves and of which you are able to take advantage. Even if you subcontract others to do certain work for you, your knowledge will keep the business and your workers on their toes.

What will make your business stand out from similar ones? Generally, such things as reliability, your job expertise, having well maintained equipment, punctuality plus an ability to co-ordinate well with other workers on the site! Such attributes should get your name on the top of the list of subcontractors.
(See also Above Ground Pools)

EXERCISE CLASSES
(See under Personal Fitness Instructor)

F

FAMILY TREE/GENEALOGY CONSULTANT

This can be a fascinating business if you are interested in genealogy…but it will only provide an income if you use your knowledge creatively. Many hours can be used up in research and, as time translates into money in any business, you may find it hardly produces the equivalent of a hobby income for you under normal circumstances.

On the other hand, if you were to launch into lectures, videos, 'how-to' books, classes and perhaps a website, you may find you are presented with a whole different ball game.

Apart from preparing the usual charts and family trees, you could offer comprehensive family histories for sale *in book form*. A simple desktop computer, printer and scanner could weave anecdotes and old family photos into wonderful family histories for posterity. The finished manuscript could then be passed to a professional printer who specialises in short runs and customised binding. The result might be a magnificent heirloom volume beautifully bound in leather and stamped in gold.

Family histories can be compiled on CD and DVD if you are handy with a video cam and basic editing equipment. A background narration may be needed so, if you yourself are not able to perform a professional 'voice-over', simply prepare the script and find a good voice to narrate. Some clients may prefer their own voice.

Combing through and collating a client's home movies, old photos and personal possessions can be time-consuming but there are people who will pay handsomely for a finished article. The trouble is, you've just got to *find* them! So your marketing techniques will need to be very finely tuned to the right market.

As an adjunct to genealogy consulting, you might be able to offer a line of heraldic products such as **coats of arms, framed family history charts** as well as **photographs** and **paintings of historical sites or landmarks** that are closely associated with the family's history.

Heraldic products can be created, researched and manufactured by you - or, you may prefer to do it the easy way by buying a franchise where most of the research and hard work will have already been done for you. Some business opportunities magazines list ads for such franchises..

FENG SHUI ADVISER

Feng Shui practitioners need to build a name for themselves if they want to succeed! Simply advertising a service and waiting for clients to visit is rarely efficacious. People need to be convinced that, if they pass over their hard-earned money, you will be able to do what you say you can do.

What patrons of this art want is an 'expert'…and you need to make yourself into one! How?

Writing a book or making a short video on feng shui could be a good start…if you really know your subject and can speak authoritatively about it. You could advertise it in the classifieds, try selling it from your home page or wangle a write-up in the local papers. Success will only come from good marketing and PR.

Ask any of your friends who sell goods at weekend markets to display copies of your new book or film (and brochures) at their stalls. You could give them a commission on sales.

Distribute leaflets to homes, health and natural therapy clinics and try to find suitable public noticeboards on which to place your brochures. Local TAFE colleges and Uni campuses can often draw clients though notices on their noticeboards.

If you are able to speak reasonably well in public, write or email the various TV stations who are constantly on the lookout for unusual subjects for their current affairs and other entertainment programs and tell them about any up-coming talks or seminars you might be having. The local library might be willing to assist you present a *Feng Shui Seminar* - or perhaps you could give free talks at charity luncheons, mothers' clubs and TAFE seminars.

Think of other ways in which your name could become more widely known. And your talks might be a great place to sell copies of your *books and videos*!

Remember, recommendations from satisfied clients will do more than their fair share to help promote your selling efforts.

FENCING

Success in this home-based business will be dependent on two main factors: clever advertising and good workmanship.

Keep a folio of the styles of fences and gates you offer and photos of finished jobs. Also, whenever you complete a job, offer to knock a few dollars off the price if the client will allow you to leave your business sign on the fence or gate for a specified period of time.

One free advertising opportunity that many tradespeople overlook is the sandwich board. Placing one of these signs on the footpath wherever you are working if permitted can be a great confidence builder to potential clients because they can see others employing your services and your workmanship is evident.

A sandwich board is especially effective if you are doing a lot of work in the one area as your name is then continuously reinforced in the mind of the community.

FIBREGLASS MOULDING

Being able to run a business in fibreglass moulding from home may depend a lot on where you live. Expect neighbours and the council to object to the pungent smells! Even if you are lucky enough to obtain council permission, you might find the EPA knocking at your door because of complaints. On the other hand, if you have a large property, appropriate zoning and the aroma poses no problems to neighbours, go for it. It can be a really creative and exciting business.

There is no end to the range of goods that can be produced in fibreglass, from theatrical and mardi gras procession components (e.g. huge animal heads) to friezes, boats, games and surfboards!

If you are creative and clever with your hands, you could do extremely well in this field. And one of the best things about this business is that, if one product line doesn't work or one segment of your market folds, you can always try another.

FINANCIAL ADVISOR

If you are qualified as a financial advisor but no longer wish to work for someone else day after day, from 9 to 5, why not work at your own pace at home? More consultants than ever are working from home these days and many are going mobile as well. Having your office based at home as well as offering to visit clients 'on site' gives you a great deal of flexibility. It might also save your working clients a great deal of hassle, particularly if they have little children.

Unfortunately, home-based workers can risk 'getting lost' in the suburbs if they do not keep their business visible. Be sure to keep your name up there in the public view by writing articles for the local press, offering regular, free seminars and producing a *regular* newsletter for clents. They will appreciate this no end.

However, your knowledge could be put to other uses as well. Could you run training courses in financial matters? A school for the financially illiterate would hardly put you out of business as an advisor and would help your clients make better, more educated choices.

Or could you educate children in financial matters? Not only would parents love you for giving their children this essential worldly knowledge: you would be helping young people ensure their financial future and security.

FISH BREEDING

- Breeding exotic or tropical fish for aquariums *(See under Aquariums)*
- Breeding fish for consumption *(See under Fish Farming, below)*

FISH FARMING

If you live on a rural property with fish-filled rivers running through it, lucky you! However, even if your land is not so obviously blessed, putting in a series of fish-filled tanks and maintaining them to a high standard could have the potential to earn you a nice extra income…plus a free fish dinner whenever you feel like it!

These days the meat, fish and poultry we eat is often so contaminated by chemicals, heavy metals and antibiotics that we wonder just what there is left to consume. Your fish could be raised on natural unpolluted feed, in clean unpolluted water. Consumers are desperate for natural, chemical free products but there is never sufficient to go around.

Gather lots of information about fish and fish farming to see just what methods are available and what fish such a market is wanting. Then you will need to assess just what would be required of you if you were to run such a business on your property. Talk to the professionals, to the local council, to your neighbours. When you have all the necessary information, only then will you be in a position to make a decision You'll find many numbers and websites that should be able to assist you with basic business information at the back of this book.

FISHING EXPEDITIONS

Here's one for the reluctant business person who would actually prefer to spend the day fishing than working. Here's a way of fishing to your heart's content *and* getting paid for it! Think about arranging fishing trips for tired tourists and overworked business folk who are not as smart as you!

It could help if you lived in a seaside area but this is not strictly necessary. Wherever you live in coastal Australia, you should be able to plan short fishing trips, day charters, stay-overs at trout farms and so forth. Or you may prefer to do things on a grand scale, taking the more adventurous clients out to catch marlin!

Even owning a boat is not necessary: they can be hired by the day, the week or longer! And, as far as running the business is concerned, technology has already taken care of that with mobile phones, pagers and so forth. So go enjoy yourself!

Your expeditions could be promoted to motels, hotels, tourist centres, tour operators, ibusiness and fishing journals as well as local newspapers, bait and tackle shops etc..

IDEA: Boats that fish the rivers and lakes could be decorated with striped awnings and comfortable cushions to promote that holiday mood. Bright, highly visible adornment is also readily seen from land and could help draw the attention of those tourists still planning their local itinerary. Throw in barbequed fish lunches cooked on quiet beaches to make the expedition a real adventure. Maybe you could give a little talk on fishing methods or recount a few anecdotes.

Whether you plan to merely putt-putt up the local river for bream and flathead or head out into the wide blue yonder, your boat and equipment should be fully maintained and well equipped with all the latest safety equipment, life jackets and so forth...plus insurance!. (Maybe you'll need to include a fish finder for emergencies!)

FISH TANK MAINTENANCE

Here's a business which can generally be started with very little capital or equipment. You would, however, require a fair bit of knowledge about the requirements and needs of various species of fish, what goes with what and when! You won't last long if you start placing pirhanas in with the goldfish!

Much of the knowledge you need should be available in your local library. Also, don't be backward in asking questions at the various pet shops which sell fish. They should also have quite a variety of specialist books for sale
(Please turn to Aquarium Maintenance for more information)

FITNESS INSTRUCTOR
(For lots of marketing ideas, please look under Personal Fitness Instructor)

FITNESS EQUIPMENT HIRE & SALES

These days, many people find they are getting home later and later from work when it is too dark to go for a run or too wet or too cold or... Think of an excuse and it will have been thought up already! However, a fitness machine can be used at any time, whether it's after dinner when the kids are in bed or early on a freezing winter's morning. You can hop aboard in comfort and even watch the telly while you run, push, lift or pull those muscles into shape!

This business can be as big or small as you want to make it but it can also require a fair outlay of capital for all the equipment, constant advertising campaigns plus van. However, there are franchises available which will hold your hand and give you most of the help you need.

FLORIST

As a home-based florist, you might fulfil orders for special occasions such as weddings, parties and funerals as well as delivery to local homes and hospitals.

If you have a web page, show coloured illustrations of your arrangements available for the various occasions and seasons.

If you already have an existing client-base collected from previous experience in the industry, so much the better. Either way, you will need lots of advertising.

Investigate placing ads in newspapers and magazines and send your brochures to motels, hotels, theatres, restaurants, reception centres, local businesses, clubs, wedding and event planners. Market your expertise anywhere and everywhere. Speak to prospective clients personally and show your beautifully produced, glossy folio of work. Then leave them a brochure from which they can order.

You might consider offering a special deal to those who want fresh arrangements on a weekly or fortnightly basis.

If you hear of a small retail outlet or kiosk becoming available in a nearby shopping centre or mall, this could present a good opportunity for sales: a family member may be able to man the kiosk while you continue making the arrangements and fulfilling the orders from home. This is a way of getting maximum public exposure from minimal space and at minimal cost. The kiosk could also accept orders from an illustrated catalogue.

FOOD VAN
(See under Catering)

As well as the necessary permits, insurance and so forth required for a food van, you will also need flair and creativity to make a business like this attract customers. An old van that needs paint or a good wash might suggest dirty food and operators who don't care! Only well maintained vans, scrupulously clean preparation areas, well groomed staff and excellent food will bring in a full complement of customers. Get a bad name and you'll spend days doing nothing but twiddling your thumbs!!!

Take your mobile food van to the beach, sporting and entertainment venues, markets, fetes and anywhere else there are big crowds and you can wangle a permit.
You may decide to specialise in just one or two items like dim sums, hot dogs, hot stuffed potatoes, soup, ice cream, gelati or donuts'n'coffee...or offer a wide variety of popular food and drinks.

IDEA: Have you ever come across a van selling Devonshire Teas in winter?! Or huge slices of watermelon in summer? What about dim sums or hot soup and crusty rolls in the winter? There are so many opportunities to explore but, above all, be creative and think up as many ways as possible to differentiate yourself from all the other food vans!

FRENCH POLISHING

French polishing can be learned at recreation classes and various TAFE colleges. Only when you are truly proficient, should you offer your services to the public or to antique and furniture stores.

The two main avenues for your work-from-home business will probably be restoring furniture as well as selling pieces you have bought and restored yourself. Furniture you buy and restore yourself could be sold privately through various sources such as the classifieds, the Trading Post, garage sales, internet auctions and so forth.As well, you will probably find that you cannot do without a permanent ad in the Yellow Pages. It may appear to be a lot of money to fork out all at once, remember that your ad will be working hard for you for a year or more.

The restoration service, however, is a little different. It will require more thought than a simple ad under 'French Polishing' or 'Furniture Restoration' in the newspaper. You may need to do some active networking among second hand dealers, auction houses, other French polishers, real estate businesses, even new furniture stores. New pieces do get damaged.

FRUIT JUICE DISTRIBUTOR

This is a job for the early bird (you'll be up before the cock crows each morning!) but a juice distribution business can bring in excellent money.

You may choose to start up your enterprise from scratch but if you do, you'll need to be on the ball to compete with others already in this market. You won't be the only person aware of how lucrative this job can be if managed well.

If you have no business connections and no idea how to get started, you may prefer to buy a reputable fruit juice *franchise*. Choose wisely: do your research *and* your math before making any commitments. You will need to be sure you have sufficient finance to cover the franchise, your van and equipment *and* to cover on-going costs for several months ahead. Your accountant and solicitor should check out all the details of your business plan before you put it into action.

Beyond this, success is generally just a matter of reliability, turning out consistently good work, persistence and a pleasant personality. And don't overlook the possibiliy of tying this business in with another food distribution business.

FURNITURE MAKING

Anyone who can make good furniture should be able to make a good living! However, you'll need to research your market and see what retaillers are selling by the truckful…then manufacture something better!

Come up with *unusual* items…creative ideas that perhaps you've seen in overseas magazines or that you see a crying need for here. Perhaps you might produce superb rocking horses or chess tables that will one day become collectors' pieces, or a line of furniture copied from the homes of film stars. (Take home an armful of glossies to browse through next time you're at the library!)

You might choose to produce reproductions from a particular period like 'Gothic' or Art Deco and become known for that specialty. Or rustic pieces made from logs and local timber. On the other hand, your forte might be the utter simplicity and practicality of flat-packed items that customers can put together themselves.

Home-based craftsmen need to be crafty and offer the market what the market doesn't already have thousands of.
(See Woodworking & Metalwork)

FURNITURE REPAIR & RESTORATION

The success of this home-based business will depend partly on your talents and technical knowledge and partly on your dedication and marketing determination. However, if you are aspiring to antique furniture restoration, you will need even further technical skills plus an excellent working knowledge of antiques. This should not put you off, however, as such skills can be acquired over time at night classes, through books and other sources.

As an absolute beginner, you might start off with night classes in French Polishing or Upholstery classes at a TAFE college or recreation centre. You can often purchse antique items from garage sales at quite reasonable prices to repair and resell. By constantly working 'at the coal face' - buying, restoring and selling while you learn - it should not be long before your increasing knowledge and experience yield results.

Trying to make a living out of everyday modern furniture repair, whether you're working from home or in a shop, may be a little harder. Our 'throw-away' society seems to have the attitude: 'if it's broken, toss it out!' It is likely that only more up-market items will require your attention and expertise, so once again, you will need to make yourself competent in many areas of the required craft and finishing techniques.
(See also French Polishing, Antique Restoration, Upholstery, Leather Repair)

FURNITURE - SECOND-HAND/REPAIRING 'OBJETS TROUVES'

This is an often overlooked yet potentially highly rewarding job, especially if you don't have any start-up capital for your home business. But how and where do you get your stock of furniture if you're down to your last few dollars? You might get it for very little outlay at garage sales or the tip...*or* you might even find much of it for *free* on the nature strip! How? Find out when the various councils' junk removal days are sheduled. Generally, the most incredible throw-outs are often to be found on the nature strips a week or so before collection, especially in the more affluent suburbs. But do check to ensure there is no law in your area prohibiting collection of these items.

You're likely to come across discarded chairs, bookcases, tables, cupboards, bedheads, scores of bikes and lots of white goods. If you don't have a van or ute, you may be able to hire a trailer from one of the local petrol stations for a day or half-day to collect your booty.

Items you collect in these ways are often capable of being well restored and could then be put out for sale at your next garage sale, advertised through the classifieds or possibly even auctioned, depending on the piece and its perceived value.

While you may be able to restore furniture, what will you do with all the whitegoods you find? Answer: look under '*wanted*' in the classifieds, the Trading Post and similar publications. Hopefully, you will find traders and second hand dealers looking for stoves, ovens, dryers and fridges who will be willing to take them off your hands for a few handy dollars...particularly if these goods are in working condition.

Of even greater interest to such people could be discarded bathroom items such as unchipped sinks, toilets, baths and shower bases. Collect the better items, clean them up and then, if you can't establish a market for selling them yourself, ring the traders who are generally willing to pay in cash.

FURNITURE REMOVAL

Take two strong individuals plus a roomy van...and bingo! you could have a furniture removal business!

You should be able to tailor this business to suit your available time and equipment. Perhaps you'll be a one-van, *'weekend removalist'* specialising in local moves only: maybe you'd prefer a multi-van, monster-sized truck doing interstate and overseas moves. When your business gets too big, however, it will cease to become a *home-based business* due to the necessity of housing and maintaining vans and storing furniture.

Regardless of the size of your business, however, you will need to make sure you, your workers and vans are fully insured! Decide, too, what you want to do about insuring the contents. Will this be the responsibility of the client? Work all these things out beforehand and state them clearly on your contract.

'Do-It-Yourself' Furniture Removal could represent a great little sideline for a van that is not in use all the time. If you own your own truck or van, you would rent it out to clients by the hour, the evening or by the weekend and let them do their own moves.

Maybe you have a van which you use during the week for some other type of business but, at the weekend, it simply sits in your garage. How easy would it be to rent it out when you do not need it and get paid for...doing nothing?

G

GALLERY OWNER

A gallery can be a most rewarding business for someone interested in art. However, from a financial point of view, art can be very sensitive to fluctuations in the economy. Even if you function at the high end of the market dealing in 'investment-quality' art, sales still reflect economic downturns.

Depending on where you live, you may not get permission to sell any artwork other than your own in your home gallery. In fact, there are some councils which will allow you to sell only what you are commissioned to produce (eg portraits). So do check on your local laws and by-laws before making plans. In rural, tourist or even outer metropolitan areas, regulations may be more relaxed.

However, don't be deterred by regulations: they can often be overcome. Many councils will encourage art centres and galleries in their midst regardless of otherwise strict zoning so, until you submit your proposal, you will never know what you can do.

If you do fail to get permission to run a commercial gallery as a home business in your area, there are a few ways around this:
1) you could *hire* local exhibition space by the week for special showings of your own works or even that of artists whom you favour and are willing to take a

punt on. If there are no commercial galleries in your area, then a hall, recreation centre, library annex or similar venue might suffice. By arranging and holding exhibitions this way, you are not bound to a lease and all the overheads of a commercial gallery. However, you will still need to consider other expenses such as insurance of the works, public liability, advertising, the cost of openings and so forth.

2) to obtain a dedicated commercial gallery at home, you may be need to buy a suitably zoned commercial premises with an attached residence.

Many commercial galleries accept paintings, crafts and other artwork 'on spec' which can make stocking the gallery quite cost effective for the owner. It means not having to *buy* stock and, quite often, gallery owners will insist that contributing artists even insure their own works. Items are generally left at the gallery for an agreed length of time and, if not sold, are picked up again by the artist at no extra cost to either party. Where work is sold, the gallery is entitled to a commission. How much depends on the type of gallery and the services it offers but it is generally around the 30% mark.

Maintaining and running a gallery can be hard work and it can lap up money like a thirsty puppy. It requires continually changing displays, consistent marketing, lots of creativity and patience even in such things as dealing with exasperating customers or the constant repositioning of works...and your network of contacts must be continuously maintained and nurtured.

That aside, owning a gallery can be a great joy for the owner, the contributing artists and the community alike.

GARAGE CLEAN-UPS

This is a business that has taken off in the U.S. but is only in its infancy in Australia. The service offers anything from a basic re-organise and clean-up to painting, building storage and a complete revamp. As homes shrink in size, many home owners are beginning to realise the untapped potential of their garage as both housing for the car and a rumpus or work room. You can capitalise on this trend in your advertising.

However, you might also like to think of what you are going to do with all the 'junk' that you are asked to *remove* from your clients' garages. If you run a sideline business renovating and decorating second hand furniture, selling old tools or holding garage sales at home, you might make quite a few extra useful dollars!

GARAGE SALES

There are restrictions on how often a garage sale can be run in certain areas, so do check this with your local council. However, even one garage sale every three months or so can make good money if you are well prepared and well organised.

Between sales, you could still continue to buy and sell items privately. Some items might be procured quite cheaply from other garage sales and car boot sales, then refurbished and sold at a profit at your own sale.

Large, expensive items that may not sell readily at a garage sale could be advertised through the classifieds, the Trading Post, the internet or through a private network of traders. Certain trading publications do not charge you for your advert until your piece is sold.

- *IDEA:* If your council allows you to hold only two or three sales per year, you might organise a group of like-minded friends to form a 'garage sale circle'. Even if you have only six members, and each of you is permitted two sales per year, you could each run one mighty sale per month using each others' homes on a rotating basis!

- *IDEA:* For extra items to sell, you should watch out for your council's junk collection days. Take your car (or wheelbarrow) and, if it is permitted in your area, collect some of those wonderful tossed out items sitting on the nature strips: you'll probably find chairs, lounges, old lamps, bookcases, white goods and more, *all for free*! A coat of paint, a bit of fabric, a nail or screw here and there - and you'll find yourself building a stock of very saleable articles that have cost you virtually nothing.

(See under Junk collection)

GARDEN MAINTENANCE
(See under Lawns and Gardens, Landscaping)

GARDEN RUBBISH REMOVAL

Constant advertising and doing a thorough job when you get the work will help earn you the reputation you want.

Distribute your pamphlets widely, organise some signage on your car if possible, place an ad in your local paper over a few consecutive weeks - and you're in business! Don't forget to put a sandwich board outside any site on which you're working, even if you're only there for 30 minutes. On-the-job advertising can be very effective.

This is a job which is capable of being run in conjunction with many related businesses.

GARDEN ORNAMENTS

From gnomes to fountains, rocks to garden lights, tinkling mobiles to awesome sculptures, garden ornaments do their bit to change any garden into a world of magic and mystery.

One of the good things about having a home business of this nature is that most of your products will be housed *outside* the house *in the garden*. However, you will need to be certain that you are permitted to sell those products from your premises, particularly those which are not directly manufactured by you. Check with your local council about zoning and permits.

If you are allowed to sell from home only those items manufactured by you *personally*, don't worry. Check with your local council. There are many garden decorations and ornaments which you could easily produce yourself:

- Simple ***moulds and casts*** can yield perfect pots and statues, fountains and fairies, gnomes and animals in minimum time and with very little experience.

- ***Iron and other metals*** can be transformed into wondrous garden trellises, gates, arbours and seats.

- ***Clay*** can be fashioned into just about any creative thing and fired at the local kiln

- And *fibreglass* can be transformed into seemingly ancient rocks and boulders that weigh practically nothing yet look as though they weigh a tonne.

- ***Wall plaques*** for outside walls can really set off a pool area or courtyard. They can be made of timber, stone, mosaics, metal and many other materials. They can be 2D or 3D and can be representative or highly abstract.

And, if you welcome your customers warmly in an attractive environment, they will want to come back again and again. Remember, customers buy garden ornaments not only for themselves but as gifts for friends and relatives as well.

GENEALOGY CONSULTANT/SALES OF RELATED PRODUCTS

There are many opportunities under this heading: genealogy consultant, sales of heraldic products, illustrated family trees, videos and DVD's, self published and personalised books and albums and so forth.
(Start your search under such headings as Family Tree/Genealogy Consultant, Personalised Books, Heraldic Products, Desktop Publishing)

GIFT BASKETS

The range of gift baskets that one can produce is limited only by the imagination. They don't all have to contain jam and crackers or champagne and glasses! Think of attractive, special purpose baskets for the *new baby*, for lovers, for the *newlyweds*, the *sports champion*, Valentine's day, the overseas *traveller*!

If you are starting up your business from scratch, you will need to find a network of *reliable* suppliers for the items you'll be using in your baskets.

Photograph samples of your baskets and their contents to display in those glossy up-market catalogues, web page and advertising brochures. Remember, success will be highly dependent on promotion, promotion, promotion! Offer to do special orders for *corporate clients*, too, for which you may need to access or produce special personalised articles! *(See entry under Personalised Products)*

When making up baskets for special *'niche' markets*, *keep to the theme*: eg baby goods, Australiana, Easter, Valentine's Day, Christmas and so forth. A basket with an *Australian theme* might hold such items as a boomerang, a plush koala or kangaroo, bush jam or honey, maybe a book of Australian poetry, native herb soaps and oils.

Art and craft baskets, instead of containing the general gear one finds in most gift packs these days, could be specifically geared to an artist's specific interest, be it painting, pottery, decoupage, calligraphy, china painting, embroidery or whatever.

Perhaps you could do the same thing for the *sports-minded*: Specific interests such as fishing, golf, sailing, karate, tennis, basketball could be catered for.
(See also Art & Craft, Sewing, Embroidery, Gift Packs)

Courier or personal delivery is safest for baskets unless they are being collected by the client at the point of sale. You may have family members or friends willing to do local deliveries for you.

Talk to various retail outlets that may be targets for selling your goods, too: gift shops, baby shops, florists, party shops, bridal, special interest clubs and tourist shops. Ask if they would be willing to keep one of your illustrated catalogues on hand from which they or their clients could order.

A web page can be a useful tool in selling your gift baskets if you can get it recognised and are able to organise an *interstate production and delivery network*. However, note that sending food by mail or even by courier can be problematic. It may be best to avoid offering food hampers until you have gained lots of experience in handling, packaging and distribution. Investigate the ins and outs of trade shows, too. These can give a business good exposure when it has grown somewhat.

There is usually quite a bit of information available on starting and running *gift basket delivery services* in various home business magazines.

GIFTS - PERSONALISED

There are so many possibilities for personalised gifts: children's books, money boxes, mugs, paper weights, baby items, key rings, diaries, jewellery, bathrobes, towels - the list is almost endless. There is also a big market in the **corporate sector** for personalised and *promotional* items.

You may prefer to create and personalise the gifts yourself or buy basic items in bulk to personalise. Depending on the product, personalising could be effected with the help of:

- a desktop computer
- calligraphy
- engraving
- screen printing
- embroidery machine
- leather tooling
- carving tools
- gold stamping
- decoupage
- sewing machine
- paints & stencils

There are several **franchises** available for Personalised Products. Some pop up from time to time in the various business opportunities magazines.
(See also: Personalised Products, Balloons, Speaking Ribbons, Embroidery)

GIFT BUYING SERVICE

Believe it or not, huge businesses have grown from this little acorn of an idea! Basically, it is a service for busy professionals who do not have the time or inclination to buy or assemble gifts, gift baskets or gift packs for their clients, or even for lovers, spouses, friends or family members. The gift buying business can take many forms…but the web is where the money waits!

Of course, you don't need to be *selling* gifts to make this business work. You might simply have your own line of gifts, package them, put on the cards and send them off. You are likely to find this way far more rewarding as you would be rewarded not only for your fulfillment service but also reap the rewards from being a manufacturer, agent or seller of the products.

Gift packages could be displayed on your website, in brochures or mail order catalogues, through a direct customer network or by personal contact with employees in office blocks and various businesses.

Many executives are content to pass the whole responsibility of their gift selection and card-giving over to a reliable service! You may soon find yourself loooking after the gift and greeting card needs of your clients' entire family as well as their client list!.

If your service and network is Internet-based and well-organised, you just might find yourself getting rich by working from your diningroom table in your slippers! *(See Gofer, Personalised Products, Gift Baskets, Balloons, Speaking Ribbons, Importing/Exporting, E-commerce)*

GLASS BLOWING

Glass blowing can still fascinate an audience as can a display of your exquisitely coloured and translucent creations shimmering under the lights of the mall. The very act of demonstrating your glass blowing technique can go a long way to helping sell the products.

Possible market: for smaller items and demos: consider weekend fairs and markets, craft and home décor exhibitions, gift shops, shopping centre malls. For more up-market, decorator-quality pieces: speak to buyers in home décor shops, art galleries and gift shops.

If you leave pieces anywhere 'on appro', be sure to check on the outlet's insurance arrangements.

Note: because of the nature of the materials and equipment used, you may need a protected, indoor spot for demos.

GLASS MOSAICS
(See Mosaics, Garden Ornaments)

GOLD PLATING BUSINESS (ELECTROPLATING)

This home business has many applications: you could find yourself gold-plating family memorabilia such as baby shoes, cutlery, trophies and ornaments one minute and automotive accessories for corporate cars the next! The process itself is fairly simple yet effective and thankfully has a fairly short learning curve.

The pages of the various business opportunities magazines usually offer good leads for suppliers of the know-how, equipment and franchises in this field.

Give quite a bit of thought to the name you will use in your business. This can make a big difference to the way you are perceived in the marketplace. A name like 'The Midas Touch' or 'Gold Dust', for example, is far more evocative of the message you're trying to put across than something like 'Brown's Electroplating Pty. Ltd.'

GRAPHIC ARTIST

While many graphic artists work from home these days, clients expect a well kept, professional studio. It should be separate from the rest of the house and have its own entrance if possible. You will also need good clear signage outside of your house plus a great logo that is representative of your design ability.

There is a great deal of competition in this field. Running costs, too, can be quite high for small business owners on a budget, particularly if clients are slow to pay...or don't want to pay at all!. However, working from home, you do not have to take into consideration high overheads in costing out your jobs.

If you produce creative, good quality work *and* you are well-priced, you could be a very welcome sight to any small business wanting graphic art at an affordable price. *(See also Advertising and Desktop Publishing)*

GREETING AND HOSTING SERVICES

This heading could encompass many types of services, from greeting and seating attendees at seminars, lectures, large sporting events and other public gatherings to actually organising and hosting events. You might even act as an agent, recruiting for such events.

Speak to party planners, wedding planners, sporting event organisers such as those responsible for the Grand Prix or the Tennis Open to find out what is available. Research and brainstorm your way to success.

GREETING CARDS

How easy is it to produce greeting cards on a computer these days with the right sort of graphics software, a printer that will handle heavier cardstock…and a sense of humour or a bit of creative imagination?

If you prefer, just forget the computer and concentrate on *handmade cards*! Or use a combination of both: the outside could be hand drawn, painted, screen printed or decorated with cut outs, stickers, buttons or bows...in fact, today, anything goes! Then the inside greeting or verse - personalised if you wish - could be computer-generated on parchment or any other type of paper and stuck inside..

If you were to take a short course in caricature and cartooning, you may find it assists your creativity to really blossom in this field. Origami (paper folding), too, is a useful skill to have in card-making.

There are plenty of card making classes in the suburbs these days and a proliferation of suppliers ready to sell you cardstock, unusual papers and foils, stencils, stickers and the rest of the paraphernalia. Your only real challenge will be marketing what you produce!

You might even decide to run *card making classes* yourself or become a *supplier of card-making materials*!

- *IDEA*: Have you thought about a service sending out greeting cards to *the clients and customers of busy professional and business people?* Help businesses stay in the forefront of their clients' minds by looking after their personalised birthday and Christmas card list for them! They simply provide you with the name, address and birth date of their clients and you do the rest.

GUTTERS CLEANED, DE-LEAFED AND REPAIRED

This could be an excellent job for a retired plumber or roofer, particularly if you live in a leafy suburb! As a home-based business, it should allow you to work at your own pace - although at certain seasons of the year and after bad weather you could find yourself a lot busier than usual.

Offer clients a full gutter service if possible: regular cleaning, mending and de-leafing.

If you always turn up at the appointed time, do a good job and clean up when the job is done, your name should spread faster than the leaves in autumn. However, good advertising and signage is vital as well – on your house, on your car, on your uniform – and on the sandwich board which you place outside every site where you are working.

Differentiate your business in some way if you can so that you stand out from the competition. Perhaps you will offer certain specials that no one else has. Or will you tie your business in with another, related essential service?

One of the easiest and cheapest ways to stand out in the crowd of competitors is to give your business a catchy, memorable name rather than just plain *John Smith, Gutter Repairs!*

H

HAIRDRESSING

If becoming a really successful hairdresser is your aim, you would do well to read *Self Made in America* by John McCormack and David Legge to learn how these entrepreneurs made it to the top in this profession! It is fascinating.

Two of the possible ways to run a home-based hair salon would be to:
- maintain a small salon in your own *home*
- run a *mobile* salon that enables you to visit hospitals, nursing homes, hostels and the private homes of elderly and housebound clients.

Home-based hairdressing can fill a big need in our ageing society as many older clients are unable get out to beauty salons and are often grateful for the personal service and ease of having their hair groomed at home.

Housebound mums and home-bound carers, too, cannot easily leave little children or dependents and are likely to appreciate your professional personal service.

Advertising and promoting your home service well will be crucial. A local publication or newsletter for senior citizens, stay-at-home parents, disabled persons, school newsletters and Neighbourhood Watch newsletters might be good targets as well as the local classifieds. If you can get yourself an editorial in one or two of the local papers as well, so much the better!

Entering hairdressing competitions can help your name become known around town…and, if you happen to win, the title of 'prize-winning stylist' displayed across your brochures and ads won't hurt your business one bit!

HAIR MINERAL ANALYSIS

If you have the equipment and training, plus some basic marketing expertise, you may decide to set yourself up as a Hair Mineral Analyst.

You would be required to help private clients and health practitioners recognise mineral deficiencies or bodily imbalances through analysing the chemicals present or missing in patients' hair samples.

This type of business could be run by Mail Order but you would need to promote yourself. Circulate information in the form of letterbox drops, network with health professionals and place classified and display ads in the appropriate publications such as the better known health journals.

Mothers clubs, charity clubs and other interest groups love to hear unusual talks and lectures so, if you enjoy speaking in public, this could be a good place to consolidate your image.

If you prefer to write, perhaps you could compose a few feature articles about your work and send them off to health magazine and newspaper editors. Published features could then be referred to in your advertising for added credibility.

HAIR ORNAMENTS

Hair combs or hairpins adorned with ribbons, feathers, diamantes and other decorations are very popular for special occasions like weddings, cocktail parties and race-going, and often take the place of hats. Consider, too, pony tail holders, bun and chignon adornments and other unusual hair accessories for your collection.

In a home-based business, it would be pointless to try to compete with the cheaply produced and imported goods one finds in the $2 shops. Instead, do a bit of research into the more exclusive accessory shops and hair salons and see what the big dollars are buying. These are the type of items on which you need to concentrate.

Some of your stylish concoctions may be accepted 'on appro' by retail stores, wedding boutiques, hair salons, accessory shops and dress boutiques but, if they do the selling, you will need to share your profits with them! On the other hand, a mail order/direct mail service would keep the profits in *your* pocket! Consider, too, the possibilities offered by party plan selling if you have a large or particularly unusual range. *(See Party Plan Selling)*

Desktop-publish some beautifully illustrated brochures for distribution and, if possible, think about setting up a website.

HANDBAGS
(See also Beaded Handbags)

Basic lined handbags can be quite simple to make, especially ***evening bags*** made of soft fabrics like velvets, silks and satins and they might provide you with a very nice business. *Ready-made patterns* plus simple step-by-step instructions can usually be obtained from outlets where dress patterns are sold. Your success will depend not only on how well the bags are made or decorated but how cleverly they are marketed!

Woven bags can be an absorbing hobby, but the finished product needs to be outstanding in some way to compete with the many cheap imports already in the shops and selling for a song.

For ***leather bags***, tooled or otherwise, you would be wise to take a course in leatherworking. This craft can be fascinating but there are quite a few tricks of the trade that need to be learned to make and finish a saleable item. If you take the time to learn these 'secrets', your work will have a professional finish! However, don't expect to make a lot of money from leather bags unless your work is particularly up-market or outstanding in some way as overseas competition is rife.

Markets and fetes are probably the best place for more basic leather accessories. Better styled, quality handbags could be offered to accessory and fashion shops either as a straight out sale or 'on appro'.

HAND-PAINTED AND DECORATED GIFTS
(See under Arts and Crafts)

HAND PAINTED FABRICS

Quite a lot of time goes into hand painting fabrics so you will need to assess carefully whether the return is going to be worth your output of time and energy.

One area in which hand painting on garments might work well is if you are *manufacturing* the clothing items yourself. Hand painting better class, well made garments destined for an exclusive market can often add tremendous value, providing the painting itself is appropriate to the type of garments and their proposed use.

Silk painting also can often demand good mark-ups if done well. Scarves, beachwear and evening wear are prime targets for beautiful hand-painted silks.

Look for markets in small boutiques and craft outlets. Many art galleries, too, are happy to place hand-painted silk scarves and hangings among their stock on 'appro'.

Good quality, natural fabrics are best for handpainting. Cushion covers, dresses, sarongs, bags, sun hats and t-shirts can be excellent money spinners when sold in tourist areas and busy weekend markets.

Note: many painted fabrics and garments can be just as attractive and certainly faster to produce if they are simply *screen printed*! So consider carefully whether the items you are painstakingly producing by hand are really commercially viable.
(See also Silk Painting)

HANDPAINTED JEANS

It's all the rage and soooo simple! If you are a jeans manufacturer or retailer, it may be worth trying a line of these! Or try painting jeans *to order*.

You will need to have a catalogue of designs available so that clients can choose a design and approve it before you start. If they want their own designs, be sure you understand their request and have the design laid out on paper, in colour - and approved! - before going ahead.

HANDYPERSON

You may enjoy performing maintenance tasks around your home - but most people hate it! Many find life is just too busy to cope with the never-ending jobs. That's where *you* come in!

Repairs such as leaky taps and other small plumbing jobs, painting, tile repairs, small carpentry jobs, removing tree branches, cutting back vines, changing light globes, refitting smoke detector batteries and removing rubbish are just a few examples of the requests that you're likely to receive.

Those with the right equipment and expertise might offer extra services such as cleaning heating ducts and chimneys or doing small concreting jobs. However, you do not need to tackle anything beyond your area of expertise. In fact, you could have a profitable arrangement with a list of professional tradespeople to do the more specialised jobs for you and receive a percentage of their fee for yourself.

The *ageing* of the population means that more and more older clients will need assistance to perform those many domestic repairs and other tasks which they cannot do for themselves. As a handyperson, you should always be able to find plenty of work assisting them, and others, to maintain their homes.

Don't underestimate the usefulness of the handyman: many large-scale tradespeople such as tilers, painters, plumbers and so forth refuse to do these smaller jobs or else keep customers with minor jobs waiting for weeks.

Your handyperson business could service local homes, flats and apartments, schools, businesses, nursing homes and hostels, clubs and Real Estate Agents.

Be alert to opportunities. If a *For Sale* or *For Rent* sign appears on a local house or apartment, be sure to drop a flyer in the letter box.

Distributing magnetised business cards for the fridge or other metal surfaces is a good idea, too, as clients are less likely to lose track of your service if your card is firmly affixed to their kitchen or laundry appliance.

It is important to give the impression that you are a caring, friendly service if you want to decimate the opposition! Turning up on time, taking your shoes off at the front door, cleaning up after a job, are all signs to clients that you respect their homes. They should repay you by using your service again and again.

HATS

Hats! They're back! And a good millinery course could see you in business in less than a year! There are private millinery courses around but check with your local TAFE or Uni Short Course centre as they often have excellent short courses.

You will probably *make* your creations at home...but it is not that easy to *sell* millinery from a home base unless you are a very good networker and have a substantial advertising budget.

Exclusive accessory and dress boutiques may be willing to stock some of your hats 'on appro'. The big negative in selling this way, however, is that your profit margins will be slashed in half. On the plus side, however, you are working from a home base and do not have to contend with the overheads of a shop owner. Therefore, you may feel it is worth putting up with a lower margin just to get started and have your work showcased in upmarket salons.

Contact some local dress boutique owners and see if they are interested in holding some fashion parades in conjunction with you for charities and schools. These functions can draw very large crowds and many clients.

If you want the best of both worlds, viz. the benefits of having a home-based business yet the glamour of owning a millinery boutique, consider moving into to a combined shop and residence.

HEALTH FOOD REPACKAGING

This type of business generally involves both repackaging and delivery, so it is most likely that you will require a van for transporting goods.

Many products like flour, nuts, dried herbs, oats, cookies and so forth can be bought in bulk and repackaged under your own label - or you might simply repackage the goods for various stores. *But be sure to check out all permits and licences required.*

HEALTH PRODUCTS

The list of possible health products for sale is almost endless, from herbal remedies to shiatsu sandals! And selling them can take many forms: mail order, direct mail, wholesale, retailing, party plan selling, selling from a web site…and even running seminars. Investigate the plethora of opportunities available to you.

You may decide to manufacture *your own products* at home or buy *already manufactured goods,* in bulk, then repackage them for sale under your own label. If home manufacture is your choice, be sure you have all the necessary permits required. Health products are increasingly coming under scrutiny and are expected to provide all the benefits that the manufacturer promises.

There are quite a few *health product franchises* that are well known and widely advertised. Some may have the potential to make you an excellent income while others may not be all they are purported to be. You need to check carefully any franchise or dealership that you are contemplating.

If you decide on a health product franchise, investigate it thoroughly. Only make your choice after you've done a lot of research, talked to others running similar franchises and talked it over with your accountant and other relevant professionals.

HEDGE MAINTENANCE AND TOPIARY

A *hedge trimming and shaping* service could be a business in its own right - or form part of a bigger concern such as total garden and lawn maintenance. You should be able to offer a level of service to suit your own physical ability and equipment.

You might also consider *growing* many of the required shrubs yourself that are to be used either as new hedges or fillers for old ones. Many of these popular plants can be very easily grown and shaped at home, bring a good price yet cost you virtually *zero dollars* to produce. They may even represent a good sideline business in their own right if you were to supply nurseries, garden centres and florists as well.

Ficus and similar plants could be shaped in hearts, initials, animals, decorative styles and sold to nurseries who may not have the time to put into this type of endeavour.

Teaming a service such as hedge maintenance and topiary with another, synergistic enterprise should help the bottom line.
(See Agriculture/Horticulture)

HERBALIST

Herbalists are well regarded in just about every community throughout the world. They treat many conditions, although reputable practitioners will not claim to treat the more serious diseases such as cancer. Treatments are generally used for minor problems, although one often sees them employed *in conjunction* with conventional medicine.

This is one of the oldest forms of healing known to man yet it is the knowledge base from which many of our modern medicines are derived. Today, herbs are made up into tablets, infusions, tinctures, decoctions, ointments and poultices.

If you are not yet qualified as a herbalist but believe it is the sort of business you would enjoy, there are many schools of Naturopathy and Herbal Medicine where you can go to learn, regardless of your age or educational level. Some schools run correspondence courses allowing you to study in your spare time.

Herbal medicine can be a great home business and many practitioners have even managed to develop nutritional and herbal medicines for sale under their own label, giving their business a dual money-making capability.

For added income, you could grow and produce many of your own herbs if you had the space.

Marketing is ultra-important in any of the alternative medicines. Put in some time, effort and research to find out just where your advertising dollars are likely to be most effective. Basic are the local newspapers, the Yellow Pages, appropriate newsletters and health related magazines.

If you are comfortable about speaking in public, you may be able to arrange a few health seminars on your subject. If this causes you to tremble with fear, you may prefer to write and self-publish a health-related book or make an info film. This could be sold at your rooms, in health shops, your own health seminars or even by mail order. *(See under Writing & Video Production)*

Are you willing to give free lectures? You could talk at local club and charity luncheons or at local libraries to boost your image somewhat. Offer your audience members a special *'discount'* voucher for their first visit to your rooms!
(See also under Herb Gardens and Aromatherapy)

HERB-BASED GIFTS

Here are just a few suggestions for herb-based gifts - some leisure-oriented, some culinary - from the many *hundreds* of possibilities:

- Sleep pillows
- Bath sachets/bottles/balls
- Potpourri
- Essential oils
- Herb soaps (hand made soap with finely ground herbs & spices)
- Herbal wreaths (made of mint, sage, rose, lavender, rosehips, lavender, pine, baby's breath)
- Mustard in little bottles, attractively labelled
- Herb blends for seasoning food
- Herb marinades
- Herb stuffing

HERB FARM
(See under *Herbalist, Agriculture and Horticulture*)

HERB GARDENS

Herb gardens can be ideal for flat and town house dwellers as they can be grown in the tiniest areas. They can also make great gifts.

- Sell your 'herb gardens' in tubs, freshly growing and ready to pick. Perhaps you could devise an attractive tub that lends itself to growing three or four of the most popular culinary or fragrance herbs.

- Pick and thoroughly dry herbs, then package or box them attractively with your own special label.

- Buy already dried herbs *in bulk,* then package them yourself in exquisite containers and under your own label. Value-add by attaching a tiny information booklet to each pack, outlining the history and various uses of that herb.

- Sell to gift shops, kitchenware shops, food stores, fetes, markets and so forth.

- Herb gardens can be fascinating places to visit. If your herb garden is on a large rural property or farm – (it doesn't have to be, as herbs take up very little room!) – you may be able to earn extra dollars by running exhibitions, demonstrations, seminars and lectures for tourists and other interested visitors. Check first with your local council.

If you do receive permission to have visitors to your property, you might also be permitted to turn a garage or shed into a simple weekend tea room from which to offer light refreshments - as well as some of your gift-packaged and potted herbs.

Note: never embark on any of these activities without approval, however. There are strict zoning laws covering home businesses. Other certification may be required, too, when it comes to incorporating activities such as food preparation and handling.

HERBS & HERB PRODUCTS

Edge out the competition with your highly creative packaging and marketing ability! Perhaps you will come up with wonderful jar designs and unforgettable labels.

Your dried herbs could be housed in irresistibly shaped glass bottles or attractive acetate boxes, each with a fascinating information booklet attached. This little book could explain the history, culinary or medicinal benefits of that particular herb and an explanation on how to use it.

This is a simple exercise in value-adding but the addition of the booklet and the beauty of the pack should help set your product apart from the rest. Differentiation can be a great business builder!

Enthuse the public about the 'miracles' of *health and beauty* that your herbs are thought to perform: could you run demos, seminars or speak at club and charity luncheons? Try promoting your products at relevant retail outlets, health stores and garden centres. Even having a little stand at a weekend market can draw interest if you are giving a demonstration.

Meanwhile, back home, hundreds more herbs will be growing quietly and obediently in your garden, without costing you a cent!

HERITAGE CERTIFICATES AND PLAQUES

Most certificates of this nature can be produced on a desktop computer. Value-add according to the frame or mount you use. A simple wooden frame will not be as outstanding or valuable as a pewter, silver or copper frame decorated with the appropriated Coat of Arms in high relief, for example.

Try marketing your products through gift stores, genealogy clubs and lists, from your own web page if you have one (mail order), at market stalls, fairs, through decorator and antique stores and by advertisements in appropriate publications and special interest newsletters.

Print some glossy, illustrated brochures of your work from which people can place orders.
(See under Personalised Products, Gifts and Desktop Publishing)

HISTORY-RELATED PRODUCTS

History buffs - especially ex-teachers – may like to research and *write books* on places of historical interest such as heritage homes and buildings or celebrated landmarks, then desktop publish this literature. The resultant booklet or manual could then be offered for sale at the actual sites and through any tourist outlets around about.

Your passion might also be of interest to schools and libraries if it is well written and well presented. If you are writing quite a few of these books, it may be worth setting up a web site from which to sell them. Alternativily, you may prefer to make audio tapes or CD's on your home computer.

Historical societies, councils, collectors and antique stores often produce their own magazines and newsletters and your unique information, if it is in the form of a written article, might be highly valued by their readers, prompting them to send for your books and audios.

Becoming known for your *feature articles* in specialist magazines will also help your credibility and should be very useful when it comes to marketing related products.

You might also contact the publishers of **school magazines** requesting a list of the up-coming syllabus subjects for the different age groups. You may be able to write and submit articles on various historical subjects for an age range of your choosing. *(See also Heritage Certificates & Plaques)*

HOBBY EQUIPMENT & MATERIALS

Retailers of craft and hobby equipment don't have to be chained to a retail store these days! The modern alternative is mail order or direct mail. You might use mailing lists, the classifieds or even display advertising in the appropriate publications, *(See Art and Craft, Bead Supplies, Embroidery, Teddy Bear Supplies, Bottled Ships, Mail Order, Direct Mail)*

HOME BUILDING INSPECTOR

If you have the knowledge and qualifications necessary to perform this service for prospective home buyers, it could provide you with a very comfortable home-based business.

You would be expected to assess the condition of a home – generally one about to be purchased, write a full report for the clients and suggest what measures will need to be taken to bring the building up to scratch.

This could be a good sideline for a self-employed builder…or even provide a job for an ex-builder.

HOME CLEANING

Do you want to be a millionaire? The way may be lined with scrubbing brushes, brooms and buckets…but for many a hard-working entrepreneur, it has led to a large pile of gold at the door of their own cleaning agency.

If you feel this business is for you but have had little experience, it may be best to work for an accredited cleaning agency for a while until you get to really understand the business. Only when you know the ropes, should you consider starting out on your own.

You may prefer to do *domestic cleaning* or perhaps you will take on *cleaning of commercial and industrial properties*.

Once fully established, a domestic cleaning business may be capable of being tied in with other *related* services like window cleaning, carpet cleaning, personal shopping services, catering, dry cleaning and so forth to form a *total personal service* for clients. You could then receive a fee from each of the services you outsourc.

As more and more business and professional people become caught up in their careers, the service industries - once considered so lowly – are becoming increasingly indispensable.

However, like any business, domestic or commercial cleaning services and agencies will only survive long-term if they are run intelligently and efficiently with trustworthy employees and an obsession to become the best.

HOME SHOPPING AND DELIVERIES

This is a sort of 'gofer service' for professionals and others who have insufficient time to shop for their food, gifts and other items and who are willing to pay others to do this for them.

There are many ways to run a business of this nature: it might be a simple 'as needs' job that brings in a few dollars occasionally…or it might be worked up to a big concern, cleverly organised and planned.

You may ultimately decide to expand your enterprise by co-ordinating with other service businesses such as dry cleaners, laundries, ironers, domestic cleaners and so forth to provide a complete home service for busy professionals.

HOME RENOVATION

Many people who have absolutely no qualifications other than a flair for home renovation and decoration have been making good money over the past few years buying *well-positioned,* affordable homes that are undercapitalised, overgrown and unloved and selling them again a few years later at a marked profit. In the meantime, the properties are rented out under various conditions. Some owners negatively gear their portfolio of homes; others prefer positive gearing. Be guided by your own professional financial adviser as everybody's circumstances are different.

The type of homes preferred for refurbishment are generally those in reasonable *structural* condition, requiring only *cosmetic* renovations such as a repainting, recarpeting, restumping, a revamp of the bathroom and kitchen plus new drapes and light fittings. A recent trend has been to rip up carpets and polish floors where possible.

This business, like any, has its risks and, while it seems to work extremely well for many people, it might also work to your detriment if you do not know exactly what you are doing or fail to gauge the market correctly when buying or selling.

HORTICULTURE

There are many ways to get your business known other than through the inevitable 'advert in the classifieds'. Consider horticultural and gardening clubs, special interest groups and local weekend craft markets.

Many clubs and charities will enjoy hearing about your expertise - if you don't mind public speaking! If you are the shy retiring type, and don't like the idea of running *lectures*, perhaps you could produce and distribute *free informative newsletters* about your plants instead!

Any talks and demos you give should be absolutely top class! Send a publicity sheet, together with a good photograph of yourself, to the local papers if you have an up-coming lecture. Editorials have rocketed many an entrepreneur out of obscurity and into the limelight.

- *Exotic plants & flowers*
  Exotic plants and flowers could be marketed to specialist retail outlets like garden shops and nurseries - or you may be able to sell them directly from your property.

  What plants and flowers could you cultivate for sale in your home backyard? Logic would suggest the rarer, the better - as most nursery and garden centres stock the common varieties. Generally, bigger concerns can't afford the space or time involved in stocking and tending rare varieties. Consider some of the plants mentioned below.

- *Weird & unusual plants* could fill a sales 'niche' if marketed the right way.

Take fascinating, 'carnivorous' plants such as the Venus fly trap for example! Relatively few people know much about these unbelievable plants so they offer scope for demos at schools, clubs, charity luncheons and shopping malls.

Could you lecture and demonstrate such plants and their behaviour? Are you able to self-publish a book about them? Stories, myths and anecdotes about your plants can fascinate your audience! There is potentially great selling power in both *demonstrating* your products and *speaking about them publicly*. The information books or videos that you produce could then be sold at any lectures you run providing the convenors permit.

- ***Bulbs*** could be a great little home-based business if run the right way. They can be so easily stored, packaged and sold through garden centres and nurseries, or offered through ***direct mail*** and ***mail order channels***! Some popular bulbs to investigate are:

    hyacinths, tulips, various orchids, daffodils and freesias.

    As well as placing your ads in newspaper and magazine classifieds and on related web sites, brochures could be sent to special interest groups and horticulture clubs throughout the country.

    While many varieties of bulbs are available, you would be wise to learn quite a bit about them and their growing conditions before you offer them for sale. Correct information on how they should be stored, when and where they should be planted, what to feed them and so forth will be extremely important to any customer.

- ***Australian native plants*** come in many exquisite varieties and some are ***indigenous to certain areas***. They can range in size from tiny, delicate jewel-like marvels to large and astonishingly beautiful blooms.

    The various species attract different types of birds and insects. For this reason, many bird lovers like to grow those natives that entice their favourite feathered friends into the garden!

    Some plants grow from ***cuttings***, others from ***bulbs*** and ***seeds***. Some can be coaxed from ***plant tissue***. (This latter method does not mean genetic modification: in fact, it keeps the original genes intact. However, it is a laboratory-based operation and can be costly.)

    Climate is crucial to many natives and this should be considered when planning your business: for example, if you wanted to start a business growing *tropical* flowers in Hobart, the added expense of hothousing would have to be considered.

As well as the financial rewards one can reap from growing native plants, there are other rewards too, such as knowing you're doing your part in saving them from extinction. The rarer they become, the more precious they will be!

Research any plant that interests you and learn as much as you can about marketing and distribution requirements before firming your business plans. You should be able to get much of the information you need from relevant clubs and associations. Consult florists, too.

Talk over your business plans with your accountant, solicitor and other professional advisers when it's time to put all the groundwork into practice!

* ***Bonsai and other ornamental or 'shape-able' trees*** (such as ficus) are always popular and are relatively easy to grow when you know the basics.

 Stock various sizes, shaping them yourself as they mature. Never throw away a tin can: use these for nurturing your seedlings.

 Bonsai, grown in ornate pots, provide a fascinating home business. They can be sold privately, at weekend markets, through garden shops, florists, nurseries and so forth.

 Advertise and market your business through your self-published books and videos, too! Lecture and demonstrate publicly if you are able to do so at charity luncheons or garden displays or consider building a fascinating, illustrated internet site full of stories and anecdotes about your products.

* ***Bromeliads*** are also popular plants and are among the easiest to grow. In fact, in Australia, many virtually grow themselves! For information, check out nurseries, libraries and talk to the Bromeliad Society nearest to where you live

* ***Rare orchids*** and other unique ***tropical plants*** are popular nearly all over the world and are grown for their ***bulbs*** as well as their flowers. While some are rather temperamental and prefer a hothouse environment, others thrive well in the open. You will find that there is a huge variety

from which to choose such as dendrobiums, phalaenopsis, cypripidiums, cattleyas, or cymbidiums to name a few.

Generally, orchids are not difficult to grow if you know the basic ground rules for each species. They can provide a good living for the specialist - although it can be a costly operation growing the rarer varieties. In fact, bulbs from some rare stock can cost *thousands of dollars*!

Australia has its own **native orchids** which, although small, can be very beautiful. Orchid growing is quite a hobby in this country, so you could cash in not only with the plants themselves but with your *knowledge* on **'how to grow them'**.

Give lectures on your favourite species at charity functions and luncheons whenever you can. Think about writing books, feature articles, leaflets and editorials, too. This type of exposure helps to build up your public image as a vitual 'expert' in your chosen field.

Any of the numerous orchid societies scattered throughout Australia could be a good starting point for gaining information if you are a beginner.

Keep an eye for up-coming orchid exhibitions and do as much research as possible before making any business plans.

Something to investigate further: while there is a big trade with the Far East in importing flowers into Australia for decorative purposes, the *export* of flowers is bigger still!

- **Herbs**
  (See Herbs & Herb products, Herb Gardens, Aromatherapy, Herbalist)

- **African Violets**
  So simple, so beautiful…and always so popular! These plants in attractive, hand painted pots can be a business in themselves…or represent a profitable sideline to many other gift or garden-related businesses.

- **Cactus**
  Hundreds of cacti can be growing in your garden or in pots, being trained into weird and wonderful shapes for future sales, with minimal effort and without it costing you a cent! How easy is this? The cactus is one of the

easiest and hardiest plants to grow and if you know how to market them, they should not be too hard to sell.

Research the species of cactus you stock: collect lots of historical or unusual anecdotes about them and compile all this information into self-published books, videos and pamphlets! Give public lectures to schools, gardening clubs, charities. These are fun ways of value-adding and money-earning. The cactus has many fascinating facts and your interesting talks might become legendary: eg 'How The Barrel Cactus Could Save Your Life!' or 'World Famous Cactus Gardens: How They Came About'.

Show your audience and customers tricks and secrets: show them how to handle these prickly plants, tell them of the mysterious, rare flowerings. Show how easy it can be to separate and propagate them. Your success will come from marketing the *mystery*, the *benefits* and the *fascination* of your product.

You may like to consider using cactus to make ornamental gardens. Use wide, flat pots, make up *fantasy scenarios* with ornaments ; train some of your cacti into really weird shapes.
(See under Ornamental Gardens as well as Hedge Maintenance & Topiary for lots more ideas.)

HOT DOG VAN

Hot dog vans are notorious for having kick-started many a millionaire into a series of incredible business franchises...but this is not to say that this is to be the fortune of all such vans.

However, if you can produce a sumptuous hot dog in an always-fresh roll with a selection of great condiments, your van is super clean and you yourself look impeccable, who wouldn't want to buy from you?

You then need only to find the best areas to locate, get all the necessary permits and insurance...and off you go!
(See also Food Van, Popcoorn Van))

HOUSE NUMBERING

If you called the ambulance or Fire Brigade to your house, would they be able to find you in a hurry? Or would they waste precious minutes cruising up and down, trying to figure out your house from all the other houses in the street all because of the lack of house numbering?

House number display is essential and you could do the community a service – and set yourself up in business at the same time – by applying easily-seen numbers to house fronts or kerbs. Your choice might be simple, stencilled numbers applied to the kerbside but it might also be solar or battery-powered, illuminated numbers that turn themselves on and off at dusk and dawn respectively. How creative can you be?

Do a bit of research and assess if any of the products that are currently available would suit you. Perhaps you will come up with a better design or method than anything on the market at the moment, thus starting your own business from the ground up.

Or you may prefer to buy a licence or franchise for an existing product.

HOUSE SITTING

Finding houses to look after for absent owners is likely to depend a great deal on *who* you know and *how* well you market your service but, if you can find yourself a few clients with itchy feet, you might find you can live for long periods rent-free, or receiving an income for your trouble. If your house sitting jobs are all in the one area, you may even be able to *retain your day job!*

House sitting can offer an ideal option for many home-based workers such as writers, embroiderers, knitters and others whose work does not entail a lot of equipment yet who need peace and quiet while they work.

The biggest plus in house sitting is usually that it enables you to live 'rent free' and often in excellent environments. The big negatives are likely to be the continual disruption inherent in moving residences and in trying to find short term accommodation in between jobs.

Occasionally you may be lucky enough to find a client who is going overseas for six months or more.

I

IMAGE ENHANCEMENT FOR PROFESSIONALS

Image enhancement can assist business and professional people (as well as job seekers) to improve not only their public image but their self image as well!

If you've had experience in sales training or consulting, you could find this type of business ideal to run from a home base. If you do not have the space or facilities at home, you may decide to organise training through seminars in hired premises.

Your own public image is important in this field so feature articles on your work for business and sales magazines could assist you no end. You might even consider writing a book or two. If you're not a good writer yourself, secure the services of a professional to turn your instructions into something eminently readable.

Consider, too, the viability of making a series of self-improvement videos. Books and videos could be sold and marketed by mail order as a segment of the business, a separate business, ...or you might decide to sell the rights to a publisher!

IMPORT/EXPORT

The import/export business is one of the world's oldest businesses. It has affected people of all countries, for the most part enriching them culturally - although history has shown that, in the hands of the unscrupulous, it has also had its downside.

One no longer needs to be a Marco Polo to know what products are being produced on the other side of the world. Today, thanks to technology, our communication and networking capability is so sophisticated that we can see, hear and appraise the world's discoveries anywhere, as soon as they are publicised. We can travel personally to the far ends of the earth for our finds and treasures - or we can make our discoveries, import them, distribute them and export them all from our *dining room table* if we wish.

There are countless import/export courses available for all levels of interest, from tertiary to correspondence: and there are franchises available to guide you and hold your hand when you are ready to begin.

Check your local TAFE or adult education outlets for courses if you're not sure where to go to learn the ropes. In the back of this book, you will find an information page with many useful contacts and websites.

Franchises can often be found in the business opportunity magazines and in the classifieds but, be wary! Some are very good; others may be shonky so do some in-depth research before parting with your hard-earned money!

Never go into any business scheme or follow anyone's advice without fully checking the credentials of those giving the advice...and talking over your plans with relevant *professional* advisers such as your accountant and solicitor.

INFLATABLE CASTLES

Whether you create fun for fairs, fetes or parties, the success of these inflatables will depend a great deal on your *marketing* ability!

You will certainly need big dollars if you intend buying the equipment outright. You may prefer to hire. Information can be obtained from the various suppliers. Look in the various business opportunities magazines or the Yellow Pages for names.

Comprehensive insurance as well as continuous and vigilant safety checks are required on any job like this.
(See also Amusement Machines/Inflatables)

INFORMATION PRODUCTS

The selling of information products in this Information Age could lead you straight to the *big money*...but success will depend a great deal on your *own* information! Can you gauge correctly what people want? Can you research all the necessary facts then come up with those facts presented in a clear yet interesting way?

Producing successful information products can be not only financially rewarding but personally satisfying as well because, in producing such products, you know that you are fulfilling people's needs and helping them to improve their lives.

Finding information these days is rarely difficult but it is certainly not for the shy and retiring. Only so much research can be done in a library or on the internet! You will need to find info that sets you apart, that gives your product an edge of exclusivity. To find the really useful 'tips and tricks' about any subject, you need to go straight to the 'horse's mouth': talk to experts in the field you are investigating. Record your interviews on audio tape, then transcribe the information then rewrite it, making it understandable and clear to the novice.

If you don't like the thought of having to arrange interviews with experts (and lots of people will do anything to get out of this!), there is another way to get products for your information business: have others do the job for you! This can be done simply by buying the **reprint rights** to already existing (but reputable) products! However, producing products this way can be expensive, will rarely give you exclusivity and furthermore, you will not be sure whether the information you have to sell is correct unless you research it all over again!

All products, whether produced, commissioned or bought for duplication by you should be *test marketed* before you do any large-scale advertising. Then, if all goes well, you can more confidently market, package and dispatch them. Here are just a few types of information services that you might like to consider:

books	e-books	audio books
audio CD's	co-authored books	transcribed interviews
video training	DVD's	special reports
newsletters	reprint rights	licensing products
e-zines	radio spot	TV show
reference material	bootcamps	introductory seminars
weekend seminars	residential seminars	continuing education
mentoring	teleseminars	correspondence courses
consulting services	speaking engagements	

(See Desktop Publishing, Writing. E-commerce, Coaching)

INFORMATION RESEARCH

There are many firms specialising in the finding of information for organisations and individuals. Even information specialists themselves will often outsource, requesting private researchers to do some of the digging and delving for them.

It will be up to you to set the parameters and style of the business you wish to run but, to those who love research, income is the minor part of this business.

INKJET CATRIDGE REFILLING

As with everything associated with technology, one has to be cognisant of the fact that huge changes are inevitable down the track. Of this business, one can only say that, *at the moment*, the market seems good for inkjet cartridge refills and appears to be expanding. The motto here is 'seize the day'!

For preliminary information on this business, browse through the various business opportunities magazines and the Yellow Pages.
(See also under Printer Cartridges)

INTERIOR DESIGN

Interior Design courses are available all over the country - and so are interior designers! To succeed in this competitive business, it goes without saying that you will need to possess outstanding aesthetic and design skills as well as good networking and marketing skills. The greater your network of contacts, the stronger will be your chance of finding clients.

If you make it in this field, the rewards can be excellent – but, as they say: 'many are called while few are chosen'! If, after a generous amount of time spent in this field, you feel that you are not succeeding despite your best efforts, don't waste your life! Move on!

INTRODUCTION AGENCY

You probably do it every day without even thinking about it: introduce people to other people. Even when you throw a dinner party, you try to match guests who are on the same wavelength and whom you believe will be most likely to enjoy each other's company. It's a natural instinct we all have - but some lucky people have it more highly developed than others.

If you have a gift for matchmaking, starting-up a well-run, creatively organised Introduction Agency could be extremely rewarding socially, emotionally and financially.

With today's long working hours, many professionals just do not have time to waste on dating potential partners who turn out to be the antitheses of what they want long term. They seek *quality* relationships in *minimum* time!

Furthermore, people are becoming accustomed to professional agencies finding them jobs, homes, babysitters, home maintenance staff and so forth. Why shouldn't they employ an agency to help them look for a life partner as well?

Many of today's more successful agencies provide quality outings for their clients: theatre groups, at-home dinner parties, dinner groups in restaurants, special interest groups, cocktail parties, supper clubs, games, dances, weekends away to mention just a few. These 'supervised' gatherings enable likely matches to get to know and assess one another in a friendly, risk-free environment without the pressures of a one-on-one date.

Here is a job that can be great fun, financially rewarding and socially stimulating for the adept matchmaker!

IRIDOLOGIST

Many schools of naturopathy run courses in iridology, some by correspondence. It is relatively easy to learn this method of diagnosis and does not require much start-up capital or investment in equipment. In fact, it would be possible to get by with just a torch, a magnifying glass and a few iridology charts! However, most practising iridologists are armed with a little more technology than this such as microscopes and special cameras.

Iridology regards the iris of the eye like a clock face with 12 sections. These 12 segments are believed to correspond to various parts of the body and any unusual markings or spots that appear on any of them can suggest a corresponding problem area.

While iridology is employed by several alternative therapies as a diagnostic tool only, quite a few iridologists have become well known in their own right. Most of the big names have enhanced their reputations through writing books or lecturing on their subject.

The more you put yourself on the public podium, the more your status in your field is likely to grow. If your presentation or public speaking skills need polishing, there are plenty of outlets for practice, such as the various Rostrum Club branches.

Warning: Iridology should never be substituted for a qualified doctor's diagnosis. It should only be used as an adjunct to traditional medical diagnosis.

IRONING SERVICE

Service businesses are the way of the future and can be very lucrative if well organised and well-run. However, relax! You do not necessarily have to do the ironing yourself! You could elect to be simply an *agent* and employ ironers to do the actual work in their own homes.

If you are indeed the prime worker, will you prefer to iron in the client's home or at your own home? And if you intend to do deliveries, you will probably need a van rather than a car as many freshly ironed garments will need to be hung from racks so they do not crease.

Ironing can be very time intensive work no matter how efficient a worker you are so, to increase your bottom line, consider tying in your ironing service with a reputable laundry or dry cleaning service. As an agent, you will receive a fee from each service provider you engage. By organising your business in this way, you would be offering almost a personal valet service: your vans would pick up soiled clothes from a house in the morning and deliver them back, cleaned and neatly pressed, in the evening,

Economic forecaster and futurist Phil Ruthven of IBIS Information Services predicts: 'the concept of pick-up-and-return laundry and dry cleaning has got to be an industry that will ultimately employ hundreds of thousands of people'! In fact, Ruthven questions whether house owners will feel it is worth while having home laundries at all in 30 years time!

J

JAMS AND PICKLES

Do you have a few secret recipes for making jams and pickles and a penchant for marketing? Then make money in your kitchen! Manufacture and learn how to market your products, devise your own attractive label...and start raking in the dollars!

Marketing suggestions: gift shops, tourist outlets, greengrocers, wineries, weekend markets, fetes and gourmet or specialty outlets.

JEWELLERY

Jewellery-making can be a wonderful home business for the truly creative, innovative craftsperson.

You will need some start-up and working capital for your materials and equipment... and more still for marketing! However, having said that, many a fashion entrepreneur has made it big with a range of unusual or eye-catching jewellery for very little start-up cost.

Precious stones do not necessarily a home-based jeweller make! There are many other less expensive materials used in jewellery, too: shells and string, metal, home-made and other beads, enamel, paste, resins, crystals, agates, buttons, gold plating, coins, medals, wire, ceramics...even wood. The list is virtually endless. What you are after is a product that is both beautiful and eye-catching!

Marketing is important in any field but in fashion, you need to get your products moving quickly as soon as they hit the marketplace because there are copycats on every fence just waiting to rip off your designs!

An illustrated web page should enable you to display your range to a huge audience and then, you could simply sell your range by mail order. Also, try to interest small, local fashion stores in your products, as well as larger department stores.

If you are a beginner, consider selling your jewellery at fairs, weekend markets, fetes and exhibitions. If you seem to be doing well, you could then consider doing a part-time course in jewellery-making to expand your horizons and bring you up to professional standard.

JOURNALIST (FREELANCE)

This is an ideal home-based job for someone who can write well and who has initiative and drive. Good writers can make excellent money if they treat writing like a business and are able to ignore the rejections: there are bound to be some!

If you have not had much experience in this field but are confident that you do write well, arrange interviews with well-known, interesting, newsworthy people and interview them. Then write articles revealing their views or experiences and substantiating with quotes.

The public thirsts after the knowledge and opinions of experts. Unfortunately, the views of writers are not so widely sought, so it is best *not* to offer your own opinion in the piece if you want to sell it!

When you have had a few articles accepted by major publications, you might consider supplementing your income by ***teaching journalism***. You could offer private tuition, correspondence courses or teach at a school or evening college if you can get a position

(See under Writing, Desktop Publishing, Coaching)

K

KNITTING

Knitting? An income-producing job? Why not? Jenny Kee did it with incredible style! Maybe you can too!

Hand knitting is regaining its popularity all over the world and has been described by some adherents as the 'new yoga'. Afficionados say it is extremely therapeutic. Gwyneth Paltrow, Madonna and Russell Crowe are just a few of the famous names rumoured to have taken up the craft so…if you are planning to knit, you'll be in good company!

For a home-based business, it would seem safer to concentrate on hand made garments rather than machine knits. Machine knitting is really the province of importers and bigger manufacturers and you'd have to be very brave - or very innovative! - to compete.

Because hand knitting is a relatively slow process, you may be wondering, 'how could I ever make money from hand knitting?' This is why you need to develop stupendous, up-market styles that can demand higher prices. Far better to work on one splendid work of knitted art for which you can charge accordingly than a half dozen commonplace woollies, the equivalent of which can be bought for a song at the local store.

One of the world's fastest hand knitters was said to be Hazel Tindell of Shetland who was rumoured to knit 255 stitches in 3 minutes - but you don't need to compete with her unless you're also targeting the Guinness Book of Records!

If you have an eye for colour and unusual, *can't-get-it-anywhere-else designs*, an illustrated website advertising your creations complete with price lists and ordering info might suit your business. Such a website might see you receiving orders from around the world so a Merchant Account would make life easier.

One of the cheapest ways to advertise is via what is called *'2-step advertising* whereby you place a small ad of a couple of lines in the classifieds and, when potential customers phone, then send them a free brochure of your designs with full information, price-list and order form.

If your work seems to be really taking off, you may decide to approach a few exclusive fashion boutiques.

Make an appointment and show the buyer your illustrated portfolio plus a few samples of your work. Some garments might be accepted 'on appro' or you might receive an order there and then. Unfortunately, the profit from garments sold through retailers will need to be shared but sometimes it is worth the sacrifice of a few dollars just to get exposure in the right echelons of the fashion market.

There are many other ways to promote yourself. For example, holding mannequin parades in conjunction with local fashion and accessory shops can often draw big crowds when these functions are for schools and charities. The parades do not need to take place in the shop. They can be held after work or in the evening in church halls, recreation centres, schools and many other venues.

Entering your knits in major craft exhibitions can boost your name, especially if you win a prize! You could then use this good fortune to advantage in advertising: *'prize-winning designer'* is a phrase that can always be relied upon to pull interest and orders!

Start your home business *slowly* and build up! Make and *test-market* a few designs first, until you see the reception they receive in the market place. What *you* see as 'fashion' may not represent fashion to *others*!

If your creations become the talk of the town, it will be time to turn your 'therapeutic craft' into a fulltime business and start raking in the profits. At that stage, you might be ready to source other home knitters willing to do piece work or knit up your fabulous designs for you.

L

LABELS

It's hard to believe the obscene amount of money that some people are making from manufacturing name labels! One woman stumbled on this occupation simply because she couldn't buy the type of coloured labels she needed to differentiate her children's lunch boxes. So she designed them herself and…bingo! Everybody wanted coloured name labels just like them! A million dollars from a simple frustration fix!

This goes for many basic products that people have been using for decades: suddenly, someone somewhere has an idea for making them *easier* or *faster* or *better* and the word spreads like wildfire.

Labels - whether they're for identifying clothing, organising files, personalising lunch boxes or anything else - can be simple, everyday necessities or beautifully designed and superbly functional in some way! They don't have to be square, oblong or round. They can be shaped like animals, birds, sports equipment. Creativity attracts money!

Can *you* find a way to be creative with label-making and search out a niche for yourself in this market?

LAMPSHADES

To make a dent in the lighting market, you'll need to produce products that are really outstanding in some way as there is so much competition both locally and from overseas.

Shades can be sold with or without bases. However, creating and selling hand-made or unusual bases can make a huge difference to your bottom line, especially if they are attractive and unusual.

Not all bases need to be outstanding works of art at the outset. Basic, unadorned bases could be bought wholesale and hand painted or decorated by you in some way to look many times their cost.

Leadlight shades are also in good demand particularly for family rooms, pool rooms and rumpus areas. There are numerous leadlighting classes available for those interested.

Marketing ideas:
Try selling *on appro* through smaller lighting retailers and home decorating shops. Perhaps others could be sold privately from a home base or by mail order from a web page.

A stall at a really busy weekend market or a stand at a home show or two might also be worth trying.

LANDSCAPING AND PAVING *(See also Concreting)*

No paint brush or canvas needed for this type of landscape artist! The title covers *total garden design:* paving, paths, garden walls, watering systems and so forth as well as the supply of plants and trees. It also implies that you're somewhat of an expert at what you do!

If you don't have all the necessary knowledge, you can acquire it at evening school.

The money to be made in this field by top landscape artists is considerable. However, to be successful, it is necessary to be forever on your toes networking and promoting your business.

Landscaping can be very strenuous so it is only for the physically fit. Even if you employ others to do the hard physical labour for you, be prepared: there may be times when *you* may have to step in to the breech when a worker does not turn up or someone goes home ill!

Wherever you are working, *always* place an attractive sandwich board outside on the footpath, advertising that you are on that site. You will be surprised at how much work can come from passers-by and neighbours who see these signs in their locality over and over again.

One of the biggest problems that most landscapers and pavers seem to face is finding and keeping a good, reliable team of workers.

LANGUAGE TRANSLATION SERVICE

Are you bi-lingual or multi-lingual, well educated and reliable? Then, you need never be out of work again, especially if you live in a big city!

Some languages are more in demand than others, particularly in certain suburbs, so it will pay you to do a bit of preliminary research on what languages are needed where and when. If you want to make translation your prime business, consider settling in an area where your skills will be in demand.

Produce some up-market brochures containing information about your service. These could then be sent to hospitals, local doctors, solicitors, government organisations, the Courts, various organisations and corporations which are likely to have overseas affiliations, TV and radio stations (particularly ethnic TV and radio) as well as publishers. Also, you might consider placing ads in the classifieds and related ethnic newspapers, newsletters and magazines.

LASER PRINTER AND TONER RECHARGING

Here is a way that might not only earn money for you – it might *save* money for your clients! And it doesn't require any diplomas, degrees or anything else!

To make the most of this job from a home base, you will need to actively promote your service as there is a great deal of competition out there. Advertising could be via the classifieds, in magazines, posters, notices, newsletters and flyers, through word of mouth and *non-stop networking*!

As you will not have the big overheads to pay in working from home, you may have a better chance of making a living out of this service than those who are running the business from a commercial premises.

LAUNDROMAT

The most obvious way to run a laundromat as a *home-based business* is to set yourself up in a shop with an attached residence! That way, you can have the best of both worlds.

Operators don't always have to be on site…but machines do break down and money does get caught in slots! So you will need to be 'on hand' so that clients requiring assistance can at least buzz you when you're needed.

You can generally add value to a laundromat service by becoming an agent for allied services such as dry cleaning, ironing, mending, stain removal, invisible mending and so forth.

LAWN MOWING/GARDEN MAINTENANCE

Does anyone have to be convinced of the viability of lawn maintenance after the phenomenal success of Jim's Mowing, V.I.P. and other well known lawn maintenance services that have become part of the scene in just about every street in the country? Australia's Jim Penman, for example, went from mowing lawns with not much more than $20 dollars in his pocket - to 'multi-million dollar franchiser' in just a few years!

Becoming a franchisee can be an excellent way to start in this business, although *purchasing* the franchise can be expensive. On the positive side, the better franchisers offer you a well respected business name plus guaranteed customers and a good weekly income over the starting period.

If you do not have the funds to buy a franchise, and prefer to start up under your own steam, view yourself primarily as a *business*person rather than a tradesperson! Learn as much as you can before you start, not just about *garden maintenance* but *business maintenance* as well! Talk to other franchisees and contractors that you see mowing lawns and let them know you're thinking of starting up a similar business. Find out as much information as you can...but be sure to tell them *your* business will be over on the *other side of town*, otherwise they may not share any secrets with you!

Most importantly, take all your plans to the professionals in your life such as your accountant, solicitor and bank manager and be guided by them.

LEADLIGHTING

This is an ancient and beautiful art where transparent coloured glass is used to transform simple everyday items like door panels, lampshades and windows into glowing, lead-veined mosaics.

Leadlighting is widely taught, both privately or in classes, at many studios, workshops, recreation centres, TAFE's and colleges.

You may prefer to work and sell privately from your own home workshop or fulfil orders for decorator shops, window/door manufacturers and retailers. You may even create a web page of designs. Network with architects and builders, too, and anyone else whom you feel may be able to help you.

While this art may not be easy to demonstrate out of a workshop environment, you may be able to give illustrated talks at clubs and other venues. Some of your finished pieces could be on display and a glossy, illustrated catalogue would show potential clients other designs available.

Even a continuously-running video or slide show on your laptop might be helpful. *(See also Lampshades)*

LEATHER REPAIR

With the popularity of leather in furniture and other goods in constant use, leather repair and restoration for the commercial, residential and automotive markets could become an excellent business if you have the skills.

You could also learn to repair and recondition other materials as well, such as carpets and plastics for a more comprehensive service.
(See also under Automotive and Upholstery)

LEATHERWORK

Leather products have many markets and are produced with various levels of finesse. Top quality garments and accessories are generally the province of the specialist, as are equine products like saddles and boots...but there are many openings for even the most basic craftsperson, too.

Stalls selling basic leather goods can be found at most fairs and markets. One of the best ways to sell at these outlets is to run a continuous demo which can draw audiences like honey draws bears! A range of products like belts and other simple accessories could be pre-cut, then *'personalised'* for customers while they wait. This need only involve tooling a name. Alternatively, the client could place a deposit, then come back in an hour or so to pay the balance and pick up the completed item.

Many tourist outlets and souvenir shops are happy to take work from creative leatherworkers. In such places, there is generally a preference for goods that are in some way connected to the locale or have a national flavour.

Many leather items such as belts, bags and other accessories could also be sold by mail order! If you can find the right *niche market*, you stand a good chance ot making a good income! Perhaps something useful but incredibly well crafted for the handyman or the fisherman? Just as an example, it might be a well-made, multi-pocketed *handyperson's belt in oiled leather* with hammer loops and 'places for everything'! It could be accompanied by a glossy pamphlet explaining where every tool and nail goes and even be sold with an appropriate bonus tool of some kind.

Brainstorm by getting all your friends, male and female, to make a wish list. *(See also under Personalised Products, Bag Making)*

LIGHTING MAINTENANCE/LIGHT GLOBE REPLACEMENT

This is only a relatively new business but it is expected that franchises will soon be available throughout Australia.

Whether you buy a franchise or start up a business on your own, you may be expected to service lighting outlets in all types of domestic and commercial premises and change anything from simple ceiling globes (particularly needed for elderly clients) to globes in commercial premises that could involve chandeliers many metres up!

Globes that are out of reach are usually changed with the use of a specially designed rod with grabber...*and* full insurance!

Your business should be marketed to…everyone who uses light globes!
But you could also search out *niche* areas for your advertising, too, like seniors' magazines and newspapers.

Wherever you are working, be sure you have a sandwich board in full view on the footpath to catch the attention of passers-by and neighbours. (Don't put it where they will trip over it, though!) A permit will be necessary.

Such simple, on-the-job advertising can be most effective as many people will not know that a service such as yours exists.
(See also Chandelier Cleaning Service)

LIMOUSINE SERVICE

A life of glamour driving VIP's and film stars awaits you if you are a good driver, excellent marketer…and have a spare limo or two in the garage!

If not, don't worry. Luxury vehicles can also be leased!

Patience is necessary, too, in a job like this as much time is spent waiting for clients, dodging parking inspectors and trying to find places to park your ultra long vehicle.

Introduce your business to all major hotels, tour organisers, airports, clubs, film studios, entertainment centres, wedding and party planners, government institutions; in fact, anywhere and everywhere you can think of where the rich and famous…and those who wish to *appear* rich and famous… might congregate!

LINGERIE

Lingerie can be made at home and certain styles can be sold quite profitably but you need to know *what* to make and *where* to sell it.

Leave the selling of those jamas, practical nighties and everyday undies to the big stores who import it by the tonne! *You* need to concentrate on exquisite, hand finished silks and satins that are the province of the glamorous and wealthy! Make up samples to test market first.

Party plan lingerie can make a mint where the garments are truly outstanding and sexy. Parties can be organised in your own home or in the homes of friends to get started. When party givers know that you always give the host or hostess a superb gift from your collection to say 'thank you', you're bound to find more and more takers! The value of your 'gift of appreciation' could be estimated according to the number of invitees or the number of sales made on the night.

Garments could also be sold directly from your home workroom if you can get council permission. As well, they may sell through exclusive boutiques or even from your own web page.

Advertise in upmarket fashion publications and in the appropriate sections of the newspapers. Distribute your glossy, illustrated brochures to all likely clients including photographers, film and model agencies and party planners.

Most importantly, make and continually update a mailing list of new brides and brides-to-be and send them your brochures and specials. Compile this list assiduously from the wedding/engagement notices that appear each week.
(See also Sewing & Embroidery for more ideas)

LOCKSMITH (MOBILE)

If you do not wish to own a shop or kiosk in a shopping strip or mall, a great alternative for a locksmith is to go *mobile*. You will need your own well-equipped van plus a home workshop. However, consider the noise factor of any machinery you need to run in your workshop: will the neighbours object? There may also be restrictions on the horsepower of the equipment you use, so you will need to check out these things with the council.

Advertising will be most important: you will need to network and advertise well. Good, clear signage on your van, your house - and on the sandwich board you erect on the footpath outside every job on which you're working is vital!

Your work might be largely *residential* or for *local business* but there are many *state and local government* needs for locksmiths, too. Top locksmiths could find themselves working at hospitals, universities, schools or offices one minute and then, being called by the fire department, the police or public works department the next. This work can be quite varied.

Maintain a *regular* ad in your local classifieds and a permanent ad in the Yellow Pages if possible. In your advertising, make a feature of the *benefits* of your service: *security, reliability, punctuality, 24-hour service* and whatever else you offer. Flyers or magnetised business cards should be delivered to as many homes and businesses in your locale as you can manage.

And be sure you have all the permits and insurance cover you need!

LOGO CREATION, SLOGANS AND JINGLES

This business could be an excellent adjunct to an advertising/desk top publishing business or for anyone selling *personalised gifts and promos*.

If you are able to create clever logos and jingles, you can earn quite a good income if you are a good marketer.

Your own logo will need to be outstanding, as it is representative of your capability. It needs to be displayed on all your literature, your ad in The Yellow Pages (a 'must'), on any signage outside your house and on your car.

- *IDEA*: A button or bumper sticker business might be a useful add-on business.

LUNCH RUN (MOBILE)

Traditionally, a lunch bar can mean 'big bikkies' for the operator but, unless your shop is attached to your residence, it is not easy to run it as a home business! However, check with the local council before giving up on the idea as you never know what zoning loopholes may exist in your area, particularly if it is high density.

Here are a couple of more attainable home-based alternatives:

- *Lunch basket run*: If your lunch run is only small scale, servicing a few local businesses, you may be able to manage with just a basket or trolley of prepacked sandwiches, rolls, cakes or biscuits and fruit.

- You might even provide a *fax order service* for clients. Regular clients could fax or ring through their lunch orders each morning while you could provide an assortment of sandwiches and snacks for casuals. Perhaps one of the office or factory workers might act as *co-ordinator*, taking the orders then ringing them through to you each morning. You could then repay this person with free or discounted lunches.

- *A lunch run* might be a good sideline for parents of school-aged children who want a job that finishes by around 2.30 p.m. each day.

- *Mobile Canteen*: If you envisage something on a larger scale looking after offices and factories or big work sites, *a mobile canteen* might be required. Will your service provide for the whole day's requirements of workers: breakfast, lunch plus morning and afternoon teas - or will you provide lunches only?

M

MACADAMIA NUT FARM

Who doesn't love macadamia nuts? This is an established market and could provide a very good little business if you can find a suitable site with the right growing conditions and zoning, sufficient capital to support its growth…and sufficient marketing nous to compete and win.

Don't go into a business like this with your eyes closed: you need to find out all you can about it beforehand. Speak to other nut farmers as well as other business professionals and those advisors whom you feel can help you weigh up your ideas.

Be prepared to formulate a *detailed business plan* and have it checked over by the appropriate people before you start. By researching your market thoroughly and planning ahead every step of the way, you can often avoid many costly errors and help make business a pleasure.

MAGICIAN

Success as a magician depends not only on one's talent for creating incredible illusions but the ability to *entertain* the audience as well! A large proportion of time is spent creating and rehearsing a really enjoyable commentary to go with their act.

If you are confident that you have a good gig that can hold an audience spellbound, you'll then need to **promote** yourself. **Network**! Talk to likely talent hiring bodies such as talent agencies, TV stations, clubs, hotels, children's party organisers and others who may be able to help you get work. You might also place ads in the classifieds, in magazines, in school newsletters and other relevant publications.

Many entertainers build up their names *and* perform good deeds at the same time by offering their acts free for charity and hospital performances. This is a win-win situation where both parties –you and your audience – can benefit.

MAILING LIST BROKER

Lists of potential targets for mail order products are compiled, bought, sold, hired and traded every day. However, good, reliable lists that are current and focus on particular groups and categories are not that easy to come by and require astute networking skills.

If you are in a direct mail or mail order business, you will have automatically built a list of clients over time for *the type of products you sell*. However, if you are starting a new business or introduce a new product, a new group of clients with a proven interest in that product may need to be sought.

How does one find ready-made clients in a hurry? The easiest, but not always the cheapest, way to do this is to engage a mailing list broker who can *supply you with a list of names* and addresses of likely buyers: ideally, those who have bought similar-type products by mail order, preferably in the very recent past.

You may decide to become a list broker if you are a good networker. If so, you will need to learn all you can about the availability and quality of lists, where and how they are obtained, the areas or subjects they cover, ways of assessing the currency and viability of targets... prices and so forth.

Some mailing lists are stale or as good as useless. Others can mean big money, for you as the middleman (or woman) and for the clients on either side of you.

MAIL ORDER
(See also Direct Mail)

If becoming a millionaire in a hurry is your goal, the mail order business is said to be able to get you there much quicker than just about anything else - *providing you have a reputable product* and *know how to market it*!

There are hundreds of products that can be sold by mail order...but dealing in anything that has a short shelf life, like most *foodstuffs*, could be problematic. So, too, could the selling of *delicate, breakable* items or certain clothing that comes in *various sizes*. If clothing is your product, try dealing in 'one-size-only' garments or 'small, medium and large' to help avoid too many returns.

Information products are among the most popular to handle. Generally, they are cheap to produce and can often be *'printed on demand'*. Thus, if a product proves to be unpopular or unprofitable after it has been tested, it can be discontinued without too much wastage of time, materials or money and another conjured up. This can then be trial marketed and assessed.

If you don't wish to manufacture your *own* products, you may decide to become a **dealer** or **agent** for another person or company's products.

In the field of information products, for example, it is possible to buy the *reprint and duplication* rights to many books, videos, CD's, DVD's and reports. Generally these require you to pay a once-off fee; after that, all profits you make from the goods are yours. Alternatively, you may be offered the opportunity of purchasing the completed product at a discount.

You need to be careful of the dealerships and products with which you associate yourself. Associate only with long-term, *reputable* companies!

When advertising your products, it is sensible to choose those publications or classifications that are *related to your product* and which present a fairly obvious target. Telemarketing and the internet can also be useful marketing tools. But there are other more *direct* ways to go if you wish.

For example, in **direct mail**, you could mail offers of your products directly to clients who have recently **exhibited an interest in similar products** or bought them by mail. Such target-rich environments can be discovered by a lot of research, networking and hard work...or by buying relevant mailing lists from a reliable list broker.

Sometimes you can be lucky. Particularly if your product is one for other businesses, you might find the very names you want waiting for you in the Yellow Pages!

Mailing lists can be quite expensive and out of the range of many newcomers but, for a going concern, they can often be invaluable if you find a good one that yields results.

You'll find more information about *mail order*, *direct marketing* and *reprint rights* by looking up these topics on internet search engines or browsing through business opportunities magazines

One word of warning: proceed slowly with any product you intend to sell by mail order, *test-marketing* everything first! Otherwise you could end up with a garage full of widgets but no takers!

- *Dropshipped Products*
  Dropshipping is a relatively easy way to sell goods by mail, providing you have a trustworthy supplier. It means that you don't need to personally handle, store, post or even *see* the goods that you're selling if you don't wish to. You merely advertise the product, take the orders...then send the names and addresses of customers to the dropshipper; the latter does the actual storing, packing and shipping.

  Note: you need to be sure that your provider is utterly reliable and timely in their delivery, otherwise *you're* the one who will be dealing with customer complaints!

MANICURIST

As a manicurist, you have several options available in working from a home base. A few suggestions are:

- You might perform your nail magic for weddings and special occasions as well as for your permanent clients at a *home salon*.

- You may work on a casual basis for a couple of days per week at *local beauty salons*.

- You could think about performing manicures for *hostel and nursing home* residents on a weekly or fortnightly basis. This could be quite a good source of income.

- If you have an artistic bent, you might offer *'nail art'* as part of your repertoire of services. Many clients love to have tiny designs painted on their nails for special occasions. Make up an illustrated folio of the designs from which clients can choose.

If you maintain a home salon, it should be professional, separate from the house, clean and *well ventilated*. Simply clearing an area in the lounge room for customers is a no-no! Look at converting a garage, an outside room or bungalow into your salon.

Advertising is extremely important. Small ads in local newspapers, posters in the local shops and several 'letterbox drops' is probably the cheapest way to start off. It may take a while for your name to become known …but *word of mouth* is a very effective form of advertising and costs nothing at all to gain you a great reputation! So, if your work is good, it should bring its own reward.

You might decide to throw in a *freebie* such as relaxing hand massage at the end of every manicure. It will make clients feel pampered and appreciated.

Note: Check on any permits, zoning, insurance requirements before you start up any business.

MARRIAGE CELEBRANT

To become a registered celebrant and receive your Statement of Attainment certificate, you will need to undergo a nationally accredited training course learning how to *plan, conduct and review a Marriage Ceremony.*

This is a respected profession, can be an excellent 'work from home' business if you have a sociable personality, a good voice and like performing in public. Furthermore, it can bring you into contact with many interesting and delightful people in some truly beautiful – and weird! - environments. People marry in a variety of ways and places: underwater in shark tanks, parachuting out of planes...but don't worry! There are plenty of traditional weddings, too, if you prefer.

Note: **Funeral and Name Giving** celebrancy courses are also available.
For further information, go to www.ag.gov.au/celebrants

MASSAGE

Some forms of massage require masseurs to be *accredited*, but there are several forms that can be started after only a short course or two. Courses can usually be located among TAFE and Uni short courses, naturopathic schools or from practising professionals.

(Check out any prerequisites necessary for the technique you are interested in with the *Association of Massage Therapists [AMTA])*

Massages are best performed in a restful, comforting environment. If you are working at home, your rooms should be spotless, warm and neat and preferably separate from the house. Do not, under any circumstances, begin operating this business without proper insurance cover.

Decide on the style of massage you wish to offer and the type of clients you would like to treat. Some types of massage are customer specific. For example, **sports massage** could bring you into contact with sportspeople, gymnasts and dancers; **therapeutic massage** might see you spending much of your day with the frail and ill; **neck massage** (see below) could have you mixing with office workers or professional business people.

Here are just a few of the various styles of massage you may like to investigate:

- **Aromatherapy**
- **Chinese, Thai, Korean massage**
- **Deep Tissue**
- **Sports Massage**
- **Reiki**
- **Pregnancy and Post Natal**
- **Trigger Point Therapy**
- **Shiatsu**
- **Magnetic Therapy**

- *Cellulite massage*
- *Relaxation*
- *Remedial*
- *Head and Neck massage*

You will need to enquire about any qualifications required.

Here are some brief comments on just a few:

- *Head and Neck Massage*: this could prove to be a great little business if you are willing to go *mobile*, which should not be a problem if you have a car as your only other equipment is quite minimal: a portable rest, hand towels, massage oil - and a soothing personality!

  As a visiting head/neck masseur, you might treat clientele in offices, factories and other places of employment where workers are sitting for long hours at their desks, computers and machines and who are therefore prone to neck strain.

- *Sports Massage* is almost a 'must' in the schedule of any sports enthusiast, to assist the body in physical performance as well as recuperation from injury. Attaining the necessary qualifications for this form of massage can take quite a long time however.

- *Therapeutic Massage* - a gentle, relaxing type of massage employing soothing strokes to improve circulation and in order to help reduce stress and tension. Many hospital, nursing home and hospice patients look forward to visits from therapeutic masseurs.

- *Traditional Chinese Massage* can take many years of training but there are also some short intensive courses available at various levels. It requires both intellectual and physical skills but even a few short weeks of training under a good teacher can place you in a position to start business in the simpler types of massage.

- *Reflexology* treats specific ailments by the pressure of various 'reflexes' or 'hot buttons' on the patient's feet (and sometimes the hands or ears). These spots are said to correspond with various organs of the body. For example, the big toe is believed to correspond to the head area: the area under the second and third toes is said to correspond to the eyes, that under the fourth and fifth toes to the ears.

  It is not the province of this book to say whether or not there is any substance to these claims but reflexology certainly has many adherents who attest to its efficacy!

- *Shiatsu* is virtually *acupressure* - thumb pressure applied to various vital points along the meridians of the patient's body. This is believed to have the effect of clearing energy blockages, allowing the body to return to normal function.

- *Reiki Level 1* can be learned over one intensive weekend of training. The hands are placed just above the body rather than actually on it contrary to most massage techniques..

  New graduates have ongoing access to a network of Reiki practitioners nationwide for continuing information and assistance. Reviews can generally be undertaken without further cost. There is also an Advanced Level available to students who wish to take their studies further.

MATCHMAKING SERVICE
(See under Introduction Service)

MATTRESS CLEANING & SANITISING

While *all* dust mites cannot be removed from matresses and furnishings, they can certainly be reduced and then kept under reasonable control by sanitising, good ventilation and air conditioning or heating the rooms in which they live. They tend to thrive in cold, damp environments.

A *reputable* franchise might be best here unless you are experienced in this field. *(Please turn to Steam Cleaning)*

MEDITATION INSTRUCTOR

Have you studied meditation? Could you teach others to relax and meditate? If so, you might be able to build a small business for yourself while helping others at the same time.

The meditation room should be clean, harmonious and quiet, with pleasant smells and soft lighting. Give a short talk about meditation and stress reduction techniques at the beginning of each class so students understand what they are doing and what to expect.

MEN'S RECYCLED CLOTHING
(See Recycled Clothing)

METAL BEATING

In the hands of an artist, metal beating can be a real art form. Whatever you are thinking of producing, be it copper plaques, silver jewellery or pewter bowls and candlesticks, you could make yourself a good business if you possessed the necessary talent and skill.

This type of craft is eminently suitable as a home business but one needs to pay extra attention to marketing the products produced. Unless you can find a way of selling direct to the public, either through your own home gallery (for which you would need to obtain permission) or some other way e.g through a weekend stall, sub-leasing portion of a gallery or selling by mail order or via a web page, you may find you need to rely on retail outlets like galleries, tourist and craft shops, decorator shops and so forth to take your work, which can eat up quite a slice of your profits.

METALWORKING

Humans have been working in metal for centuries. It has been used for utilitarian purposes as well as for artistic and decorative work and it is impossible to list the thousands of items that a metalworker could fashion or the many ways it could be used!

Many technical schools offer tuition for beginners. Knowledge you may have already gained in this medium should be capable of being channelled into some type of home manufacturing operation.

Metalworking is suitable for the home workshop but there are a few provisos: in many areas, there are strict noise and power-machinery restrictions placed on residential businesses as well as the number of assistants you can have working for you. Once you start using lathes in the peace of suburbia, neighbours could turn nasty!

However, metalwork today does not *have* to involve noise, heat, sweaty foreheads and large biceps. It can be a pleasurable activity using lightweight machinery that can bend, twist, scroll and fold your materials into saleable and useful items without all the hassles of the past.

Ornamental wrought iron objects like gates, house numbers, wine racks, candelabras and chandeliers, bird cages, furniture, aquarium stands and so forth can be a great start for the home operator.

MINIATURE GOLF – MANUFACTURE & HIRE

Miniature golf courses are used indoors and out and can be *permanent* or *portable*. Mini golf provides excellent entertainment for both adults and children at amusement parks, fetes, motels and B&B's. One of its main attractions is that it takes up little room yet can offer so much enjoyment.

Mobile courses are fairly easily transported, erected and dismantled.

While there is a business in portable golf course hire, there is another in the *manufacture* of these courses. In fact, they could be quite readily home-manufactured by the clever handyperson.

The building of permanent courses might be a good sideline for an ex-builder or concreter.

MIRROR SPECIALIST

While mirrors are often bought fully framed, they can also be cut and made up in the home workshop if you have the right equipment and knowledge.

Frames can be made up in wood, copper, plaster, silver, pewter, wrought iron and many other materials in unusual or popular designs. They can be carved, gilded, beaten, moulded, painted, decorated with plaster, adorned with shells, dried flowers, mirror tiles, mosaics or even intricate decoupage. Real silver is used for the backing of the mirror itself.

As a home business, you will need to produce items that are way ahead of what can be bought in the stores, and that are outstanding or unusual in some way. For example, what about *special purpose* mirrors, with frames aimed at golfers, tennis or basketball players, dancers, art deco afficionados? Frames for children could illustrate favourite stories like Cinderella or Puss-in-Boots and could even be personalised (with a stencilled-on poem containing the child's name). Your stock might also include an inexpensive line of quaint or unusual smaller mirrors to encourage gift-buying customers.

Home decorator shops often accept work to sell 'on appro'. You could also try selling at weekend markets. (Be sure you are fully insured, however, as transporting and displaying mirrors in public can be risky.)

Mirror repair could be a useful sideline, too. If you are unable to do this to a professional standard, it may be worth taking a short course or two.

MOBILE BOOKKEEPING

Outsourcing business services such as accounting and bookkeeping has become part of our way of life in the new millennium. If you promote yourself well as a *mobile* bookkeeper and run a tight ship, organised and timely, you should end up with all the business you can handle.

MOBILE DOG WASH

With a well-equipped van and a flair for pet grooming, you may decide to start up this business on your own...or you could buy a reputable *franchise* that provides the 'know-how' - plus what you *don't* know! - and throw in ready-made customers as well! Franchises can be expensive to buy, however, and somewhat restrictive in their operation but, if you are just beginning, it is sometimes the best way to go.

If you are adamant about starting up on your own, then learn everything you can about the job first. Invite a mobile dogwash to give your own pooch a pampering session at home while you observe and ask lots of questions. Do this with two or three dogwash companies if possible. (What a spotless dog you will have!)

When you have drawn up your business plan, talk it over with your accountant and any other professionals whom you feel could help you. Don't be backward about getting *information* from franchisers, too, even if you do not intend buying a franchise from them. What you need is lots of information before going it on your own in this very competitive business.

MOBILE DJ

Love music and the party scene? Then be prepared to accept *satisfaction* as part of your pay packet because this job - unless you have masses of talent, a great *personality and a wide network* in the industry - is hardly the quickest path to riches.

On the other hand, it may be that you are a very special person - one of a rare species who just happens to have been born with the magic 'it' factor that catches on with a crowd! You may have an easy-going, natural spiel, a certain 'magnetism' that impels an audience to listen and enjoy. If this sounds like you, don't pass up the opportunity. Give it a try!

MOBILE LOCKSMITH

As a mobile locksmith, advertising will be your best friend (by flyer, letterbox drop, the local classifieds as well as the *Yellow Pages*.) You would also do well to go the extra mile in *service*, too: can you offer *24 hour service, 7 days a week...* or *service within the hour*?

You'll need to check on any restrictions on noise levels and machinery in your area if you intend to work at home, as neighbours often protest at the whine of motors, lathes and other machinery.

This work can offer a great variety of technical challenges, working environments and interaction with all types and classes of people in often amazing situations.

MOBILE HEALTH CARE

A *mobile* naturopath, masseur, podiatrist, acupuncturist, reflexologist? Why not? Everything else is going mobile these days!

Whatever your field may be, ***advertising*** and top quality ***service*** will be two factors vital to your success.
(See various entries under Naturopath, Herbalist and Massage, Beauty etc)

MOBILE VEHICLE INSPECTION/ MOBILE WINDSCREEN REPAIR
(See under Automotive)

MODEL & FILM AGENCY

As with any business associated with the media or entertainment, the more people you know in the industry, the better. A model, ex-model or actor might find this an excellent home-based business.

It requires hard work to build up an agency...plus lots of resilience and unlimited persistence!...but as a successful model yourself, it is most likely you will have already developed these qualities.

You may decide to specialise. Are you interested in promoting children, animals, the fuller figure or some other 'niche' in the market, depending on your interest and network of contacts? You need an eye for *people with potential*. One way to find new talent is to start your own ***modelling school*** in conjunction with the agency. *(See Casting Agency)*

Here are a few ideas that you might like to toss around:

- ***Children's Agency:***
  Unless you have been in the industry for a long time and have built up a network of contacts, running a children's film or model agency from your home is not the easiest task. However, if you yourself are a fairly well known media personality, running such an agency 'on the side' could be a piece of cake!

- ***Model Agency (General):***
  A home-based film and model agency may have smaller overheads but again, unless you are *well networked*, you're unlikely to have the clout, accessibility or even the credibility that a city-based agency has.

- ***Agency for Animals:***
  An agency offering clever animal talent to the film, modelling and entertainment industry should be capable of being run from a home base. Don't leave anything to chance! Always audition the animals first and satisfy yourself that they are capable of doing what you say they can do; never take their ability on hearsay!

MODELLING

Fashion models don't necessarily have to be extraordinarily beautiful or pencil slim to become successful. Some fashion houses and magazines specialise in fuller figures, the mature aged and so forth. Well manicured hands and feet can also find work if their owners are persistent!

The work itself can be fun, glamorous and exciting…but unfortunately, like everything else, it has its negative side: that is, *finding* the work! Breaking into modelling is *not* glamorous, *not* fun and *far from exciting*. However, if you are as persistent as a blowfly at a barbeque, you might make it. And, if you do, you could be in for a marvellous period of your life!

If you can get yourself on the books of a reputable agency. so much the better. But how to do this?

If you have the funds for a modelling course at one of the major modelling schools, it could be your quickest way to stardom. Some schools run their own modelling agency. At the very least, they are usually very well connected in the industry and are usually adept at spotting talent.

Beware of the occasional small 'agency' or scoundrel that preys on innocent young hopefuls, luring them into paying out fortunes for a folio of photos then disappearing with their money! There are many of them and generally, they prowl the classifieds. Deal only with *well respected agencies* to avoid being taken for a ride!

You may have contacts of your own, too. If so, use them. If not - and if you can't afford a modelling course – plunge right in and make appointments with the various agencies, photographers and fashion magazines, taking along a folio of your very best photos.

If you cannot land an appointment, *send* your photos with a covering letter, a short CV and tear sheets (if you have any) of jobs you have done…and keep your fingers crossed!

- *Artist's model* is one alternative for those who have a reasonable figure, and can hold a pose for a fair time. Generally, it can provide quite a reasonable living. Apply at reputable art schools, TAFE colleges and art societies (don't forget the *specialist* art societies like pastel societies, watercolour societies, realist art societies and so forth).

  Caution: It is not recommended that you take private modelling work for anybody unless you are 100% certain of that person's reputation.

MODEL SHIPS AND PLANES

If you are skilled in making ships, planes and other models in wood, make patterns of your prototypes and have a trial number cut from plywood or balsa wood. (You may be able to do this yourself if you have the right equipment!)

The pieces can then be packaged under your own attractive label. Include a desktop published booklet of ultra-clear instructions and any accessories needed.
You could try selling a few of your models at weekend markets or 'on appro' through toy, craft and model shops to see how they go. If your test market goes well, you'll know it is worthwhile making a larger quantity.

MOSAICS

Mosaics have been a popular art for centuries and, in many instances, have given us valuable pictorial histories of past civilizations and cultures. They have withstood earthquakes and tempests, wars and even time. You can virtually assure yourself of a place in the future with this most permanent and beautiful craft if you are artistically inclined.

Mosaics can be produced for *artistic* or *utilitarian* purposes. Today, they are set in walls as panels, in swimming pools, on plaques, lamp bases, tables, floors...in fact, anywhere that totally durable artwork is wanted.

Glass mosaics are extremely popular with craftspeople and a nice little mail order business could possibly spring from selling supplies for this craft: patterns, glass, fusing materials and so forth.

Browse through the glossy, up-market craft magazines and the Yellow Pages for suppliers and ask them to send you brochures as a first step to developing ideas.

MOTEL

A motel can be a fantastic 'home business', if it is well situated and well run. It can also be a very quick way to lose thousands of dollars if it is poorly run.

Your choice of locations is almost endless: seaside, mountain, rural, major highway, tourist spots...even the CBD! You also have a choice of size, from little cabin retreats to multi-roomed megaliths. It's all a matter of lifestyle preference...and availability of funds!

Motels are no piece of cake to run, particularly for beginners. If you firmly believe this is the business for you but are lacking in experience, it could be worth your while to do a hospitality course and/or try to get a period of employment in a motel for a while to observe and absorb the way it is run.

If you intend to buy a going concern, make the sale conditional on the vendor giving you generous assistance during the hand-over period.

Owning a motel can offer many opportunities for expansion into areas not generally considered. For example, do you have seminar facilities that are being under utilised? If so, you may be able to run your own week long *residential courses for artists*, *writers* and other *special interest groups* at certain times of the year. It is a matter of engaging specialist teachers, supplying them with room and board plus a spacious tuition room and then, advertising for students in relevant *special interest* magazines.

While your residential seminars are running, you could still continue to accept general motel guests if you have sufficient unused rooms.

- There are yet other possibilities for would-be motel owners, especially those who have a medical or nursing background: *a health or weight loss retreat*.

- Those with a background in alternative medicine, such as naturopathy, might consider *an alternative healing centre or meditation retreat.*

There are so many possibilities in the hospitality industry for lateral thinkers and entrepreneurs that it would be impossible to list them all.

MOTIVATIONAL SPEAKER

There are few occupations so satisfying as motivating people and giving them the skills that are required to succeed in life.

While it is possible for skilled people to build up a business on their own, it may be possible to join an organisation which specialises in offering seminars and lectures of this type. If you do this for a while until you get experience in organising and running seminars, it might be the best way to go.

Alternatively, you may prefer to obtain a franchise…or perhaps you are already well enough established in the speaking circuit to become a franchiser yourself.

MOULD MAKING AND CASTING

Making moulds for - and reproducing - chess pieces, bird baths, garden gnomes, garden pots, statues and so forth could be turned into a great home-based business if done the right way.

Create *some* lines that cannot be purchased anywhere else! Even basic items can often be transformed into the *incredible* through decorating or painting! *Personalise* your way to success!

You may prefer to sell your moulds by mail order. The cast objects might also be sold through various retail outlets like garden shops, nurseries, decorator shops and smaller home stores 'on appro'.

There are many materials and methods used for making moulds but you do need to be sure you are not infringing copyright when copying an original. Of course, you might decide to make an original piece yourself, then clone it by the score for sale!

One of the most basic ways to mould items is with plaster, thickly coating the original but leaving a 'seam' all around to allow the cast to be easily removed in two halves after the plaster is set. The empty mould halves are then sealed together and a quick-setting liquid material – (metal, fibreglass, plastic, even slip or liquid clay) - is poured in through a hole left in the bottom. When dry, the resultant mould should be an exact copy of the original.

Moulds of small articles can be formed by applying several applications of *latex* over the whole surface of the original article. The latter needs to be specially prepared to protect its surface. When set, the resulting mould is flexible and can be pulled off and used over and over again.

Fibreglass moulding can sometimes be a problem for home business, however, because of the odour. In suburbia, neighbours are likely to object to the strong smell when you are working with the material on a continuous basis. You should check with your local council and the EPA on the advisability of working with fibreglass at home. In a rural area, it may not present a problem so it is worth checking.

Some moulds can yield hundreds of copies. Choose from gnomes, chess pieces, 3D wall plaques, huge boulders for gardens, giant animal heads and masks for Mardi Gras parades. theme park figures and so forth.

MOWER REPAIR

Service your clients' temperamental and broken mowers…or sell them a smooth running beauty from your stock of reconditioned models…which you've bought for a song and transformed into excellent working condition! Always offer a guarantee with your reconditioned mowers – 3 months at least.

Your servicing might include cleaning the filter or replacing blades or small parts which you could do in the comfort of your home garage or workshed.

If you don't want customers wandering in and out of your home, you could offer a local pick-up and delivery service.

MURAL PAINTING

You don't need to be the world's greatest artist to be a mural painter as you can have someone else design the mural for you if necessary. However, if you are able to do the artwork yourself, all the better.

All you will need apart from the design, the paints, brushes and a ladder is an opaque projector for projecting the image or photo onto the wall several times its size. Some people can dispense with the projector but, unless you are accustomed to drawing and painting on a large scale, trying to keep proportion can be rather daunting.

If you are unable to buy an opaque projector, you may be able to work by placing grid lines over the original design and *transferring* it, *to scale,* onto the wall. This is far more laborious, however.

Have the design worked out on paper before you start so your clients know exactly how their finished job will look. This way they will have a chance to approve of the design and make suggestions before you begin.

Until your work becomes known, you'll need to market yourself relentlessly. Introduce your work to restaurants, cafes, delis, shops, hotels, offices, architects, home decorators, building advisory centres, motels, airports and tourist centres. Advertise, too, in whatever publications you can afford: *The Yellow Pages* advertising generally more than pays for itself. Produce brochures for distribution to up-market homes and new or planned offices.

You will also need to prepare a quality folio of your work to show clients. But how do you accumulate a folio of work if you haven't yet had any jobs?

One way is to perform a few good deeds in your field: offer to paint a mural at a children's hospital or for a charity or two. This type of philanthropy benefits both the giver and the receiver of the service. It gives pleasure to the needy, it gets your name known quicker, gives you an immediate history…and provides you with a work of art to photograph for your brochure. When the next potential client asks you what jobs you've worked on, instead of blurting: 'Oh, I'm only just starting out!' you'll be able to say: 'as a matter of fact, I have just completed a mural for the children's wing of the Northwest Hospital! And here are a couple of photos.'

Write yourself a press release and send it off to the papers when you've finished a major work.

MUSEUM OPERATOR/CURATOR

If you live in a tourist area, a museum could be a great attraction, even if you house it in a garage or workshed on your property.

You might consider a rock and fossil museum, sea shells, local pioneer artefacts, old planes or trains. Much will depend on the size of your display area, your interests - and the zoning of your property. If you are permitted to include a small on-site tea room, it may enhance the museum's interest to tourists.

You will need to advertise, advertise, advertise! As well as signage, make up desktop published literature and books for sale about your exhibits as well as any interesting information about your locale.

Let local motels, hotels, tourist information centres and other local tourist attractions know about your museum and give them brochures to distribute. (Offer to distribute brochures for *them* in return)

If you enjoy public speaking and your museum starts to pull in small groups, you might have ready a *short*, well-rehearsed talk on some of your exhibits and history.

MUSHROOM FARMING

This could be a very satisfying business for someone with a large property and spare sheds. Furthermore, it need not be made overly time-intensive and could possibly be run in conjunction with another home business.

You may decide to operate on a small scale for local distribution only or perhaps you will be brave and go for the market in a big way. Much will depend on where you live, your zoning, the capital you have to invest and the size of your land.

One good thing about most mushroom farming is that you are not necessarily dependent on environmental concerns such as soil quality or weather - as mushrooms can be grown indoors, in sheds!
(See Weatherproof Crops under Horticulture)

MUSICAL INSTRUMENTS MANUFACTURE

Many musical instruments can be manufactured and sold from a home garage or workshop.

However, whether you make didgeridoos, violins or flutes, your pieces need to be truly outstanding if you are to do well as a home business. *Check with your local council if you are using noisy equipment.*

MUSICIAN

If you have been a performer for some years and are well-networked in the industry, you will already know the vagaries of the music industry: that it can make loads of money for some and loads of frustration for others. For the canny, however, there is a middle ground. They're the ones continually on the lookout for opportunities and who seem to find a way to *make* those opportunities happen.

If you have a soundproofed studio at home - (not so expensive to arrange if you already have a spare room or garage!) - you may be able to record your own CD's, tapes etc. Digital technology has thankfully made the impossible relatively possible! Even though technology costs, a group of dedicated musicians can sometimes manage to pool enough resources to get it all together.

It hardly goes without saying that, if you do not intend performing your own compositions, you will need to check on copyright laws before recording a note.

- *IDEA*: There is another avenue for musicians/composers that few seem to consider. Many smaller media producers need royalty-free music for short films, ads, audio productions and so forth. If you can produce good original music for them, let them know! You will *not* need to give away your copyright: they wish to buy only the *reprint* rights to your composition for their productions!

  This means you can sell your work *over and over* to as many buyers as you can find. Not only that, but you will have the satisfaction of knowing that your recordings are being used and getting noticed by lots of people. But don't forget to protect that copyright by having purchasers sign a contract! And...ensure that your name appears in the credits!

  You could even devote a web page to your royalty-free music! Act as an agent, too, for your friends' compositions, selling it the easy way 'on the web'!

N

NATUROPATHY

It is possible that many of the benefits offered by naturopathy could help not only your patients but your family and yourself as well.

Excellent accredited courses are available for which no major prerequisites are necessary. Contact some of the better-known schools of naturopathy and ask them to send you their brochures. Also, just to familiarise yourself with the many courses available, peruse the ads in the back pages of the many Health journals and magazines. Your *Yellow Pages*, too, carries a large helping of offerings.

Some colleges of naturopathy offer courses by correspondence which means that, if you are currently in a job, you will not need to take time off for classes.

Once you have gained any qualifications needed, you can work from home or from your own professional suite. However, it's easy to become lost among the competition if you do not actively market yourself! You will need to get out and about, spreading your name and talking about your services if you are to do well.

If you are able to write well and use a computer, you may be able to self-publish a few books on your particular healing methods - or even make some audio tapes or videos on various health-related subjects. If you enjoy speaking in public, arrange seminars and lectures for charities, hostels for the aged, clubs and schools.

The local papers might give you a write-up! Send them some interesting information about your public appearances.This type of exposure can do wonders to enhance the public perception of your name and business.

Give lectures whenever possible at club luncheons and other organisations. Spending a couple of days a week as a *visiting consultant* at a local Health Food store or pharmacy might also help boost your income and, at the same time, remind the world that you are there!

Naturopathc subjects also experience quite high popularity at evening courses held by TAFE colleges nd other recreational venues Could you teach a few short courses?

O

ONLINE AUCTIONS

Some people are making soooo much money from bidding and auctioning goods online that it's hard to envisage why any sane person would ever bother going to work again! But...it's not an area for the unwary. Generally, those who do well in this incredible trading heaven are those who learn the ropes slowly and surely and steer clear of the more dubious online auctions.

EBay is probably one of the best and most reliable place to start. It has been growing steadily and constantly improving its site for over years.

There are many tricks and strategies to winning yet it is possible to educate oneself in these. The best teachers seem to be personal trial and error: so start off bidding on some small item, then maybe selling a couple of items. Do this a few times with merchandise of various categories. As your experience grows, you will see how easy it can be. It can also be incredible fun!

Envisage standing in an auction room that is as big as the world itself. There are millions and millions of bidders. Each of them will place their bids on the little computer sitting before them. Each person there is registered and each item is categorised. The bidding then begins but forget those old paddles! This bidding is handled by 'proxy' software taking into account the seller's minimum price and the incoming bids.

Want to know? Try reading one of the *absolute beginners* guides or books on eBay from vatious eBay sites or Amazon.

ORNAMENTAL GARDENS

These can be a wonderful source of enjoyment for apartment dwellers as well as home owners. They not only give visual pleasure; they also give the owner the enjoyment of maintaining and shaping the growing artwork.

These gardens can be very small yet still suggest another world to the owner. Indoor or outdoor, they can be decorated with small ceramic figures, animals, houses and so forth to emulate a particular environment.

(Also look under *Apartment Gardens.)*

Here are a few ideas to set you thinking:

- *Ornamental, oriental-type gardens* complete with tiny bonsai trees. Rivers can be suggested with tiny pebbles or a mirror spanned by a tiny bridge.

- *Ornamental water gardens.* These could be tiny gardens with small recirculating waterfalls or fountains among the foliage. They could be given an oriental, tropical, classical or any other theme.

- *Ornamental cactus gardens* can be a popular choice and can certainly make a lovely display but they are not the best idea for children as there is always the danger that little fingers will end up covered in painful prickles!

- *Fairy gardens* might be a fascinating choice for children: for example, a leafy backdrop could give way to a forest clearing sprinkled with tiny spotted mushrooms. (Make mushrooms yourself from simple-to-use materials such as Das or Fimo, then paint them brightly.)

  Place a few fairies and elves around the garden! They, too, could be made out of Das if you are 'crafty'; if not, simply dress up tiny plastic dolls (procurable from most toy stores) with tuille dresses and wings.

- *Nursery* and *fairy-tale gardens* might be leafy mini-worlds containing well-known and well-loved characters from children's stories. For example:

- *Red Riding Hood* tip-toeing down a path in the woods, carrying a basket of goodies for Grandma. You might have the wolf lurking nearby in the bushes and Grandma's house in the background. In another forest, the *Seven Dwarfs* could be returning home to their quaint little house while Snow White waits by the door.

- *Hansel and Gretel* finding a gingerbread house in the forest.

- *The Twelve Dancing Princesses* coming home through the forest.

Note: When offering any of your fairytale gardens for commercial sale, always check the copyright implications first if well known characters are portrayed.

P

PAINTING

- *Domestic*
  This home-based business can be as big or small as you want, from a single 'handyman' enterprise to a large, going concern subcontracting dozens of workers and fulfilling scores of contracts. Much will depend on your organising/marketing-ability! However, be assured that really big money is there for top-notch tradespeople who know how to run a business!

- *Commercial*
  The bigger you are, the more they'll want you! While it's not that easy to break into commercial painting, when you do and you finally land on your feet, the rewards (and the competition, unfortunately!) can be substantial.

PANEL BEATING *(See Auto)*

PARTY HIRE

This business has great potential but, like any venture, it is dependent on your ability to market yourself and network with people who matter. There can be quite a big outlay for equipment such as glassware, cutlery, silver bowls, trays, candelabras, marquees, outdoor lights and so forth. You will need to have a large, waterproof storage area and a display area to show samples of your wares and set-ups.

However, your storage, office and showroom do not necessarily have to share the same premises. The showroom might be housed in a small commercial premises in a local business area where you could arrange to meet clients *'by appointment'*, yet your office and storage could be at home. This arrangement may not be as convenient as having the whole of your establishment together in one place but it might get over a few zoning problems. It would certainly save you many dollars on running the whole show from one large commercial premises! However, check out your plans with the local council.

There are many synergistic businesses that could be tied in with a business such as this: caterers, wedding planners, 'events' organisers and so forth could all be of possible assistance to you - and you to them.

PARTY PLANNER OR EVENTS ORGANISER

If you like meeting people and love organising events – while, at the same time, making money! - this one could be for you.

Parties can be held, day or evening and in all sorts of places. They can be in clients' homes, hired venues... in fact, anywhere, so here's the chance to do what you enjoy most without having to clean up the mess afterwards.

Weddings, engagements, birthdays, end of year office parties, seminars, lectures, bucks' nights, showers, cocktail parties, balls, reunions and other big events can cause one big headache for busy people! Do the planning for them, and you should be rewarded handsomely.

In planning your business, ask yourself what type of function you prefer to be involved in: anything and everything...or will you *specialise*?

As an events planner, you could find yourself in the most amazing places: the venue could be anywhere from a mansion to a private yacht! What a life you're in for!

When you consider the hundreds of parties, events and seminars that go on every week, you will see that there is, potentially, plenty of work out there. To ensure it comes to *you*, you'll need to market and promote your business widely.

You'll also need to build up a *reputation* for reliability, punctuality, faultless organisation and perfection in everything you do.
(See also Wedding Planner, Catering, Children's Parties, Children's Activity Centre)

PARTY PLAN SELLING

Through party plan sales, people are selling everything and anything: kitchenware, toys, gifts, exotic lingerie, cosmetics, swimwear, jewellery...the list is endless.

Parties can be held in your own home or at the homes of friends and acquaintances.

Generally, the host provides the refreshments but you, the organiser, will be expected to provide the entertainment and bubbling commentary to make it all fun. You will also be expected to provide the host or hostess with either a gift or one of the articles from your collection.

Sometimes items are sold on the spot but generally, orders are taken at the party and the goods are delivered subsequently.

For some reason, many people tend to equate party plan selling solely with *women's* groups. This is a pity, because so many goods can be effectively sold to *male* groups and *mixed* groups.

Only use suppliers that you feel you can trust. They must be able to provide you with goods when you need them and without delay. In fact, it is far better organisationally (and from a profit point of view as well!) if the product you sell is of your own manufacture.

PERSONAL ASSISTANCE SERVICES

- *personal services for busy professionals:*
  Long hours at the office leave little time for busy people to clean their homes, shop, pick up dry cleaning/laundry/ironing, cater for parties, cook, buy gifts, collect children from school, supervise homework...there are so many jobs that could be fulfilled by you.

  This could be a fantastic business if run the right way. Such assistance for harried executives can only expand!

However, business professionals are not the only market for a service such as this. One of the biggest potential markets is likely to be:

- *personal services for the elderly:*
  As the community ages, there will be an increasing need for services designed for the elderly: cleaning services, carers, shopping services, handyperson services, drivers and day-tour organisers, maxi-taxis (for the wheel chair bound), mini tours, escort services for day or evening outings, even changing the light globes!

  Often overlooked is assistance for those with failing eyesight: simple, light duties such as letter writing, sending cards to relatives at Christmas, buying and wrapping presents, having someone read the daily newspaper and many of these services might be of enormous value to residents of hostels and nursing homes. It would also be more time effective for you to offer your services where there is already a concentration of elderly residents with similar requirements.

  Many such services already exist but not specifically for the aged. It is projected that such services will become more and more essential in the future.

PERSONALISED PRODUCTS

(See also under Personalised Children's Books, Personalised Chocolate Bars, Photos on Plates, China Painting, Embroidery, Deck Chairs Personalised)

Personalised items are required for gifts as well as for promotional use for businesses, clubs, schools etc. They cover a range of small gift items and can be hand painted, screen printed, etched, embroidered and so forth.

You may not want to produce the basic gift items yourself, so you could simply buy basic, undecorated products wholesale and personalise them to order.

Here are just a handful of *personalised product* ideas for you to consider:
- *books*
- *poems*
- *combs*
- *clocks*
- *umbrellas*
- *money boxes*
- *photo frames*
- *keyrings*
- *songs*
- *mugs*
- *plates*
- *hats & caps*
- *mouse mats*
- *mirror frames*
- *surname history certificates*
- *T-shirts*
- *framed pet pedigree certificates (illustrated with the pet's name and photo)*

You may prefer to buy a *franchise* to provide you with guidance in the particular field you choose, or you might simply search out products yourself and organise the business from scratch.

There are some very long-standing and reputable franchisers of these products, both in the U.S. and Australia, who are generally able to supply their franchisees with everything they need. The cost of the franchises can vary from hundreds to thousands of dollars, depending on the product and the level of input that goes with it.

PEST CONTROL

There is a lot of pesky competition in this field but you might leave them all for dead if you can find a creative *niche* in the market.

How popular would you be if you were to offer the public *'non-toxic'*, humane pest control? After all, poisons and dangerous chemicals can be picked up not only by the pests, but by children and pets as well! Research the alternatives and talk to other pest controllers.

You will need to offer your clients a generous guarantee with every job in order to compete.

PET CEMETERY

A pet cemetery fulfils a deep need in some pet owners who become as attached to their pets as parents are to their children. Therefore, this business needs to be run with all the care, seriousness and sensitivity of a human funeral home.

Your property will need to be in a suitable area with the right zoning, and be sure to obtain council permission for your project.

Immaculate and well landscaped premises are very important. You may decide to include a little chapel - or even a summerhouse that could function as a chapel – for your services. Learn the words of your commemorative speech off-by-heart and practise delivering it fluently and with compassion.

Your basic costs would cover the casket, the service and burial or cremation of the pet but you could also offer **on-going maintenance** of the plot. You might also consider offering for sale some of the following:

> a range of **personalised pet products** such as illustrated *pet pedigrees*,
> a hand painted *portrait* of the deceased animal
> a beautiful glossy photo
> a framed personalised *poem* as a momento.

However, any retailing of goods from the property should have prior council approval.

PET FOOD DELIVERY

While pet food deliveries are generally performed by pet shops and pet food outlets themselves, there are quite a few sole operators who do not have time to perform this service and must subcontract others to help.

Generally, pet food delivery is not a highly paid job but it might tie in nicely with some other, pet-related business that you run or provide those few extra useful dollars that you could need.

PET MOTEL

If you are a pet lover and live in an area where there are several motels and B&B's, you might consider establishing a *pet motel*... 'for 4-legged guests only'! Many pet owners like to take their little friends away with them on holidays and often choose a

holiday resort or town where they know they can board their animals nearby.
If you would like to start up a Pet Motel, check on zoning and local regulations.
Many rural areas are relatively relaxed about this type of establishment providing it
does not threaten the peace and quiet of the surrounding populace.

If you already own a motel - or plan to do so - perhaps your property will be large
enough to *add* a 'pet motel'. Such an annex to your business could make it a must
for pet-loving holiday makers. However, the furry guests would need to be placed far
enough away from the main buildings so as not to annoy their human counterparts.
Canine accommodation poses a potential problem because of the continuous barking.

Your marketing might include the Yellow Pages, travel and tourist magazines, motel
and tourist literature, canine and cat magazines, clubs and breeders as well as the
usual media advertising.

PET PORTRAITS

Pet portraiture can be an extremely lucrative field of painting (or photography) as it
represents what is commonly called a 'niche' market.

While pet *photographers* are fairly numerous, few *artists* seem to be doing this
work - which is understandable as this form of portraiture requires a special talent.
However, if you have this gift and you like animals, the work is there...and the
money is virtually sitting there waiting to be collected!

- *Paintings of pets* can be executed in oil, acrylic or pastel...and are preferably
  painted from life in order to capture the animal's personality. However, if you
  are not up to working with live models (and some of them *can* be rather large
  or over-exuberant!), ask the owners to keep their dogs - or cats! - on a leash!
  You can also take some photos of the animals to supplement your sketches
  and colour notes.

  Cats can be difficult to subdue in a studio and want to explore every nook and
  cranny. Sometimes a little mechanical toy can help keep them occupied or
  they may even settle down after a while on their owner's knee.

  The portrait itself, particularly if it is in oil, may take anything from days to
  weeks to complete, depending on its size and complexity. This must be taken
  into account when giving clients a finishing date.

- *Pastel and pencil sketches* can often be done in just one sitting.

Your studio could be set up in your garage if you have one, away from the main house. It is neither professional nor advisable *for health reasons* to have strange animals coming into your home on a regular basis.

A proposal for this business should be submitted to council first. It would also be wise to consider taking out public liability insurance. Simple as your business may be, clients can still trip over a garden hose.

PET-RELATED BUSINESSES

Pets are big business in much of the western world. To many pet owners, their animals become part of the family: for some, their pet is their *only* family!

Pet lovers are generally a great group of people to work with and appreciate their animals being admired or catered for. More and more pet-related businesses are springing up every day.

- *Pet products – Mail Order*
  A pet shop (in the normally accepted sense of the word) is hardly suitable as a home business. However, you may still be able to function profitably and legally from your house selling pets and pet products in a slightly unconventional way.

  For example, you may be able to **breed and sell domestic animals and birds** on a very limited scale! (Check this with your local council.) Or if you are 'crafty', you might also be able to make and sell **animal accessories** such as collars and coats and sell them from home. *(See under Pet Accessories)* Look into the possibility, too, of selling **pet-related products by mail order/ direct mail**.

  (Please note that, in some areas, you may only be permitted to sell from home those articles that you yourself manufacture or which have been consigned)

- *Pet accessories*
  Some astute entrepreneurs who have realised the potential of the pet products market have made themselves *millionaires* through manufacturing **pet accessories** at home.

  The big money spinners are up-market, stylish and unusual fashion accessories such as coats, caps and hats, raincoats, leashes and collars that cater to the canine 'rich and famous'. Some manufacturers have even produced doggie shoes and sunglasses!

You might try selling your goods through pet shops, grooming parlours, veterinary clinics, by mail order, through pet shows and exhibitions.

When you get on your feet with this business, you may be able to afford to hire a salesperson to look after sales and marketing while you concentrate on the design and manufacturing at home.

Many fashion items can be made by home sewers and several major pattern books carry patterns for pet clothes and accessories.
(*See also Dog Life-jackets*)

PET SITTING

What an easy way to make a little extra money…if the pets are well-behaved and you're insured!!

Looking after other people's pets in your own home while their owners are on holiday could be a nice little 'sideline' to some other home businesses. The pets will not feel lonely with you around all the time, and are unlikely to interfere too much with your other activities. There can be a few drawbacks, however, if you are running a home business that requires you to be on the phone a lot: barking dogs during a business call can be a problem.

Secondly, there may be restrictions on how many dogs you are permitted to have on your property at any one time. Generally, you are allowed only two.

You may prefer to look after local pets in *their* home while their owners are away. You wouldn't need to be there all the time, of course. Just take the animals for walks to the park, play ball, feed and groom them and they should look forward to your visits. Caring for local pets in their own homes enables you to look after many more little charges in a day than you could if they were actually staying with you and is thus far more profitable.

PET TAXI

If you enjoy being around animals and also like to drive, one option might be to start a pet taxi business.
- You might offer pet transport to vets, grooming parlours and others who need such a service.
- Pick up and deliver animals to boarding kennels for pet owners heading off on holidays.

- Your service might also be hired by the boarding kennels and catteries themselves for their *own* pick ups and deliveries.
- Don't forget insurance!

Running a Pet Taxi might be a stand-alone business or merely present a useful sideline to another home-based business...like a pet model and film star agency?

PHOTOS ON PLATES

Glazing photographs onto porcelain plates is just one delightful and popular method of producing personalized gifts and promotional items. The machine that is generally used (small enough to fit on a table at home) and the simple instructions to run it should be fairly easily procured. Check out some of the adverts in home business opportunities magazines.
(See also under Personalised Products and China Painting)

PHOTOGRAPHY

Professional photographers have the potential to make excellent money, but their success depends as much on their ability to locate *niches* in their markets as in their technical and creative ability.

Not all photographers need a degree or diploma to get into business. With a good digital or SLR camera, a steady tripod plus a short course or two at the local TAFE, an intelligent beginner should find ways to a good career.

- *Travel photography* may be at the top of your list but it is also at the top of many other photographers' lists as well! Why fight the competition? Look for less competitive areas when you are starting off. Make money first - *then* go on your holiday!

- For professionals, **glamour photography**, **wedding photography**, **babies'** and **children's** portraits are generally capable of paying the rent several times over providing the work is of good quality and well marketed. *Specialise* wherever possible, feeling out a *niche* in the market, then exploiting it for all you're worth.

- *Pet portraits*, *equine portraits*, *car rallies* and *sports* photos can all be money spinners if done the right way.

- Think about producing *special interest coffee table books* of superb photos, be they of shipwrecks, lighthouses, antique cars, vintage planes, cat and dog breeds, waterfalls, rivers, surfing, pioneer homes, wildlife parks and so forth.

- For beginners, a good quality Polaroid or a digital camera plus portable colour printer might see you working your magic at fairs, weekend markets, livestock shows as well as tourist areas.

   You might wander through the crowd, offering to shoot the usual *photo-on-the-spot* portraits for those who want it...or go one better: perhaps you could erect a stand with a *background mural* of some kind such as a pioneer cottage, a famous landscape, a jungle, mountains, a well-known landmark! Photograph your clients in front of this. Will you offer them the option of dressing up in appropriate gear for the occasion?

- Perhaps you could produce a series of life-sized cut-outs of *famous people* with whom your clients could shake hands whilst having the momentous occasion photographed by you for posterity! Such photos might even be capable of being printed on the spot with a portable printer. *(Note: You would need to get prior permission if you decided to use photos of well known people.)*

- Alternatively, go for a few *digital fantasies*: you might decide to photograph your clients against a plain blue drop sheet, then use a little digital magic to superimpose their image onto a photo of an exotic or dangerous environment. Digital photos can take a little time to manipulate particularly if they have to be superimposed, so you could have customers prepay, then post them their photos a few days later.

PHOTO RESTORATION

If you have a computer, a scanner, a good quality colour printer and some type of photo manipulation software - plus the 'know how' to go with it (short courses are usually obtainable at TAFE), you may be ready to start a *photo restoration* business.

Scanning and enhancing old photos can be time consuming but, if you know your business, it can also be quite absorbing watching darkened and faded images reappearing from the past!

Realign, crop, adjust the hue, saturation and perform other feats of magic, then print out onto best quality photographic paper and - voila! You have manipulated time itself!

There are a lot of people doing this work so, to compete, you will need to do some fairly active networking. Talk to businesses whom you think might like to offer this service to their customers but who don't wish to perform the work themselves such as photo processing labs, chemists, gift shops and major stores.

PERSONAL FITNESS COACH

'On-site' personal instruction in this field is becoming increasingly popular with clients and instructors alike. After all, why pay to rent premises when you can use a client's home for free? When the weather is good, some instructors arrange exercises in the local park or make a supervised jog part of the lesson.

You may prefer to run classes at home. A garage-turned-gym might suffice but be sure you obtain council approval, have all the necessary qualifications and obtain insurance cover.

If dollars are in short supply when you're starting off, it may help to apply for a part-time job at a local fitness centre. Even working a few hours a week can help put food on the table during those initial slow months when you're recruiting clients.

Local media advertising will be important in getting your business known around town but there are other ways to promote yourself as well, such as giving *free lectures* on health and fitness at local clubs and charity luncheons.

You might even decide to *write a book* on health and exercise. Or make a *video*! Technology has made home media production fairly simple these days.

If you wish to write a book on your subject but don't know where to start, why not enlist the services of a *professional* writer to co-author your book? If you cannot afford to pay a writer, perhaps you could offer them *reprint* rights to the book so that they, too, can print and sell copies for profit. Extending your distribution arm in this way can expose you to a much wider audience!

As a home-based instructor, you may decide to specialise in training just one type of student e.g. *'the over 50's'*, *'exercise for the elderly'*, *'exercise for men'*, *'exercise for women'*, *'post natal'*, *'prenatal'* and so forth. If you need to gain further qualifications, study in your spare time. Such intelligent, focused effort toward an ultimate goal usually pays off in the long run.

Following are two 'niche' ideas you may like to think about:

- *Fitness For the Over 50's:*
  While fitness instructors are generally in the younger age bracket, an older instructor might be preferred by the over 50's. Seeing a superb physical

specimen of their own age, so vital and healthy, may reassure older students and give them the belief that they, too, might achieve similar results by following your example!

Apart from offering individual instruction in clients' homes, you might also run 'Fitness for the Over-50's' classes in recreation and community halls, hostels...even in nursing homes! Before you scoff at this latter suggestion, read the book *Strong Women Stay Young* by Miriam E. Nelson Ph.D and Sarah Wernick Ph.D (Lothian Aurum Press). Then ask yourself what you're waiting for!

Whether you elect to offer private or class tuition to your clients, you will need to be *well qualified* in what you do and be prepared to show empathy, understanding and loads of patience. This is especially important when dealing with older clients.
(Full insurance for you and your clients is of top priority!)

- ***Fitness for Housebound Parents:***
  They can't get to classes because they have an armful of squealing babies or toddlers! She's gained weight since the birth of her last child! He feels guilty for contemplating taking time off for himself...but they all long to get their bodies into shape! Can you help them? You bet!

  By visiting the housebound - not only ***stay-at-home mums and dads*** but ***housebound carers***, too, who have elderly or incapacitated dependents! - you can help them regain their self-respect and their health!

  In tailoring exercise programs for those under this type of duress, you might also offer stress-relief training or meditation techniques. However, while you are transforming the shape and fitness of your clients, you may have to deal with an audience of noisy children and a few annoying interruptions, but that's all part of the job.

  If you are able to speak well in public, it should help your business enormously to give ***talks on fitness*** and health at various charity functions, mothers' clubs, TAFE seminars and so forth. Generally, this type of soft-sell marketing can help get your name around the neighbourhood pretty quickly.

Marketing any service needs creative thinking. You may be able to convince local offices and factories to hold exercise sessions for their ***stressed-out employees***. This could be supplemented with meditation or relaxation exercises. A large staff room should suffice as an exercise venue; all you'll need to provide is a tape recorder - and yourself!

Even if you are instructing clients in their nice, seemingly safe homes - or yours - you should always ensure that you are both insured.
(See also under Fitness Instructor)

PICTURE FRAMING

This business could be run from a home workshop but, as in any business, you would need to market your service constantly. Obtaining work from local galleries, print shops, photographic studios and gift shops would help boost your income. Try to form an arrangement with these business owners by giving them a good deal on their framing needs.

You might also try to rent out 'work space' or a spare work room in a commercial art gallery a couple of days per week. This would help increase your exposure as well as your income. If the gallery owner is willing, demonstrate your craft as you work. Demos of anything can attract customers, particularly in a busy area and this might be good for both you and the gallery.

Info brochures could be mailed to galleries, print shops, private artists, art schools, art groups and photographic outlets. Advertising could be in the local classifieds, school newsletters and other publications.

It's unlikely that framing, as a business, will make you a squillionaire but it could be an excellent adjunct for painters, portraiture artists, art or print galleries as well as photographic studios,

Alternatively, you may be able to offer a do-it-yourself framing service where people can come to your workroom to make their own frames - but with your expert guidance. There are many of these do-it-yourself framing outlets but you would need to talk over the implications of this type of business with your insurer.

PIZZA PARLOUR
A pizza parlour…in the parlour?

It is hardly likely that you will be able to wangle starting a pizza parlour in your home…but, if you own or rent a food shop with an *attached dwelling*, you might be able to have your cake (or pizza!) and eat it, too! Food can be a tiring business and, with the family taking turns serving, then resting, it could make a hard job easier.

Of course, there are hundreds of pizza parlours with attached residences. What is going to make *your* pizza parlour stand out from the others? The answer, apart from your fantastic pizzas, might be your imaginative 'theme'!

For example, one idea could be to make your pizza shop look like a little corner of Italy, with wrought iron tables and chairs, checked cloths and an Italian mural. (The mural won't cost you an arm and a leg if you paint it yourself. Just project a photo of Tuscany or the Amalfi coast on the wall, trace it and then carefully paint the scene following the colours in the photo). A few potted plants, a background of Italian music playing and your business could be lifted from a mere 'suburban pizza shop' to something quite magical.

If your shop is spotless, your food great and you are friendly to customers, what more could a customer want? Maybe it won't be long before you can afford that trip to Italy for an *authentic* pizza!

- ***Mobile pizzas:***
  More realistically for those who want to work from home, make those pizzas in your home kitchen (after obtaining council permission, of course!) and deliver them in your ***pizzamobile***! They should arrive at the customer's front door 'piping hot'.

  If you remain at home making the pizzas, a family member might take on the deliveries…dressed in *chef's regalia.* (Your son? Father? Uncle Alvo? Better still if he has an Italian accent!) Dressing up may seem a lot of trouble for a pizza driver to go to but it is often 'out of the ordinary' touches or 'gimmicks' like these that can help separate business successes from business failures.

  It is said that, some years ago, one rapidly failing Australian pizza producer tried delivering his pizzas on hot tiles for effect. It wasn't long before he was media news!

  Use some creativity and see how long it will be before *your* pizza delivery personnel are followed by the paparazzi!

PLANTS FOR HIRE.

Restaurants, hotels, motels and offices do not always want the hassle of having to look after those pots of lush green jungle that decorate their main rooms and foyers.

If you have a green thumb, a van plus a garden in which to grow and revive these reminders of the natural world that brighten up our concrete and steel environments, this could be a good part-time job.

It could also be a useful adjunct to a business already engaged in some aspect of growing plants and horticulture.
(See under Horticulture)

PONY RIDES

Animals are greatly appreciated wherever there are children; pony rides are no exception!

You might decide to operate your rides at fetes, exhibitions, showgrounds and parties as well as parks at weekends (with council approval of course!) You would need quiet, well-mannered and well-maintained animals for rides. You will also need adequate insurance; don't leave home without it!

It's unlikely that this business will develop into a big concern as it can be quite expensive to run. However, if marketed the right way, it should bring a useful income – and even be a good add-on for a related business such as children's parties.

Consider, too, training your ponies and getting them on the books of various talent agencies. They might get occasional TV commercials, modelling, or work in films.
(See Children's Parties:Wagon Train Parties)

POOL & SPA CLEANING & MAINTENANCE

Apart from giving excellent and reliable service, you will need to advertise your business widely, particularly at the beginning of your venture as there is a fair amount of competition for this type of work. After a while, you should find local word-of-mouth doing a lot of the advertising for you.

If you are new to this business, it would be well worth your while working for a large pool maintenance company for a period in order to learn about cleaning and testing methods, chemicals used and the various types of equipment you are likely to come across. You will also need a van to transport your equipment.

If permitted, always put a sandwich board sign outside any property you are working on. It may seem a very small contribution toward marketing but you would be surprised how potential customers are drawn to using products and services that they see others using, particularly their neighbours.
(See also under Above Ground Pool Maintenance & Repair)

POPCORN STAND

Can you really make money from popcorn? The answer is 'yes' if you make your outlet attractive, position it right and build up a name for quality, cleanliness and creativity.

You will need a permit, of course, and there is a small matter of being exposed to all weathers but many people do not mind this. Often, one can wangle a good sheltered position in a crowded mall where the aroma of the cooking popcorn attracts passers-by like honey attracts bears.

PORTRAIT PAINTER

Painting and drawing offer many opportunities for a talented artist to make excellent dollars. You may think this is a strange statement considering the numbers of starving artists that we read about. However, the truth is that while artists may be creative in what they produce, they are not always creative in a *business* sense.

With portraiture particularly, if you are both technically skilled *and* commercially minded, you can make a *super* income doing what you love best.

Some portrait artists might work all day at places like markets, fetes or shopping malls doing portraits of passers-by for a few paltry dollars per job. Yet an equally talented but more *commercially-minded* artist might turn the garage or lounge room into a professional studio, market themselves in the right way, make sittings 'by appointment only' and *charge* like a professional. Same job, different approach!

Portraits of children and animals are notoriously difficult to paint and draw...unless you are fortunate enough to 'have what it takes'. If this is you, exploit it for all you're worth!
(See also under entries under 'Art and Craft' and 'Pet Portraits')

POTTERY
(See under Ceramics and Art & Craft)

POULTRY FARMER

You may live in a rural area and know eggs and poultry backwards - but how does a small farmer like you compete with the big guys at the supermarket?

Relax! You should be able to find a niche for you and your feathered friends - and it is most likely to be in the area of organically fed, naturally reared, free-range livestock.

People are becoming increasingly wary of eating produce from filthy, overcrowded and stressful batteries. If you can convince consumers – particularly the locals - that you breed natural, super-healthy, free-range eggs and poultry, you should find yourself building up a faithful and increasing following of customers.

Check on all permits needed!

PRINTER CARTRIDGES - RECHARGE AND REPAIR

It is not necessary for shops, offices and homes to throw away those expensive 'disposable' cartridges from their inkjet and laser printers or photocopiers these days. Generally, cartridges can be cheaply and easily recharged...by *you,* in your home business. But your clients will know that you exist only if you tell them you're there!

Advertise, advertise, advertise...by classifieds, by flyers, by introducing yourself to large, local businesses, by notices in local shops and a notice on your fence. Make it easy for local businesses to become your clients by collecting and returning cartridges to their doors. You may need to charge a little extra for this service. *(See under Inkjet Refilling)*

PRINTING

These days the catchcry of successful home-based entrepreneurs is 'look for the *niche* market'! While general printing assignments may be your bread and butter, there are many niche markets to be explored. All possibilities should be brainstormed and researched.

One market is short-run printing: home computers have made many shy writers game enough to self-publish their works. However, most are not game enough to risk forking out thousands of dollars to have a mountain of copies printed that may end up unsold and mouldy in the garage. They would rather pay more per copy and go for short runs.

Many students, too, need theses bound - and sometimes in a hurry! Docu-tech machines make it all so easy.

Advertising: the internet, on notice boards around the Uni campuses, in writers' newsletters and literary magazines. Place an occasional display ad in the literary supplement of newspapers if or when you can afford it.

If there are services that you need to perform in your small home printery but do not have the time, 'know-how' or equipment, outsource!

PROFESSIONAL SERVICES

So many self-employed professionals are working from home offices, studios and surgeries these days that clients and patients have come to accept this as part of the norm.

While your professional rooms should be separate from the house with their own entrance if possible, a large garage can often make a perfect home office, studio or surgery.

Doctors, dentists, chiropractors, osteopaths, naturopaths, dermatologists, financial advisers, accountants, real estate agents...it is hard to think of a profession where at least some of its practitioners are not working from home.

The decision to function this way may have been made due to a longing for a more relaxed lifestyle, low overheads, a preference for autonomy, an end to commuting, closeness to family or any one of a hundred reasons. Whatever the reason, the home-based business offers an opportunity to start making positive changes to your life!

However, for some professions and in certain situations, the home office can have a few drawbacksl. For example, when working at home, there are no knowledgeable colleagues sitting at the adjoining desk ready to assist you! So the more self-sufficient you can make yourself, the better. Also, you can be a sitting duck for friends and family who need a talk, a coffee and a bit of TLC. So you need to establish strict working conditions right from the start.

You may also need to outsource certain tasks from time to time as it is not always permissible to employ extra help or use certain equipment when working from home.

Check your plans with the appropriate bodies, including your local council!

PROMOTIONAL ADVERTISING AND VOUCHER SERVICE

This can be a simple job for someone with basic desktop publishing experience and who likes selling. It will involve a lot of marketing and PR in order to encourage local businesses to buy advertising space in your book of promotional tear-out vouchers. Speak to shop owners in the local shopping strips. (Always have a sample to show them)

Organising the delivery of these voucher booklets to each home in the area can sometimes be a bit of a headache - but if you get enough business, you may be able to hire someone to do this for you.

If you do hire help, be sure you know where you stand legally, what insurance cover you need for the person and what workplace regulations you need to abide by.

It's always wise to start off something like this on a small scale to test your market first.

PROMOTIONAL PRODUCTS
(See under Personalised Products)

PROOF READER

With today's highly sophisticated software, proof reading is often left to the computer but, as you will no doubt have discovered already, computer spelling and grammar is not always to be relied on.

Mistakes appear in even the most up-market publications. Generally, a spelling error is recognised by a computer only if there is one form of the word. If there are two or three forms, *context* becomes critical and, fortunately for you as a proof reader with an excellent knowledge of grammar and spelling, context is not yet something that computers understand too well!

Proof reading will appeal to a literate, alert person who just loves reading. If this is you, you could apply to the various publishers - small and large, book and magazine - and advertise your service in the trade magazines as well as writers' magazines and newsletters.

This job is unlikely to make you a millionaire but it may fit in well with other activities in your life bringing you an extra source of income.

PROPERTY MAINTENANCE FOR RENTAL/REAL ESTATE AGENTS

If you already have a home cleaning business, you may like to consider extending your services to include a few other services like lawn maintenance, tree lopping, pool maintenance and so forth.

You might even tie your business in with other already existing home services to offer a *full cleaning and maintenance* service. Such a service may be of interest to real estate agents and others who lease houses, holiday homes and flats.

PR CONSULTANT

You're going to need to use your PR ability to promote *yourself* if you're just starting out in this business and have determined to become a big success. Some people take to PR like a duck to water and make a good living out of it, both in financial and lifestyle terms.

Your job will be to help promote people and businesses who do not have the knack or the time for self-promotion. Many professionals hate it and regard it as an unpalatable necessity!

The amazing thing about PR is that nobody has to wait to be discovered: a talented PR consultant can make it all happen for you! Like a spider spinning a web around a fly, they will spin legends about you, write press releases, organise your concerts and seminars, get your products onto radio and TV and cocoon you in stardom. They can make sales go through the roof or turn even your next door neighbour into a hero!

If *you* get on well with people, love organising, are convincing and are a good networker, this type of consulting work might be a super job for you, bringing a good income and a most exciting lifestyle.

You don't need any real qualifications other than business nous, an irresistible personality, the ability to network, well-developed intuition, lots of determination and a hide as thick as a rhinoceros! And experience helps a lot, too!

PUBLISHING
(See under Desktop Publishing)

Q

QUILT MANUFACTURE

Bed quilts have been used for warmth for centuries and examples of early quilts can be found in the finest museums. They became quite an art in Europe around the 14th century and really flourished in North America by about the 18th - 19th century. The early settlers carried the designs of their homelands right across America but as time passed, the traditional designs and methods tended to evolve into a form unique to America.

Today, sewing machines with computers and quilting attachments make the work of the quilter an enjoyable craft or hobby...or an enjoyable business. For a while, quilters might have gone through an uncreative phase, copying traditional designs and producing only utilitarian products but today the new machines have sparked off a real revolution in modern design.

There are many books available on this subject so, before deciding if this is something that could interest you, do some research at the library and in educational bookshops as well as talking to some of the sewing and craft shops where demonstrations and classes in the art are often held.
(See under Sewing)

R

RAMP MANUFACTURER

One of the main uses of portable ramps is in industry to enable small vehicles like tractors and forklifts to access higher floors and larger vehicles. Or attach them to the rear of your van when loading and unloading goods. They are generally made of metal, are lightweight and sturdy and are of various designs depending on their use.

However, there is quite a market, too, among those who care for the disabled to enable wheelchairs to access steps and higher floors. Many 'maxi-taxis' which carry wheelchair-dependent passengers find lightweight portable ramps indispensable. Not all drivers are able to afford hydraulic lifting equipment in their vehicles and such ramps are easy to handle.

There are many different commercial uses for these ramps that could be investigated. Do a bit of brainstorming and reasearch, then talk to could-be clients about their requirements and needs.

If you do not wish to manufacture the ramps yourself, you could simply purchase them wholesale or have them specially made to your own specifications.

REAL ESTATE

This high-tech age of mobile phones, networking facilities and home computers can assist in putting a home office within the grasp of many small businesses.

For a qualified real estate agent, a home-based agency may turn out to be a boon. It can offer a more relaxed lifestyle, longed for autonomy, no commuting, flexibility of time, low overheads and no lease to worry about...unless you *rent* your house, of course.

Working from home can also offer you the opportunity to integrate more with the family...but one needs to be extremely disciplined in mixing home and work activities. The potential problems are as legendary as the benefits, as there are temptations to procrastinate at every turn!

If you do not yet possess your real estate licence but aspire to running a home-based agency in the future, you may decide to go back to school for a period and attend evening classes at your nearest TAFE.

Perhaps, while studying, you will decide to take a job as a receptionist with a local realtor for the privilege of simply working in the environment and having the opportunity of listening to and watching the way the business functions and how their various problems are encountered and overcome.

In running your own home-based business, you may find you are not permitted to employ outside assistants. Check this out in relation to your area and situation when obtaining council approval for your venture.

RECIPE CREATION

Are you a great cook? Do you love making dinner parties and producing unusual dishes for your guests? Perhaps you have a secret recipe or two handed down from your great grandmother? Then how about writing and illustrating a ***cook book*** revealing those secrets?

If you can't write or don't have a clue how to go about producing a book, there are many writers who would, no doubt, love to team up with you. Advertise for a writer willing to *collaborate* on your project by placing a 'wanted' ad in some of the writers' newsletters. You could possibly find a professional photographer to work with you by this same method.

If you have a good quality camcorder and know how to use it, you should be able to *video* those wonderful dishes being made up, step by step. Cooking videos are really quite simple to make. Be sure to have a spicy, running commentary or voice-over and, if you can't do a really great voice-over yourself, find someone who can!

These days, **videos** are used to great advantage in teaching. Many information seekers are unable to attend classes for reasons of time, distance or work restraints and are grateful for these training films which can be watched over and over again 'in the comfort of their own homes'!

As a video presenter, you may need practice. You may also find that you photograph better with a different hairstyle or more flattering makeup, but the time you spend in perfecting your presentation skills before the mirror and the camera may ultimately result in minor fame... even fortune! Who knows?

It is important to be *creative* about what you are doing. Don't try to compete with what's on T.V. Find some way to present the unusual - or present the usual in an unusual way! Single yourself out from the crowd by revealing unique information that you think the crowd would love to know about!

Consider **special interest dishes** such as **ethnic, Pritikin, low fat, diabetic, time-saving, vegetarian, children's party food, no-fuss cocktail parties, cake decorating, chocolate making and so forth.**

Be creative when it comes to **titles** for your books or videos. Titles such as: *'Fat Free Meals Means a Fat Free Body!'*, *'Delicious Diabetic Desserts!'*, *'Fast 'n' Fabulous Finger Food'*, *'Makin' Money Makin' Muffins'* or *'Never Reveal Your Sauces'* would certainly be more interesting than a title like *'Clarissa Smith's Fruit Cake Recipes'*!

It is easy these days to self-publish information products and, if you do happen to come up with a really popular book or video, it might prove to be an 'evergreen', continuing to bring you a good income for years to come. However, it's important to start such a project slowly, step by step, testing the market as you go.

Advertising ideas: the classifieds, your own web page, school newsletters, the local papers or, if you *do* make a hit, perhaps you could try a display ad in a glossy national magazine. You may even like to try your luck with the T.V. stations.
(See also Information Products, Desktop Publishing)

RECYCLED CLOTHING

Consider how easy it would be to fit into certain 'niche' markets with this business, offering second hand *sportswear*, *baby clothes*, *children's wear*, *millinery*, *menswear, wedding and evening wear*. The latter might even evolve into an up-market *Wedding and Evening Wear Hire* business one day.

For this type of business to be run from home, you will need to check with the council on zoning, get all necessary permits and insurance and then, advertise well.

If you are unable to run this business entirely from home, you should be able to at least *prepare and repair* the clothes there, saving precious commercial space. To sell the garments, you might prefer to take a stall at a busy weekend market. Many markets draw big crowds and the cost of stalls can be very low.

Your display should be first class with clean, ironed clothes and clean, polished and well laid out accessories.
(See Wedding Hire)

REFLEXOLOGY

Some people believe in the efficacy of reflexology - and others don't! However, for the believers, it's one of the first methods they turn to when they encounter a physical problem.

What do reflexologists do? They massage certain areas on the feet and around the ankles which are believed to correspond with various organs and parts of the body. This massage is thought to clear blockages around the target area.

For example, if a patient has a problem with the eye area, the reflexologist might press around the base of the second and third toes - the area thought to be in some way connected with the eyes; if the problem were headaches, the massage might be centred around the big toes, the area thought to correspond with the head. This concept may sound incredible and far-fetched - but many people say they have been cured of all sorts of ailments through this ancient art!

However, as a practitioner, you should always suggest that your patient see a qualified medical doctor in conjunction with your healing methods for any serious problem.

RESTUMPING

If you're stumped for a home-based business, this one could be ideal if you know the trade…or are willing to learn.

Certainly, restumping or reblocking can be dirty work often performed in damp, mouldy and cramped conditions but, for those tradespeople who build up a good reputation and work efficiently, the rewards can be generous.

Advertise your service to builders, renovators, home owners and real estate agents and place good, clear signage on your home and vehicle, too, if possible. You will find that an eye-catching sandwich board to place outside each site on which you are working will attract the attention of the locals and passers-by.

Your core advertising will possibly be a permanent ad in the local classifieds and *The Yellow Pages* if you can afford it. This might be supplemented by leaflet drops in all surrounding suburbs, shopper dockets and local 'money saver' coupons.

RESUME PREPARATION SERVICE

This could be an excellent adjunct to a home-based personnel/recruitment agency. It could also represent quite a good 'stand alone' business for anyone who has already had experience in HR.

However, the art of writing a resume is not a difficult skill to acquire and there are many evening courses available where a clear-thinking person can learn this art very quickly.

Generally, knowledge of one's client is gained through a personal interview: you ascertain his or her work history, achievements, goals, educational background… even hobbies, personal traits and characteristics and work from all this information plus your own observations.

Clients often expect to be given an all-purpose CV that can be used over and over again for many different job applications but such a document would never compete with one that is *tailored* to suit a particular job. For this reason, you might offer to tweak the initial resume to suit each new job application for a small extra fee.

Resumes should never be sent without a *covering letter*, so you may be asked to prepare this as well. Just two or three paragraphs, this letter serves to separate your client's application from the slush pile of resumes that is the usual result of most job adverts. It presents the employer with the 'personal face' of the candidate and should sum up just why the applicant feels he or she is right for the job as well as giving some indication of his or her personality.

Many clients feel quite lost when it comes to on-line job search. Be sure you are conversant with the various options and formats used in producing eResumes as this way of job hunting has now become very popular and your expertise in this area may help to differentiate your service from the many other resume preparation businesses that are out there.

RETAIL KIOSK/MARKET STALL

It is not necessary to be big to be successful. Many well-heeled entrepreneurs are functioning extremely well working in weekend markets or from tiny kiosks.

The important thing is to be where the customers are! And for sure, there are plenty of potential customers at the busier markets, even if they do only operate at weekends.

Customers will feel more confident buying from you if they see you at your little stall *every* weekend and it will certainly help if your products are always attractively displayed and your service is outstanding.

After a while, you should find yourself becoming part of a 'family' of traders at your chosen market and, from this, further channels for expansion could open up quite naturally.

RIDING SCHOOL

Be warned! Running costs, equipment and particularly insurance can really add up in this business! Make sure you have all the necessary permits and can afford the insurance costs before you start planning.

Generally, this is a business for rural or outer metropolitan areas but if you know horses and love riding, have all the facilities …and the mounts!…it could prove an ideal opportunity to earn an income whilst indulging your passion.

Value-add to your school wherever you can. You may be able to *sell* equestrian-related books and accessories to students - or even *write an instruction manual* yourself and self-publish it! Also, consider organising *lectures, competitions and film nights* at your school to make it more of a club.

You could try to obtain permission to **sell posters, jewellery, ornaments, T-shirts, sweats and anything else** relating to horses and riding. But, before retailing anything from your property, check with your local council. For example, you may be permitted to sell goods that *you* manufacture yourself on your property but not goods manufactured elsewhere. Each council has its rules and regulations, zoning and other issues so check everything before you begin.

Perhaps you could consider establishing an agency for **equine portraits**, either painted or photographic. You should be able to do this quite simply by engaging the services of a couple of local equine artists and photographers and acting as agent for them.
(See also Pet Portraits)

ROADSIDE STALL

If you are in a rural area and grow **fruit, vegetables** or other produce, you may be able to set up a roadside stall right outside your front gate. To make this venture worthwhile, your property should be situated on a busy highway or well-traversed tourist road.

Permission will be required for this type of enterprise, whether you are selling from within the property or out on the roadside. You'll also need public liability insurance and, possibly, other permits depending on what you sell.

Flowers, honey, eggs, home made chutneys and jams could all add to your income.

If you want a *weekend* business only, a stall selling **cut flowers** may do well, particularly if it is situated near a major hospital or cemetery. Small useful kiosks like these are often permitted in busy city and suburban sites; you will not know until you apply.

The big negative about roadside stalls, of course, is the weather! In mid-winter when the wind is blowing and the rain is beating down, it is quite probable that you will be thumbing through this book looking for another, more comfortable home-based business!
(See under Agriculture and Horticulture)

ROCKING HORSES
(See under Babies' & Children's furniture, Carpentry)

ROMANCE WRITER

If you have a gift for creative writing, there could be a host of publishers out there happy to receive your books. However, *Romance Writing* is a genre in itself and trying to get it published is not always as easy as you may think. Certain publishers insist that you write to a strict formula to fit their particular style so, if you want to let your creativity wander off the leash and will not be told how or what to write, prepare for a hard journey.

To discover what publishers *do* want, send for a set of 'writers' guidelines' from the various publishing houses and see if their requirements are in line with what you are willing to subscribe to. You may also be able to get these guidelines from their web sites.

Consider, too, joining a reputable writers' club as their newsletters can be very helpful: many list the various publishers who are currently looking for manuscripts. They also list publishers that do *not* wish to receive unsolicited submissions.

A further benefit is that most list up-coming writing competitions, which can be a good start for any new writer. The phrase 'prize winning author' could be a great asset for your next dust cover!

Unless you are comfortably off financially, however, it may be wise to look for a more lucrative business than writing as your 'day job'…and write as a *hobby* until you've clocked up a few prizes or received an offer from a publisher!

Note: Self publishing *Romance* novels can be risky and marketing them can be a real test! It can be a quick way to see your money disappear down the drain…so, if you simply *must* self-publish this genre of book, consider publishing it electronically! *(See also under Writing)*

ROOF RESTORATION

There are several ways to organise a business of this nature from home: do you want to work on the jobs yourself, become a subcontractor or start a series of franchises? For sure, as the weather gets wilder, good roofers will be more in demand.

List your various services in your advertising: ***tile replacement, re-sheeting, high-pressure cleaning and demossing, re-bedding, re-pointing, recolouring, glazing, guttering repair*** and so forth.

Placing your ads in consecutive issues of publications for a few weeks at a time will allow readers to familiarise themselves and become comfortable with your name.

Potential clients tend to feel more secure about a brand name they see advertised repeatedly.

The Yellow Pages is almost essential. Useful, too are local classifieds, pamphlet drops, shopper dockets and coupon advertising.

Generally, clients expect a 10-year guarantee on a roofing job! Also, safety-on-the-job is of major concern for you and your workers, so be sure you have all the necessary safety equipment, permits and insurance.

ROOF SCAFFOLDING - SUPPLY AND ERECT
(See under Scaffolding)

ROOM/FLAT LETTING IN YOUR HOME

Sharing your home with anyone can be dicey and should only be agreed to if you are entirely comfortable with the tenants - and after you have thoroughly investigated them. Be sure you get them to sign a tenancy agreement before moving in or you may never get rid of them!

If you have a large enough home with a spare room or two, you may be able to rent out those rooms to add to your weekly income, providing you can obtain the necessary permits.

You will be far less inconvenienced if you have a bathroom of your own. Sharing bathing facilities with strangers can sometimes be troublesome. If you do not want to share kitchen facilities, you may prefer to provide breakfast and a hot dinner for them.

IDEA: Overseas students are generally a good way to make a small income and help young students at the same time. It can be quite educational learning about their countries and customs, and you may even pick up a few free language lessons.

Overseas students are always searching for accommodation plus breakfast and an evening meal. Naturally, they prefer suburbs not too far from their universities and colleges but if they cannot get a suitable place nearby, many are prepared to go further afield.

 Most of these young people are very serious about their education and spend a great deal of time quietly reading and studying.

Make sure they know the ground rules. Many are quite happy to share a room if necessary. However, do consider their *dietary preferences* when preparing their meals.

If you have *a self-contained flat* to rent out, this can be much more comfortable than having to share your whole house. Once again, however, you will need to apply to the council to see what is permitted. A special application may get you over the problem so it's worth asking.

Any tenancy agreement should clearly state your conditions. After all, your home is your home and you don't want the place trashed! Nor do you want your peace disturbed by loud music, drug-taking or unsavoury visitors. If you don't approve of certain behaviour, make this clear at the beginning.

RUBBER STAMPS

Many big office suppliers and printers now offer this service at a very competitive price. Craft resellers and card-making schools, too, have such a range of ready-made creative stamps, so don't expect to make huge dollars from a home-based business of this nature unless you can come up with *a very unusual or innovative idea.*

Whatever great ideas you have will also need to carry right through into the *marketing* and *selling* of your products.

RUBBISH REMOVAL

Rubbish removal can be a dirty job - but it can also be exciting! What is rubbish to your client may turn out to be a *'find'* for you, especially if you run a second business ***refurbishing and reselling second-hand goods!***

While most rubbish will be…well…rubbish, there is always the thrill of coming across some great item for resale in a pile of throwouts. You will be surprised at the number of tables, chairs, lounges and whitegoods you can accumulate from ***domestic rubbish*** removal! While you are out and about, watch out for items you see piled up on nature strips, awaiting the local council's disposal truck; that's where many a potential treasure can be found!

There is quite good money to made in commercial rubbish removal if you can get the contracts. Like every other business, your success in this one is most likely to come from reliable service, good marketing, a pleasant disposition…and good networking! *(See also Second-hand furniture)*

S

SAILING INSTRUCTOR

Here's a chance to do what you love...and get paid for it, too! However, it's not all 'plain sailing' as there are issues re insurance, marketing, advertising and so forth to be thought through!

Ask yourself why people should come to you to learn sailing? What makes your tuition stand out? Are you known to have excelled yourself in the maritime arena? Did you sail around the world alone? Or do you just have a long history of making expert sailors and fun classes? Think out what your special strength is and what your students will get from *you* that they can't get anywhere else. Then emphasise that quality in your advertising.

Talk to various sailing clubs, scout and sea scout groups, local schools, the local council as well as anyone whom you feel may be able to help you and whom you may be able to help.
(See also under Coaching)

SANDING AND POLISHING OF FLOORS

Today, polished floors are *in*! In fact, builders, decorators, renovators and owners of all styles of homes are polishing their act and getting rid of germy carpets that stain and collect mud, dust and dirt! Actively network and advertise among professionals in the building and decorating industry, as well as home owners and investors.

This, together with excellent work, reliability and sensitivity to your clients' needs should ultimately seal your success.

SAUCE MANUFACTURE

Paul Newman did it! Dick Smith did it! Can *you* do it?

Everybody loves sauces and, if there is an outstanding one on the market, it will soon be found. However, *your* job is to get into the overcrowded food market in the first place!

You need a great, catchy brand name. Think hard about this. Maybe you will go for a fun name like "*Straight To The Sauce*' or '*Saucy Sauces*'...maybe you will prefer something that suggests fine dining and elegance. If you are not a film star or a well-known VIP, then your branding will be crucial.

You will also need all the help you can get from the press. Chase PR, editorials, offer free tastings, give lectures and media appearances. It can be hard work for the creative sauce manufacturer who is after the sweet taste of success!

SAUNA MANUFACTURE
(See under Woodworking)

SCARF MANUFACTURER

Silk, satin, organza, wool, cotton...handpainted, knitted, embroidered, crocheted, woven...you could give full scope to your creativity, producing a wonderland of scarves in various colours, weaves and fabrics.

It would be wise to produce new designs in *small numbers only* at first to test what works in the market and what does not. You may need to try several different approaches and markets before you get styles that 'click' with the public. Taking a stall at a weekend market here and there should give you a fair idea of whether you have a product worth pursuing. .
(See also: Silk Painting, Knitting)

SCRAPBOOKING SUPPLIES

This craft has gone crazy! If you are considering a craft on which to base a business and would like to know a little more about the popular art of scrapbooking before making a choice, take one of the many courses available ...then scrapbook your own family's life. If you enjoy the process and think you would like to teach others how to go about recording their lives and family escapades in this creative way, then you may have found a business.

The books of instruction, tools and craft components used in making up the albums could be sold, by *mail order*! These include the albums themselves, adhesives, scissors, templates, cutting tools, stickers, laces and various cardstock.

Many suppliers of these materials run *scrapbooking classes* as well! Teaching can often help boost your income and may bring potential customers right to your door. Get really creative and show your students new ways and methods of filing and presenting memorabilia!

Write you own scrapbooking book and self-publish it, incorporating some of your - and your students'- more unusual ideas. You would need to get the students' permission before publishing their ideas - and acknowledge their ideas in your book.

If you *really* want to compete in this business, you may ultimately need some display advertising in the up-market, glossy craft magazines. Unfortunately, this can be quite expensive so wait until you are on your feet before risking any hard-earned dollars in this way.

Start your business slowly and cautiously. You'll know when the time is right to get into the big league!

SCREEN PRINTING

These days, compact little machines are taking a lot of the headache out of this business, although many artists still like to use silk screens and work the old way.

Some modern screen printing equipment will now fit neatly into a small corner of your garage or spare room... and will print hundreds of articles just as easily as a handful. Compare this with some of the giant, old fashioned machines of decades ago!

Screen printing is almost unlimited in scope. Clothing and accessories...even fabric by the metre - can be printed with *unusual, elegant or even humorous designs* for many different markets, from beachwear to children's requirements.

Bigger money still could come from printing *corporate names and logos* on the various *promotional accessories and other items* distributed by major companies. *(See Directors' Chairs and Personalised Products)*

Make sure the company from whom you buy your equipment is willing to throw in some basic training, even if you know the craft backwards. You need to know that you are comfortable using the particular equipment that you have purchased.

If you find a successful 'niche' in the market, you might be surprised to find that screen printing makes you more money than you ever dreamed of. The key to success will be *your own creativity*: that is, creativity not only in designing but in *marketing* as well.

Brainstorm all consumer and promotional markets. Investigate the possibilities offered by *tourist outlets, theme parks, animal park kiosks, schools, sporting clubs, gift shops, surf 'n ski shops, fashion outlets, weekend markets.* Talk to any business that uses promotional products

SECONDHAND BOOKS

Who needs a *real* bookstore when they can visit a fascinating web page showroom right in their lounge room? The web can be a great way to trade, particularly if you are interested in *hard-to-find* books.

Another is to hold garage sales for books, perhaps in conjunction with friends' garage sales. *(See Garage Sales)*

You can often buy stock for a song from other garage sales, from on-line auctions, trash and treasure markets and through the classifieds. Harder to find books may need to be fossicked for through personal networks of bookworms, the Trading Post, special interest clubs, the web and newsletters.

SECOND-HAND FURNITURE
(See under Furniture - Used)

SECURITY

Security is a booming business with a myriad of avenues. Many big companies have moved into this industry but don't let that deter you. There is still room for small, home-based entrepreneurs with low overheads, providing they know how to market themselves...and take care of themselves! For security can often be quite dangerous work.

Are you interested in becoming a *bodyguard*? Do you prefer commercial *surveillance*...or even *domestic surveillance*? Would you prefer something really low-key but useful such as offering an escort service to *older clients* when they go out in the evening?
(See Escort Services for the Aged and also Security Products)

Those expert in the martial arts are often drawn to becoming *a bodyguard*, not just at nightclubs and parties but for big-name entertainers and visiting VIP's who must often place their lives in the hands of their security personnel. As a bodyguard, the people you meet and the venues you get to visit can often make life incredibly exciting…if a little hair-raising!

However, be warned: Security offers *little* security! In fact, it can be a very risky business, so thoroughly investigate any job you contemplate taking on, be sure you know what you are getting into, ensure that you have all licences and authorisation necessary and that you are comfortable with what you must do.

This is such a wide-ranging job that it would be well worth your while to talk to various firms offering various levels of involvement in the security business (as well as franchises) until you can assess just what aspects you find most impelling, then research those.

SECURITY PRODUCTS

These run from deadlocks, door chains and bolts, peep holes, window locks, alarms, sensors of all sorts, 'guard dog' tapes (to play when someone rings at the door), lights, cameras, smoke detectors, personal alarms, books and videos on security…to full home security systems where your clients' homes are connected to a centralised control centre.

Selling your products door to door will wear out your shoe leather…and you! Instead, try selling by Mail Order: advertise through the classifieds, the Yellow Pages, your web page, Neighbourhood Watch newsletter…even on shopper dockets.

You might respond to enquiries by sending clients your well illustrated and comprehensive brochure, listing your products, services and price list in detail. It would be a nice touch to include information on recent crime statistics and explain how the products you sell could have been instrumental in protecting victims from many of these crimes.

If yours is only a small concern, you might decide to take a stall at a weekend market to sell your items and services. If you have a security personnel uniform, you might decide to wear this as it could visually enhance the importance of what you do!

Perhaps you could decorate your stall with information about recent neighbourhood crimes and add a few Neighbourhood Watch statistics for the area.

If you speak well in public, you might decide to run a few seminars on subjects such as self-protection and home security. A self-published book or video might add to your image.

Perhaps you could be an agent for a unique line of imported security products suitable for sale through martial arts shops, schools, martial arts magazines, seniors' groups and their newsletters or magazines.

SELF DEFENCE
(See under Security & Martial Arts)

SEMINARS - PROFESSIONAL/EDUCATIONAL

Do you have expertise in a subject which you believe people would like to know about? Do you enjoy speaking in public? Do you just love to impart your knowledge to others and see them benefiting from it? In giving a seminar, however, it is not only the audience that is likely to benefit but the presenter as well! By dint of imparting specialised knowledge in this way, a good presenter generally becomes regarded as 'an expert' in his or her field!

Many small business owners do not realise the potential of giving seminars and lectures on their expertise. A public talk, a seminar or even an editorial written about a fascinating event has rocketed many a small business to fame almost overnight.

Could this happen to you? Maybe. Much will depend on your public speaking ability, your target market and your *marketing ability*. But, if you are satisfied with the viability of all these elements, you only need organise the event itself - or have someone do it for you.

Seminars have come a long way. An information-hungry public is now paying thousands to learn the finer points of everything: real estate, share trading, writing copy, selling, making millions, starting a business, self-improvement, health, diet, weight reduction...you name it! If you have expertise which you believe will interest others and can present it well , it may be worth giving some thought as to how to package and sell that knowledge in a public arena.

Talk to those professionals whom you believe could help assess your ability and who might advise you in arranging and giving seminars. If you can get a job on the seminar circuit working for someone else for a while first, it will give you needed experience in organising this type of business as well as stage craft.

SEWING

Anyone who can sew well should *never* have to be without an income! The avenues here for making a good living are endless but, as in any business, good marketing, creativity and intelligent self-promotion are vital.

It's amazing how many excellent sewers underestimate their money-making ability and who waste time and opportunity by taking on such trivialities as 'piecework' for large clothing companies. For this, they receive no more than a pittance! The rationale is often that it gives them the chance to work at home and look after their children! These people do not seem to realise that if they were working for themselves as *entrepreneurs*, they could make many times what they make from their virtual slavery to big manufacturers! Working for themselves, they'd still be able to remain at home with their children – and so, too, would the *profits* from their work remain at home.

Several potential income-generating ideas for a home sewing business are:
- *local ballet and dance schools*: ballet schools are always looking for people to make dresses and costumes for their concerts. Think of the orders that just a chorus line might yield: 12 cygnet tutus for the Swan Lake finale could net you...? Wow! Watch those dollars add up! This could be big, big business.

- Make to order for *Fancy Dress Hire.*

- Great designed clothes for *Mothers-To-Be*. Talented people are making millions out of this one! And many have started in their own homes.

- Cater for overweight people who need *larger garments*.

- Make and sell unusual and beautifully decorated *baby clothes*, quilts, rugs and pillowslips.

- *Brides* and their entourages need dresses for the wedding.

- How about something *unusual* for the fashion market, under your own label... like beautiful warm *bridal capes* or jackets? So often, brides have to shiver in the cold when they go to the park or the beach in their sleeveless gowns for the photography session! How it spoils the whole look if they are wrapped in the groom's jacket between shots! No more goose bumps for the bridal party!

- General *alterations* and repairs

- Small exclusive fashion shops often accept unusual lines or commission home sewers to make certain designs. But how do you get your foot in their door? Answer: by initially offering your services *for alterations*! Then, a few weeks after starting your alteration service with them, show them your wonderful illustrated folio of unique fashions!

- Perhaps you could have a ***web page*** devoted to the special lines you manufacture such as '***clothes for relaxation***' , '***slinky silks***' , '***gorgeous sleepwear***' or '***bikini covers***' (preferably in '***one size fits all***' so you don't have the hassle of returns).
- Would you enjoy making up exquisite accessories like ***beaded evening tops and jackets***?

- If you don't wish to make clothes, there are thousands of other money-making avenues for your skills:
    > ***evening bags, curtains and pelmets, quilts, bedspreads, birdcage covers, beanbag covers, cushions, pot holders, place mats, tablecloths, table runners, unusual and appliquéd pillowslips, oversized toys, teddy bears, dolls clothes, rag dolls, scarves, ponchos, bridal veils*** ...the list is endless!

- If you love counting money, you're likely to have lots of it to count if you make clever ***accessories for pets***. This can be *big, big, big* business for the good marketer! *(See under Pet Accessories)*

- How about developing a 'Sewing Circle' ***newsletter***? Your information could be sourced from around the country or around the world – from fabric shops, sewing academies, boutiques, recyclers, sewing clubs and craftspeople and woven into your publication in an interesting way. The newsletter could be published monthly or even quarterly.

Advertise your business. Attractive flyers and brochures are cheap and easy to produce on the home computer. Also, a small weekly classified in your local paper or local newsletter - run over several weeks and costing peanuts - might result in voluminous work for you.

SHEEPSKIN PRODUCTS

You will need to check with your local council if you plan to manufacture sheepskin products from home as there are often strict limits to the amount of power machinery one is permitted to run in a domestic dwelling as well as limits on the size of workrooms, signage and other issues.

Articles such as slippers, hats and other accessories are constantly flooding into the country from overseas so it's hardly worth trying to compete with these markets in the more basic items.

You may find it far more profitable to concentrate on producing *up-market products* such as coats and jackets or tailored car seat covers. Research your market thoroughly before making any plans.

SHIATSU

This form of natural healing is easy to learn and can be a good source of income if you know how to promote yourself, relate well to many types of people and are able to show genuine sensitivity to their needs.

Clients expect professionalism in a business such as this. The work area and waiting room need to be neat, clean and comfortable and the massage you give them truly effective, making them want to come back to see you again and again.

Put a few shiatsu charts on the walls so you can explain what you are doing and why, and give patients literature in the form of brochures to take away to read.

Ensure you have any permits, insurance and qualifications necessary.

If you speak well in public, you may be able to run a seminar or free lectures on shiatsu at clubs, luncheons, aged hostels, public libraries and other suitable venues.

Could you write and publish a book or videos on this subject and sell it through mail order?

SHOPPING SERVICE - FOR TODAY'S BUSY EXECUTIVES

It's a busy, busy world out there and overworked professionals can only do so much. They have homes to run, families to cater for, friends to entertain…but who's going to do all the shopping? Who? Why, *you* of course!

And you don't have to stop at the shopping! You could extend your service to deliver and collect dry cleaning, ironing and laundry, buy and wrap gifts, organise flowers, send mail, collect and drop clients' children - the more services you can provide, the more you will be paid. In fact, you could offer a ***full personal assistance service,*** subcontracting other services where required.

Consider catering, party planning, child minding, domestic cleaning, lawn maintenance services etc. It could be as small or big a business as you want it to be. Or you may prefer to simply be an *organiser or agent for other services*, hiring specialised service operators who take care of the jobs for you.

If handled correctly, you could conceivably receive not only the fee from your client but a percentage from each service provider as well. Alternatively, you may prefer to keep the business small and personal, accepting only those local contracts that you can deal with yourself.
(See also 'Personal Services' and 'Gofer Services')

SIGNS AND SIGNWRITING

Signwriting skills not up to scratch? Is your hand not as steady as you would like it to be? Don't worry! A great deal of signage these days - even large outdoor signs - is now fully computerised.

Equipment can be bought or leased but the returns are generally good for creative people willing to intelligently promote themselves.

If you are new to the signwriting business, you may find that buying a franchise or a complete business package will save you time, frustration and dollars in the long run. If this is your preference, you will need to search out a *reliable* franchiser who offers both equipment and training...and insist the purchase be covered by a guarantee.

If you are an old traditionalist with the incredible skills and experience needed for painting signs direct, you can still speed up your business by introducing technology where it is useful.

There is one piece of equipment that will probably not be given you however, but it's one which every signwriter should have at every job: a dictionary! Don't leave home without it as it can save you money, time and reputation!

SILKWORMS

Unless you own a silkworm factory, it is unlikely you will make much of an income out of silk worms in this country!

However, you might be able to generate a business in producing educational *'silkworm farms'* for sale to children and sell them through pet shops and schools. (Advertising might be most effective in school newsletters and children's magazines and comics.)

A pack could consist of a colourful illustrated booklet about these short-lived pets and their life cycle, some cocoons, a small specimen booklet of silk illustrating the different stages of silk manufacture through to samples of the finished dyed and woven fabric.

You would also need the worms plus a source of mulberry leaves for your clients new pets. (Most important as these leaves are the worms' food!)

Thoroughly check out the viability of this venture before making any plans then speak to your local authority to see if there are any special requirements or permits you would require. Such an untried business as this would need to be tested out.

SKI INSTRUCTOR

A great seasonal job…if you live around the ski fields (lucky you!)

Your services could be offered to the various hotels, chalets, ski hire outlets in the area; as well, start your name circulating via local advertising and an editorial in the local paper if you can.

Could you make a short instructional ski video...with your contact number at the end and on the cover? You might even give these free to the tourist hotels and chalets to lend to their guests! It would be excellent promotion for you! After all…who wouldn't want a ski instructor who's a film star?

SNAIL FARM

Feel you need to slow down? Then, don't get a snail farm because, despite its name, it could turn out to be a very fast-paced business if you succeed in marketing those tasty little delicacies the right way and market them to the right places.

Of course, the snails we speak of are not of the everyday, backyard variety; far from it! These are delicious haute cuisine delicacies that have been in vogue gastronomically for years.

There is quite a lot of information about snail farms on the internet: just put in a search for Snail Farms. Further information should be available at your library.

SOAP MAKING

Soap is so easy to make, you will feel you are indulging in a hobby instead of a business. Most craft stores and books will show you how to make basic soaps which you can then embellish with fragrances, colours and even dried flowers or herbs.

Presentation is as important as is quality for many of your creations will be bought for gifts rather than personal use. Your soaps could be made up into irresistible sets of two or three, in ribbon-tied acetate boxes...or silk pouches or...! In planning, let your mind wander and follow its progress with a pen and pencil, jotting down all the ideas that come to you on presentation and marketing possibilities. Maybe you will package your soaps with fine lingerie, towels or bath gowns?

Creativity is the name of this game!

SOFTWARE TRAINER

Let computer schools and stores know of your training services by issuing them with brochures and a short run-down on your experience and qualifications in this area. Many corporate clients and computer shops need teachers willing to train employees and clients 'on site', singly or in groups.

While many computer stores themselves offer in-house training sessions they cannot always teach on-site. Others do not have the facilities for teaching anything beyond the operating system and some simple word processing. Much graphics software is way beyond the everyday salesperson.

Tuition could be offered at the client's home or office or at your own home, if you have a suitable area.

Request computer stores to insert one of your training brochures in every computer purchased: your literature might include an offer of discounted tuition fees for customers of participating stores.

SPACE WALKS

These rides are popular at shows, fetes and birthday parties. However, before going into this venture, be sure you've weighed up all the plusses and the minuses such as the costs of buying or leasing the equipment, transporting it, erecting it, repairing it and insuring it and those who use it? Have you thought of such things as the emotional costs of long days in bad weather or rainy days where few turn up?

But your love of being at fairs and fetes and out in the open, among children and those having fun, may be enough to compensate for any drawbacks.
(See Amusement Machines)

SPEAKER

If you have the 'gift of the gab', you could have a varied and interesting life as a speaker or lecturer at a variety of functions: MC weddings and parties, give talks at clubs and meetings. Your success as a speaker will depend as much on your networking and self-promotion as it will on your speaking talent.

Advertising ideas: newsletters and magazines (corporate, special interest, clubs, charities); the classifieds. Send brochures with your CV and tear sheets (i.e. copies of write-ups that you may have received in the press) to wedding planners, clubs and party organisers; if possible, obtain some complimentary promotional material in the form of letters from previous clients whom you've delighted.
(See Speech Writer)

SPEAKING RIBBONS

These ribbons can be fun and could be great adjunct to a gift business such as gift baskets, balloons or personalised gifts or even a card manufacturing business. However, you might also tie them in with another business such a photography: could you produce photos of loved ones containing a personal spoken message from the subject to the recipient?

The product itself is generally a plastic ribbon inserted or attached to the gift, card, frame or other object. When rubbed, it is supposed to make any novelty appear to talk. However, there are other methods of producing talking tapes as well.

Companies selling certain types of talking ribbons are sometimes advertised in the business opportunities magazines.

SPEECH THERAPIST

This could be an excellent home business for a *qualified* person and your hours of work can generally be tailored to suit yourself.

Lessons could be held at a hired venue if you prefer students not to come to your home...or you could go mobile, visiting clients on site.

Giving free public lectures, writing features and books and obtaining good, continuous advertising are important if you want your name to get around.

Signage on your property plus a professionally equipped separate room or studio are also important if you are working from home. And don't overlook insurance: your students may trip over the dog or fall down the front steps on their way out. Your home insurance *may* cover these contingencies but check with your insurance company to be sure!

SPEECH WRITER

It takes a while to get known in this business but when you've made it, there is usually plenty of work for the talented, especially if you have a clever sense of humour.

You might start off writing speeches for weddings and other everyday functions - but end up writing for the Prime Minister; who knows?

Take every opportunity to practise your skills, even if you have to write a few speeches for free...and be sure to advertise your skills in the right quarters! Good marketing takes research and hard work.

There are a few potential possibilities for speech writers that may not be obvious at first. One is copywriting, particularly for direct marketing or mail order advertising campaigns. Here, down-to-earth, plain, write-it-as-you-say-it copy is highly sought after - so, if this is your style, be sure to promote your writing skills in these quarters.

When not writing for others, why not do a public speaking course and become a speaker on whatever niche inteests you and can find a market for - and go on the lecture circuit yourself? r
(See under Speaker)

SPORTSCLOTHES TO MEASURE
(See under Sewing)

SPORTS EQUIPMENT – USED
Second hand sports equipment might make a first class business: golf clubs, tennis

racquets, hockey sticks, basketballs, skates ...many of them hardly used...can often be bought for a song at garage sales, cleaned up and profitably resold. Exercise machines and equipment also turn up from time to time at such places.

A couple of other sources for these items may be the *Trading Post* and the classifieds.

Learn to negotiate on price when buying items. You can often resell them at many times their cost to you!

Pre-loved sports clothes are usually good sellers. New sports clothes and accessories can be quite expensive to buy - a handicap for beginners who are often not sure whether they will want to continue the sport they start. Others just love the worn look, believing it makes them look like old pros. Most sports people love to wear the same *big names* and styles worn by their heroes. Who cares if the garments and footwear are a bit worn?

If the business grows too big to remain home-based, you might be able to take a local shop, have it manned by a young sports enthusiast while you continue to base yourself at home, buying the stock and repairing, cleaning and renovating it.

(Note: You may need an O.K. from your local council to sell these items from your home (unless it's from a garage sale or your business is mail order.)

SPORTS GIFT PACKS

Sports gift packs could be made up of colour co-ordinated towel, headband, wristbands and water container in nice little waterproof carry bags. If you have a sewing machine with embroidery attachment, you might also add value by embroidering the name or logo of the sport on the towel and bag.

Test market your packs to gyms, sporting shops, sporting clubs and complexes. You may find they sell well at markets, gift shops and fetes, too.

STAMP DEALER – MAIL ORDER

Unless you are into rare stamps and are exceedingly well-networked in philately, don't expect to make a large income from this venture as a home-based business! However, it might represent a comfortable *hobby* business that is both absorbing and educational and could be quite easily run by *mail order* from home.

To widen your business name and image, think about giving free talks and seminars to various stamp clubs, schools and charities.

How about producing your own newsletter, too, detailing all the latest finds, prices paid and news from the various interstate and international stamp exhibitions. Newsletters can often be good money spinners and excellent image-enhancers.

You don't have to try to compete with Stanley Gibbons! Just make your information interesting through doing extra research and keep in touch with other dealers.

STEAM CLEANING

From carpets, lounge suites and mattresses to car interiors, the wish to remove dust and germs from around the home is becoming more widespread as people are starting to realise just how many health problems and allergies they can cause.
Dust allergy affects thousands of people. However, dust does not come from dust mites and dust mite dung alone. It can form from simple sloughing of skin scales, hair, certain fabrics and many other sources. Nor is it solely house-born. It can originate in factories and offices and arrive in your home unbeknown to you. So your steam cleaning service will be doing the community a great service.

Good marketing often includes a freebie or two: perhaps you will offer 'free deodorising and sanitising' or 'one hallway free'. Try to think of some bonus that will make your service appear just that little more attractive than your competitors'.

Unless you've been in this game before, you may feel more confident obtaining a good, *well-respected* franchise right from the start.
(See also Mattress Cleaning/Carpet Cleaning)

STORAGE CONSULTANT

Could you devise solutions to storage problems for busy householders? Could you build or reorganise their cupboards, robes and closets, their garages, workshops, bedrooms and playrooms? Many working people are just too busy to reorganise their possessions and end up living in chaos.

While much of your work is likely to be in *re-organising existing storage*, you could also be asked to build or erect *new solutions, such as shelving, cupboards or converting attic space,* particularly if you are a carpenter or handyperson.

You may also find clients who are going overseas or interstate and wishing to rent their homes. If these people are working all day, they may not have time to ***pack, sort and store*** all their possessions for long-term storage. Could you do this for them?

Advertise the services you offer! Send off your brochures to all the big companies, to real estate agents and to newly sold properties. Letterbox drops could also go to all local suburbs.

You may decide to become an agent for a local ***mini store***, arranging for rarely used items to be safely stored *away* from the house.

STRESS REDUCTION CLASSES

Stress! It's the disease of the new millennium, eating away at people's happiness, health, hopes and dreams. However, there are many effective stress reduction techniques like *progressive relaxation* and *meditation* that can assist tense, overwrought workaholics and others to relax and cope a little better with all that life demands.

If you have learned stress reduction techniques that you can effectively pass on to others – and get paid for doing it – then what are you waiting for?

STUFFED TOYS

Producers of stuffed toys have lots of competition with overseas imports. However, if your toys are *unusual* in some way. they could be quite good money spinners. Many toys can serve a dual purpose such as cushions, pyjama bags or comfy bean bags. Some stuffed toys even tell stories.

You might like to read the now-famous story of a talking bear manufacturer in The One-Minute Millionaire by Jack Canfield. Yes, it's fiction but it gives you a great eye-opener into the competitive world of toy manufacturing.

SURFING INSTRUCTOR
(See under Coaching)

T

TABLE MATS, RUNNERS & NAPKINS

If you have a reliable sewing machine capable of basic embroidery, you could let your creativity go wild with several lines of place mats, runners and napkins.

Think of *unusual* designs: ethnic designs, bright colours, pastels for baby showers or parties, wonderful place settings for special events organisers, unusual fabrics such as sari fabrics for decorator shops, embroidered wedding napery in voile over taffeta and so forth.

Make up a few of these sets into various categories, photograph them and compile a beautiful, glossy brochure for your marketing campaign.

TAI CHI TEACHER

Tai Chi is a form of exercise which originated in China many hundreds of years ago. Because the exercises are not physically demanding, they suit most people of all ages and most levels of physical ability. However, it is always wise to have students check with their doctors before beginning new exercise regimes.

The movements are performed very slowly and gently. Mind and body are taught to work in unison and coninuously, leaving no time to think of the problems of the day. For this reason, Tai Chi has often been called 'moving meditation'.

However, you don't have to be an Oriental Master to offer classes in Tai Chi. You do need to be proficient in one form of the art, however. If you are a beginner, take a couple of terms with a local Tai Chi school then let the teacher know you would like to teach. Most schools are happy to allow their advanced students to take the occasional class. If you do well, you will most likely be permitted to teach a class for a whole term. Placing students in charge of classes like this allows the teacher to move on and expand the business by opening other classes in other venues.

When you are thoroughly familiar with the Tai Chi form you have chosen, you should then be able to start your own school.

Market it as widely as possible and see if you can net an editorial or two in the local newspaper. Obtain permission to put up small posters in various shops, shopping centres, on community noticeboards, at health practitioners, naturopaths and health food stores - and on tertiary institution noticeboards. *(You will need to obtain permission for this.)*

Perhaps you might consider producing a Tai Chi newsletter if you have enough knowledge of what is going on in the Tai Chi community. DTP equipment can produce quite a professional looking publication. It might be an excellent image enhancer.

If you have a video camera and editing equipment, you might consider producing an instructional video as well . This might turn out to be a good source of income *if done well*, making you somewhat of a celebrity in the shortest possible time!

You may decide to run classes at home, in a hired hall, a local recreation centre or even in the local park. And the great thing is…no equipment is needed for most forms!

TAILORING

Your market for tailored suits, jackets and coats will generally be among executives so make sure your pamphlets and brochures make their way into local business corporations of all sizes. Advertise, too, in local club newsletters such as Rotary, VIEW, Rostrum and similar rather than just relying on one home sign plus ads in the local classifieds.
(See also under Sewing)

TALKING RIBBONS
(See Speaking Ribbons, Balloons)

TASSEL MAKER

This could be quite an absorbing hobby and a good little business if marketed the right way. However, only *unusual and beautifully made* tassels need apply as cheap 'ho-hum' imports can be found everywhere!

You may find it easiest to sell through mail order: test the market first, however. You might place a little two or three-line ad in the classifieds of various newspapers, craft and sewing magazines or decorator magazines, offering an illustrated information brochure.

You may even decide to give *tassel-making classes* to boost your income. These classes could be held at home or you might teach at a local craft shop or school, paying the owners a weekly rental for the use of space.

TATTOOIST

If you have artistic ability as well as the knowledge essential for tattooing, you might start your own home-based tattooing studio. If your zoning does not allow this type of activity, perhaps you may be able to go mobile. Check with the local council.

Some customers come back time and again for tattoos. There are quite a few afficionados who regard themselves as living artwork, entering themselves (and the tattooist's work!) in various tattooing competitions around the country.

There is also a market in the Beauty Industry for *eyebrow and lip tattooing* (and tattoo removal), so this may be more your scene.

Be sure you have all the permits, qualifications, insurance and *knowledge* necessary before you start. Tattooing carries a high risk of infection if not done correctly.

TAXATION CONSULTANT

This could be a great little business for someone who is good at figures. Of course, you may already have the necessary experience and qualifications for this type of work but, if you have not, it can be obtained.

One long-standing tax firm offers short courses in this area from time to time and are quite reasonably priced. They often advertise upcoming courses in the windows of their offices or in the classified section of local newspapers. If you then wish to become a consultant, you can sit a test on the material you have been taught. If you pass, you can then apply to become one of their tax consultants. Later on, when you have acquired all the necessary knowledge, you may be in a position to continue on your own.

For the beginner who ultimately wants a home business as a taxation consultant, this might be an excellent way to start off.

TAXI SERVICE

Believe it or not, there are some people who just love driving through all the traffic! If you are one of these - and you'd like to start a business - a taxi service might suit you.

As a private service, you will need to find creative ways to expand your business. Could you make up mini tours for hotel and motel guests? Ask if you can leave pamphlets and tour brochures in hotel foyers.

Watch for up-coming seminars and exhibitions in your area, too, so you can be on hand to ferry participants around from hotel to event and, at the same time, promote organised tours of local attractions.

There are never enough *'maxi taxis' for the disabled*! This can be highly rewarding work but these special cabs can be quite expensive to fit out, especially those with hydraulic lifts for the wheel chairs.

Maxi-taxi drivers need to be physically fit as it can often be hard work pushing disabled passengers up ramps or steps to their destination. As well, every wheel chair-bound passenger needs to be secured by a multitude of straps for every ride. In winter, it can be very unpleasant waiting in the wind and rain for chairs to be slowly raised and lowered by lift.

However, there is also a lot of satisfaction to be gained from this work and you may form some very pleasant relationships with permanent clients and their families.

As a maxi-taxi driver, you may decide to work for a centralised booking agency for a while until you to get the hang of the business, then go out on your own when you are ready.

TEACHING/TUTORING

If you're a good teacher, know your subject well and teach a popular subject, you can be assured of a home-based income no matter how depressed the economy. However, while many teachers know their subject, not all know how to present it in an interesting, easily assimilated way. Others have no idea of how to market themselves. All these aspects should be looked at and brought up to scratch if success is on your agenda.

For those teaching educational, arts or hobby subjects, your flyers could be placed in the classifieds of various local papers, in local school newsletters, as well as on noticeboards at nearby colleges, universities and supermarkets (if you can obtain permission for this).

Some subjects of a more specialised nature may need to be advertised in relevant club, school and corporate newsletters or magazines. Advertising is essential and should pay for itself many times over if you have the ability to deliver the goods.

Tutoring can also be given in your own home, the student's home, a university foyer or library, a rented room in a church hall or recreational centre…or you may prefer to work on a casual basis for a TAFE, college or university. And don't overlook the possiblity of correspondence lessons: quality, well organised correspondence courses can bring big dollars!
(See also under Coaching, Seminars, Desktop Publishing)

TEDDY BEAR TRADER/MANUFACTURER

You've heard the stories: 'I sold my great-grandfather's teddy bear to an antique dealer for $3000…yet the stuffing was coming out and it had lost one of its eyes!'

What *is* it about teddy bears? Who knows? It's enough to know that children (and antique dealers!) love them dearly and always have!
Of course, there are teddy bears - and teddy bears! Overseas imports have now flooded the shops with bears of all shapes and sizes so, if you are going into teddy bear manufacture, you will need to produce work that is truly outstanding and targeted at the connoisseurs.

TEDDY BEARS - CRAFT SUPPLIES

Teddy bear manufacturers need to obtain their supplies from somewhere: why not *your **mail order*** business? You would need to offer all major components like patterns, fabric, paw pads, eyes and noses, joint sets and so forth in your catalogues. You could even offer clothes and accessories: teddy jamas, dresses, bear schoolboy and schoolgirl outfits, jumpers, pants, hats, socks and shoes for these furry little friends-to-be.

TELEMARKETER

Most telemarketers employed by a company or organization do their marketing from commercial premises but there are also those who do this work from home, offering a very competitive service. Some of the smaller direct mail entrepreneurs could find this cheaper service very useful, so you could approach them.

In fact, if you have a product or service of your own that you would like to sell, you might decide to do your own telemarketing as well!
(See Telephone Answering Service)

TELEPHONE ANSWERING SERVICE/ CALL CENTRE

There are many small businesses which require their telephones to be manned during the day but cannot afford extra staff for this purpose. If you are home all day, a couple of small businesses might be very happy to switch their phones to your number for a fee.

You would need to supply callers with simple information such as names, addresses and telephone numbers. Occasionally, you may be asked to take orders. At the end of the day, you would fax all the details to your client who would pay you per call received - or a flat fee for a pre-calculated number of calls. If this number is exceeded, you would then expect them to pay an excess.

If you take on a service such as this as a home-based enterprise, you will need a quiet environment in which to answer your phone as your clients rely on you to present a professional image of their business to the public. You can hardly do this if you have a baby crying or dogs barking in the background.

TOOL SHARPENING SERVICE

Not a huge business on its own, perhaps, but it could be a useful adjunct to some other (related) home business.

TOUR ORGANISER

You will be intelligent, good at organising, have great PR and marketing skills, be well networked and preferably, will have had quite a bit of travel experience. Your interest could be local, interstate or even overseas travel.

IDEAS: but how are you going to compete with all the other travel agencies and tours available? One answer may be to specialise in a particular area! Consider arranging *special focus tours* for people who have specific interests. You might consider tailoring your tours for:
- *art lovers*
- *musicians*

- *gourmets*
- *chocolate lovers*
- *historical societies*
- *history enthusiasts*
- *wine lovers*
- *dolphin watchers*
- *whale watchers*
- *bird watchers*
- *koala watchers*
- *horticulturalists*
- *world of finance*
- *shopping enthusiasts*
- *bargain shopping enthusiasts*
- *would-be Egyptologists*
- *gold seekers*
- *shipwreck and lighthouse aficionados.*

Consider, too:

- *religious tours*
- *architectural tours*
- *Great Homes tours*
- *Aboriginal cultural tours*
- *theme parks of the world tours*
- *eco tours*

Whether you arrange large group tours far afield or simply the occasional local mini tour for clubs and private clients, you are quite likely to wangle a free ticket for yourself if you recruit sufficient participants! Lucky you!

But…how do you find clients? Through good marketing! Notify likely prospects of upcoming trips in the newsletters or magazines of special interest clubs. Advertise in the classifieds. Send notices and brochures to travel agencies, transport organisations, airlines, hotels and motels. Synergise with other tour companies! Brainstorm!

Be forever on the lookout for events and seminars that could tie in with a special interest tour.

You could start your business small and slowly work up to larger, more involved tours as you gain experience. Ultimately, you may find you have created a real niche for yourself in the marketplace! A good operator builds valuable databases of repeat clients.

Although you may never have been to a particular tour destination yourself, every minute detail needs to be worked out before you leave. Tour operators have people's lives in their hands: in organising and running the show, you can't afford to be laid back in your approach or take unnecessary risks.

In this business, success is retained for the perfectionist who is alert, caring, intuitive, energetic and thoroughly dependable.

- *IDEA*: If you own a mini bus, have you thought about using it to run *special interest mini tours* for local motels and hotels? You may be able to organise day tours or even run some over several days, getting a slice of the action from motels, restaurants and attractions en route. Much will depend on where you live, what the area has to offer and how many tourists and travellers frequent the locality.

  You might also arrange tours and outings for *companies, clubs, schools, universities, special interest groups* and so forth. These could involve anything from a *day's outing* in a hired bus - to fantastic, up-market *interstate or overseas tours* lasting weeks or months. In fact, if you're a good organiser, know the industry well and love travel, life could become one idyllic, well-paid travelogue

Be sure to check on where you stand with insurance and other issues before taking on anything such as this

TOUR GUIDE

This can be a great job for anyone who is reasonably fluent in other languages. Particularly if you speak an Asian language, you should find loads of work taking you around the city, the state, the country…or even the world!

Contact all travel and tour organisers to find out if they are interested in *subcontracting* your services for their passengers. In fact, as a bi-lingual, *self-employed* tour guide, you may ultimately decide to plan and run your own tours. *(See Travel Organiser)*

TOY MANUFACTURER
(See Babies'/Children's Merchandise, Dolls, Sewing)

TRADER

Buy and sell goods via classified ads in publications such as *the Trading Post*, garage sales, second hand shops, internet auctions.
(See entry under Garage Sales, Furniture)

TRAVEL AGENT

Do it all online from the comfort of your armchair at home. However, you will need excellent phone and negotiating skills plus a firm understanding of the travel industry.

Apart from obtaining the necessary registration and certification, it will help to have travelled considerably! To understand the various cultures and different requirements of foreign countries and ways of overcoming possible hurdles before they eventuate are all part of being a good agent. After all, you have people's lives in your hands.

This job would work as a home business for a retired professional with a pre-existing client base or someone who has already built a good reputation in the industry..
(*See Travel Agent, Tour Organiser & Mini-tours*)

TRANSLATING

If you are fluent in another language, contact hospitals, language schools, legal and local government institutions, overseas corporations (those having business with the country whose language you speak), universities, tourist centres, your local ethnic radio and TV stations. Put small ads in various writers' newsletters.
Advertise your services as widely as possible...including *The Yellow Pages*.
(*See Language Translation Services/Tour Guide*)

TREE SHAPING AND LOPPING

This would be a suitable sideline business for someone in Garden Maintenance or a Handyperson. If you have the necessary equipment, permits and knowledge of tree lopping, it's mainly a matter of self-marketing.

T-SHIRT PRINTING

This can be 'big business' if run the right way, with business nous, creativity and an eye to good networking!
(*See under Screen Printing*)

TURTLES AND TORTOISES

There are many thousands of minor businesses that people could run in their homes simultaneously such as breeding cats, dogs, birds,...turtles and tortoises! These little creatures that children find so fascinating are not hard to rear and could be marketed to pet stores locally and in surrounding suburbs.

Think about all possible markets then make enquiries from the Department of Agriculture as to the viability of your plans.

TYPING/WORD PROCESSING

If you can type to a professional standard and have a reliable computer and printer, you need never be without a business. There are many companies outsourcing...and what happens when staff call in sick? Who can they call? You of course...providing you've let them know you're there! Many business people work from home now, too, and need assistance on a permanent or ad hoc basis.

Your work may come in as a result of ads you have placed in the classifieds or through word of mouth, posters on public noticeboards, flyers in letter boxes etc.

If there is a Uni or TAFE in your locale, put a flyer on *every* noticeboard in *every* faculty building (check with Union admin. first) as well as in the the library. Such ads should outline your services, show how they can benefit busy students and save them time for study. Maybe you will be able to wangle some PR for your service in the local Uni magazine.

Believe it or not, there are still people out there who cannot type, even though they may have a computer! Many more simply do not have time to devote to typing reports and correspondence...and this is where you can make yourself indispensable.

However, nobody will be using your services unless your persistent marketing push informs them that you are there - so promote yourself at every opportunity! If work grows to the point that you need to employ others to assist you, *you* could outsource.

As a word processing concern and with a growing network of office staff, you might consider expanding your horizons to include *a home-based personnel agency* specialising in *receptionists/typists and office staff*. This type of recruitment operation should not be overly difficult to run and may prove to be quite lucrative... as well as supplying you with a ready pool of typists. Experience will teach you what to look for in candidates; then, all you will need to do is match them to your client's brief.

Think, too, about starting up a typing school in your area. You want to buy up some reconditioned computers or typewriters if you are running classes or simply make do with a couple of machines and give private lessons.
(See also Word Processing, Desktop Publishing and Recruitment Consultant)

U

UPHOLSTERY & RE-UPHOLSTERY
(See Furniture Restoration)

V

VENDING MACHINES

Vending machines *can* make good money but they need to be in the appropriate location in order to attract customers. In fact, location is just as crucial to profitablilty as is product.

It is also important to research the behaviour of the *people* who live in or use the area in which you propose to site the machines. Is it an area most likely to be frequented by children, thirsty sports people, senior citizens, smokers, tired and hungry commuters?

When you have thoroughly checked out the types of machines available and the viability of the site, you might prefer to try out just one machine and see how it goes. If possible, try to lease the location for a *trial* period first. If machine and locale reward you with the sort of return you were expecting, then it will be time to consider your next step.

The type and variety of vending machines available today is astounding, many of them affording entertainment through just watching them in operation!

Machines vend...well...you name it: food, drinks, nuts, gifts, toys, sweets, gumballs, tea and coffee, personal items, newspapers...even socks! And they are found in all sorts of locations. Investigate all possibilities: inside and outside shops, pizza parlours, tertiary institutes, railway and bus stations, public toilets, bowling alleys, rest rooms, malls, restaurants, theatres, shopping strips, airports, sporting complexes and hundreds of other places!

Once the machine is in its posse, all you need do then is maintain it regularly and... oh, yes! Clean out all those shiny coins! Consider the following possibilities:!

- Sweets
- Sandwiches
- Nuts
- Toys
- Children's rides
- Pinball games
- Videos
- Jukebox music

- Driving & other games
- Shooting games
- Air hockey
- Soccer tables
- Tea and coffee
- Trinkets
- Personal items
- Food items

(See under Amusement Machines as well as the above notes on siting machines)
VENETIAN BLIND CLEANER
(See under Blind & Shutter Cleaning)

VENTRILOQUIST

Do you have the ability to throw your voice and make it appear as if it is coming from an inanimate object? If you can perform this fascinating trick and like entertaining an audience, perhaps you might consider becoming a ventriloquist.

Your first step would to make or buy for yourself a ventriloquist's dummy. Write yourself (and your inanimate new partner) a humorous, fascinating script or repertoire of acts and practise until you are both faultless...then put on a few shows for family and friends and assess the feedback.

If your act turns out to be a success, it might be worth marketing. You could try advertising through the classifieds, do letterbox drops in various suburbs, try to get your brochures or posters on party and toy shop windows, put ads in club and school newsletters and talk to a few entertainment agencies if the act really takes off.

Do a good deed (building up your name at the same time!) by offering your act *free* to various charities and children's hospitals. This is the way to get your name widely recognised and hopefully, pull in more work.

VIDEO LIBRARY

This business could function as a home-based *mail order* business. However, certain big companies are already running their video (DVD) libraries this way, so you might have some fierce competition.

You may choose to run a *mobile video and games delivery* service if you live in a smallish town. Alternatively, you could even set yourself up in a *shop and residence* in order to run a video library legally from home.

Much will depend on the facilities already offered by the area in which you live, your zoning and the type of lifestyle you are after.

VIDEO PRODUCTION AND MARKETING

Question: how could an entrepreneur make money with a camcorder?
Suggestion: how about filming some or all of the following:

- *will readings*
- personal presentations by *job candidates*

- clients' presentations for *matchmaking and dating* agencies

- *homes for sale & rent* for real estate agencies

- *Valentine's Day* messages for lovers

- *Cooking lessons*

- Christmas Day and other *greetings for families overseas.*

- While most maternity hospitals allow approved photographers to take still photos of the newborn, rarely do we see a professional cameraman making a *video of the baby*.

  Nor does it seem there is ever anyone on hand to film one of the most *important* days in the life of the new Mum and Dad: i.e. *leaving hospital* with their bundle of joy, waving goodbye to the nurses and introducing their little one into the big wide world for the first time! It may be worth investigating this angle as this is one time that can be very difficult for the new parents to film for themselves. Mum's usually carrying the baby and organising the siblings, if any - and Dad has to carry all the luggage out to the car.

- One tried and tested way that many people make money from video production is to produce *information videos*. You may decide to film certain experts talking about...whatever they are 'expert' in! However, these people would need to be capable of speaking well in front of the camera and presenting their subject at a level that viewers can easily follow.

  You would then edit and package the resulting film and try to sell it to an information-hungry public. Your marketing would need to be carefully matched to the type of people most likely to have an interest in the presenter's subject.

  Where could you advertise? Apart from the classifieds, you might try any relevant 'special interest' clubs, magazines and newsletters and other avenues closely related to the particular subject that the film is about.

- Also, of course, there are *special events* like weddings, graduations and other celebrations that are filmed for posterity but...you will need to apply particularly good marketing strategies to stand out from the crowd and make it all work for you.

Consider *unusual* avenues, too. You might come up with a brilliant idea after a bit of lateral thinking!!

W

WALKING TOUR ORGANISER

This type of business can have you meeting many fascinating people from all over the world as well as those from your own city. You might decide to run only one tour, several tours - or *organise other tour* leaders to take walks designed by you.

There are many tours possible in a big, historically interesting city. However, if you remain within your field of knowledge and expertise, you will enjoy your work more. Your focus of interest can always be expanded and enhanced while your clients will appreciate the depth and authenticity of your knowledge.

What *is* your interest? Will your tours lean toward **history**, **geography**, **art** and **galleries**, strange **legends**, **architecture**, the **macabre**, **shopping**, **dollar saver**, **gourmet**, **chocolates**, **myths and legends**, houses of the **rich and famous, convicts**?

Become an avid collector of stories and anecdotes about the area and its history. The more you research and learn what is not generally known about your 'precinct' or subject, the more sought after you will be.

WALL PLAQUES

There are many possibilities available to makers of wall plaques but one of the most lucrative is an antique or art deco style, reminiscent of the old posters and pub signs. Generally, some feature of the poster or sign is made to stand out in frieze fashion, and is often moulded in fibreglass or treated plaster. The plaques are very popular hung over home bars in family rooms and billiard rooms.

While many people are making these plaques, there is quite an appetite for them among home owners, antique dealers and interior decorators. One needs to be adept at painting and lettering, however, to attain the degree of authenticity and prefessionalism required.

WARDROBE/CLOSET ORGANISER

Some people just can't organise themselves or their belongings. Their robes and cupboards are in such a jumble, they don't know what clothes they have hanging in their wardrobes, nor can they even find their socks in the morning!

Much of the time, the solution is just a matter of better organization; sometimes it's a case of insufficient storage and you will need to provide more cupboard space or subdivide the available space with partitions or extra shelves.

If you are an organised, meticulous person who likes everything in its place, you will see at a glance how your clients could better utilise their wardrobe and closet space. If you have a carpentry background, you may even be able to provide the necessary drawers and shelf sets or partitions yourself: if not, subcontract.

WASHING/DRYING MACHINES
(See under Laundrette)

WATER-SAVING PRODUCTS

No doubt, this type of franchise or dealership will become more and more highly sought after as water becomes scarcer and thus more valuable!

There are many types of water saving products from shower roses and taps that *restrict* water flow (while retaining an adequate amount of pressure) to products that actually clean our cars, carpets and other possessions! Some of these products can be obtained wholesale; others may require you to buy a franchise or gain a licence to sell them.

Information on such products can usually be found in many magazines published for the home business and franchise markets.
(See also: Waterless Grass, below)

WATERLESS GRASS

Synthetic grass requires no watering, no mowing, no fertilizer, no chemicals and no seeding. Why would anyone have anything else? That's the question you'll need to get into your customers' heads if this is to be your business.

Synthetic grass can be used in many areas, both commercial and domestic, where growing and maintaining real grass could be a headache. It can be found around *pools*, *putting greens*, *apartments*, *hotels and motels*, *driving ranges*, children's *playgrounds* and hundreds of other places including *suburban lawns*.
Franchises and dealerships are available but you may decide to start up on your own. Find out all you can about the products available before making a choice.

Talk to the professionals in this industry as well as others on whom you will depend for business advice such as your accountant and solicitor before you go too far in your decision making.

WEAVING

When the conversation turns to weaving, listeners generally envision straw baskets or rugs.

Of course, hand weavers do make these items but there are many potential uses other than these. In fact, it's unlikely that traditional hand woven items would provide you with much of an income at all as imports have such a large part of the market! So what could you possibly weave that you might turn into a business?

If you have a flair for design, explore what happens when you try weaving your way to success with *one-off up-market garments*! For example, you might come up with a line of exquisite and unusual evening and bridal vests and jackets made from raw silk or uncarded wool interwoven with unusual threads.

Hand weaving can be extremely therapeutic and is so easy that a child could do it. Wonderful garments can be made quickly and easily on a plain, home made frame that can be knocked up for next to nothing. If you are using beautiful wools and threads, the result can be a stunning work of art!

If you're sufficiently creative *and* marketing-savvy, you might find you are lining your pockets with dollars in no time!
(See under Crafts)

WEB SITE PUBLISHING AND DESIGN

There are many different levels of web publishing and design. Excellent financial rewards are possible for those who are prepared to take the time and trouble to learn their way around the cyberworld.

Qualifications are not strictly necessary, providing you know what you are doing.

If you are a beginner with aspirations and want to get the feel of the web before deciding whether it might be your scene, set up a free web site through your provider just to get the hang of how it all works first.
Check their services and see if they can offer you a site as part of your subscription: many do. Prices vary for different levels of usage but you should get at least one web site free. This would provide you with some experience and let you assess whether it is the job for you.

At least, by using a basic site like this for a while, you'll come to understand links, navigation, how search engines work, how they can be made to prioritise subjects to the searcher, and so on.

Generally, anyone going into business in cyberspace is required to learn a whole new set of rules, from web page layout to web psychology, as well as becoming familiar with basic programming languages in many instances. But...the rewards will be there for a long time: millions of potential customers are there for the taking...and growing daily!

The fact that so much can be accomplished from any location in the world - from your kitchen table, your motel room, the airport lounge or the beach at Acapulco - makes web-based activities a boon for home businesses!

In the first instance, check your server. As well, browse through various home-based opportunities and business magazines and send for any free web publishing info offered to familiarise yourself with some of the opportunities around.

WEDDING GARMENT MANUFACTURE

This business has proved itself over donkey's years. Brides love to have the opportunity to design their own fairytale wedding dress and the exquisite dresses for their bridesmaids. But how can you make a paying business out of something so laborious?

Have you thought of getting other home sewers to do some piece work, finishing off, beading or embroidery for you in their own homes? This could speed up your work considerably.

Take a look at your workroom: is it as organised as it could possibly be... or is it a chaos of paper patterns, ironing boards, half-made clothes and mountains of tuille?

No matter where your workroom is, even in the garage, if it is neat and completely organised, fully carpeted so dresses can sweep the floor without soiling and so structured that you can work smoothly and comfortably and within reach of everything, it will save you precious time and therefore money.

A clean, organised workroom will also give customers confidence when they entrust to you their beautiful silks and satins.

WEDDING GARMENT HIRE

B*ridal wear* that has only been worn once is almost always in good condition! On the other hand, evening wear may have been worn many times and may require more attention. Most bridal garments are of good quality fabric and can generally withstand repeated dry cleaning without too much trouble.

If you have sewing/tailoring experience, you may be able to re-make, restyle and repair many pre-loved gowns.

To buy second hand garments, you will need some capital behind you but there are economical ways to go about filling your 'showroom' such as the many offerings in the classifieds, op shops and garage sales as well as the response you should get from those 'wanted' ads you place yourself.

New bridal wear and evening wear can also be made to supplement stock. However, keep an eye out for stock clearance sales and warehouse sales and samples. Many very basic *off-the-hook* garments can often be restyled, beaded or decorated to look a million dollars so, like in any other business, it pays to get creative!

You will need to check on zoning if you wish to hire out garments from your home. You may be able to get around any red tape by having only a display area at home and delivering garments by courier. You would have to check out the regulations governing your area in relation to what you want to do.

If you are working as a *couple*, you may prefer to set up a small commercial showroom nearby. That way, just the cleaning, repairs and sewing could be done at home.

WEDDING PLANNER

Who has time to plan a wedding these days? *YOU* do! Welcome to the big money! Weddings are getting grander and more complex every day...while *time* for planning them is growing scarcer!

Your service could look after just the reception - or it could encompass the couple's every need: the location, the venue, the invitations, the wedding gown, bridal party outfits (maybe you could have an arrangement with a bridal shop or wedding hire establishment!), church, bells, cars, catering, beauty consultants, hairdressers, flowers, musicians and photographer! You might even make travel and accommodation arrangements for the honeymoon!

This can be a *huge* business for the 'with it' entrepreneur who is organised to the nth degree! You can't afford to put one foot wrong and you need to be prepared to cope with anything and everything, as this event is to be (hopefully!) *the* big day of a lifetime for your clients. Goof it up and you'll soon be out of business!

Ideally, weddings should run as smoothly and painlessly as a well-oiled machine. If you can make this happen, you should receive more work - (and megabucks!) - than you can imagine.
(See also Events Organiser, Party Planner)

WEDDING PHOTOGRAPHER

If you are a skilled and creative photographer, don't fret about the massive competition. Fret instead about any lack of marketing knowledge and make that your first priority to overcome!

Wedding photographers need to be more than just photographers. They need to be mindful of the value of PR and the necessity of maintaining a strong network. The winners in this game are punctual, courteous, well organised and ready to cope with anything! They certainly cannot afford to forget one item - like film! Nor should they turn up to a wedding with one camera - it might malfunction! Or overlook photographing anybody - like the mothers-in-law!

It pays to list the photographic requirements of couples and their families well before the big event and physically tick off your list as you complete each task. A wedding is a once-only event and you, the photographer, have just one chance to record the occasion for the participants and for future generations as well.

The photographer who goes that little bit further in his or her studies, who can offer outstanding or unusual results and knows how to go about getting the business is the one who will be making the biggest money. There's little room here for amateurs. *(See also Photography)*

WHEELIE BIN CLEANING

No, it's not the nicest job in the world but somebody has to do it! And get paid for it! And help keep homes and businesses relatively germ-free and sweet-smelling!

Cleaning could be done in situ or the wheelie bins could be taken by you to a central location, cleaned then returned.

WELDING
(See under Metalwork)

WINDOW CLEANING

Virtually anybody can start a business such as this with the most basic of tools if necessary - a bucket, a ladder, a squeegee and some water! However, as in any business, you do need certain essentials such as insurance. After all, what if a passer-by trips over your bucket on the footpath?

If you find your business is doing well and you start feeling adventurous, you might even decide to tie the window cleaning service in with other cleaning services such as blind and shutter cleaning, wall and ceiling cleaning, even domestic or commercial cleaning. However, it's best to start off one step at a time, getting the window cleaning business on a solid footing first.

Build up your bank of clients through reliability, thoroughness and good service.

Perhaps you could start off your advertising campaign with simple flyers and a few small classified ads in the local papers to attract the attention of businesses and homes in your area.

While working on any job, you will find it should help attract the attention of potential customers if you place a sandwich board sign outside…preferably where nobody will trip over it!

Well run cleaning operations generally make excellent money these days if they do a thorough job and know how to market their business. Everybody has windows - and everybody wants to see through them!

WINDOW DRESSER

This could be *called* a home-*based* business…yet most of your work time is likely to be away from home creating imaginative display windows for stores.

Good marketing, design and networking skills will be vital to your success. Unless you are already well connected through having had previous experience in this field, you may find that it is not so easy to get assignments…although reception can often be kinder in smaller towns.

If you are a novice, you might be willing to offer stores a free initial display. Then, if they are happy with the result, they may consider contracting you to do all their work. Admittedly, working for free when you are starting off can mean long, hard hours of work but sometimes a little sweat equity can go a long way to growing a business and keeping it alive.

Remember, too, that once you have one client, it often makes it that much easier to gain other clients in the same neighbourhood.

WINDOW REPAIR

There are thousands of older homes with windows that are warped, rotted, swollen or just will not budge for some reason. If you have the skills to unjam or refit them, your clients will love you...and pay you as well! Some of your clients may want their old windows replaced entirely.

This would be a good 'niche' business for a retired builder or clever handyman.

WINDSHIELD REPAIR
(See Automotive)

WINDSURFING INSTRUCTOR
(See Coaching)

WOODWORKING
(See Carpenter, Furniture Making, Babies & Children's Furniture)

WOMEN'S CLOTHING

If you sew well, you may decide to make clothes for 'niche' markets such as *'extra large'* sizes, *'maternity'* or *'fancy dress'*. You may even arrange to have other home workers like yourself do *piece work* for you or just the finishing off. Your very productive sewing machine could be going flat out from sunrise to sunset if you strike the right market!

(For more comprehensive suggestions, see under Sewing, Leather Clothing, Weaving, Wedding Garment Hire and Screen Printing)

WORD PROCESSING

To gain attention, you might place catchy advertisements in the classifieds and distribute lots of elegantly produced brochures to those offices and businesses most likely to need the use of a word processing service. But there could be quite a few potential clients that you might overlook.

- *IDEA*: For example, in *TAFEs, Unis* and *colleges* there are students who are hopeless typists. Yet they need to type up papers and theses for assessment, - sometimes at breakneck speed! Many would far prefer to be putting their time into more interesting pursuits! Perhaps you can help them to this end...and help yourself as well: ask for permission to place your literature on every noticeboard and building on campus and you may be surprised by the amount of work that comes your way!

Consider *all local businesses* and *local newsletters (including the local school newsletters)*, contact *recreation* and *sporting clubs*, *special interest groups*, *churches* and other groups in your area, offering to produce their newsletters for them and do any other word processing tasks they may require.

Other suggestions:
- You might start a home W.P. service on a *website,* receiving and returning your clients' material electronically. Alternatively, the completed work might be sent back to the client by courier.

- Many writers do not have – or do not like *using* - word processors: of those who do, many don't know how to produce professional looking *manuscripts or scripts* for submission to publishers and T.V. stations.

  It would not be too difficult to arm yourself with knowledge of the various formats and layouts required by major editors, publishers and producers, then advertise your W.P. service in all the *writers' newsletters and magazines*.
(See also under Typing & Desktop Publishing)

WORM FARM

Breeding lowly worms can be a highly profitable business - and can be *very* friendly to the environment. Furthermore, worm farming is so simple that you'll be able to run another home business concurrently!

If worm farming is new to you and you'd like to give it a trial, you can simply buy a worm farm for domestic use from one of the larger hardware stores and try it out.

Worms don't take much looking after and are sought largely by gardeners to aerate lawns, gardens and compost bins. Fishermen, too, use them for bait.

Advertise your little *'Friends of the Earth'* in the local classifieds as well as to nurseries, home hardware stores, pet shops, local bait and tackle shops, waste management outlets and professional landscapers...and don't forget to put a catchy sign on your front fence, especially if you live near a fishing spot like a lake or river. If so, your business could start up just as soon as you – and the worms - are ready.

You might also go into selling *worm farming kits* by mail order. Or perhaps you will make an *information video* on worm farming for those do-it-yourselfers who are starting their farm from scratch.
(See also Silk Worms)

WRITER

Writing is one of the greatest pleasures a human being can have: however, *finding a publisher* is one of the greatest pains! But don't let this put you off! There are certain 'byways' to success if you are willing to look for them.

- *Feature Writing – Non-fiction*
  For beginners intent on publication, *non-fiction* is generally the easiest genre in the writing arena to break into. All you need to do is find an 'expert' in some field, tape and interview him or her answering loads of your questions, then write a transcript of the tape. Do a bit of creative editing, then peddle the result to a few magazines or newspapers who might be interested in the subject.

  If they're impressed, then...voila! You could become a published writer overnight!

  Generally, publishers are not interested in novice writers or their opinions. So, if you are just starting off, hang around the 'experts' and the V.I.P.'s with your little pad and pencil. Their words and opinions, providing they are well handled and well crafted, could be your path to fame.

- *Fiction writers* are likely to find publication a little harder than non-fiction writers.

  If you join a writers' club, you will be informed in their newsletters of many up-coming competition dates and other opportunities. Take advantage of these competitions, entering your short stories to see how they go.

  If you prefer to write novels, send off a synopsis of your manuscript plus a couple of sample chapters to a likely publisher. Include a well-crafted covering letter. Whatever you do, *don't* send the *whole* manuscript

Unsolicited work is usually thrown onto a 'slush pile' of hundreds of other unsolicited manuscripts to gather dust over months! If you receive a rejection slip from the publisher, don't waste your energy on tears! Simply send your work to the next publisher… and the next…and the next until...

- *Children's writers* are currently having a hey day. Be prolific with your writing but send in only *quality* work.

  Look in writers' newsletters for the names of those publishers who are on the look out for manuscripts for children, taking note of the age groups that various publishers wish to cater for.

  One good entry point for children's writing might be school magazines. Write to the appropriate publisher and ask for a schedule of subjects that their magazines will be covering over the coming months, and the age groups they are catering for, and try your hand.

  The worst that can happen is that the editors will say 'no, thank you!'; the best that can happen is that they say '*yes, please*'!

- *Romance writers* can be paid handsomely for their writing. But don't get your hopes up…because many of these publishers specialise in certain writing '*formulae*' which must be adhered to: e.g. boy meets girl, they fall in love, something goes wrong, enter the plotting antagonist - the seemingly insurmountable obstacle! Then, miraculously, the problem is solved and the hero asks for the heroine's hand in marriage. The End! Do you want to write to a rigid formula like that?

  Send for a set of Writers' Guidelines from the various *Romance* publishers and *follow it closely* in writing your novel.

  Or will you be game enough to risk writing an *unusual, individually-styled* novel irrespective of tested formulae…then try publishing it yourself? You might even try publishing it electronically!

  Historical romance sets the love story in a particular historical period and is extremely popular with a following of readers from teens to centenarians - but it must be done well if it is to be done at all.
- *Historical writing* can be either *fiction* or *non-fiction*. It could be sritten as Romance, a scholrly treatise, a play, a specialised guide book and so forth. In the *fiction* category, historical *romance* or *adventure* stories are popular

with a variety of ages. In *non-fiction*, the new writer might be wise to start off with short features for magazines and newspapers, moving on to longer works when your name as a writer and historian becomes known.

For the accredited historian, if you find that your writing ability does not match your academic knowledge, you can always hire a professional writer to write your book or feature article as either a *ghost writer* or even as a *co-author.*

- *Script writers* are one group of writers of whom there are *never* enough. Are you one of those lucky, gifted geniuses for whom the world is waiting. How will you test your ability?

One way is to write an episode or two of your favourite TV sitcom, preferably local. Ask the relevant channel to send you a **set of writers' guidelines** for the particular programme before you attempt this...then submit it. If the script is good, you could become famous very quickly!

If you do not want to write sitcoms and have your own creative ideas, you could try sending your scripts to the many script writing competitions and readings that are run by various theatre and cultural groups. You'll find many of these listed from time to time in your writers' club newsletter. The readings are usually performed by professional actors and outstanding work can often find its way to the right people!

Alternatively, send a synopsis of your play, together with a covering letter, to those producers whom you know work in your chosen field.

- *Travel Writing*
(For more ideas on writing possibilities, look under Information Products)

This can be one great perk - *if* you've got what it takes. Imagine it! Free travel (occasionally!), free accommodation (occasionally!), free meals (a little more likely!) at some of the best hotels, restaurants and resorts...providing you know your way around the industry. And publication to boot!

You don't need any special qualifications to become a travel writer but, to ensure you receive at least some of the above kick backs and freebies... or, at least, *publication*...you'll need to exhibit loads of talent, have had some experience *marketing* your writing...and display a hide as thick as a rhinoceros', especially when it comes to negotiating the free travel and accommodation!

- *Comedy* writers and scriptwriters are almost an endangered species! If you are a writer who can make people laugh at your words, the world will repay you handsomely. Everyone's desperate to laugh but human beings seem to be fast losing their sense of humour simply because they're not exercising it enough.

  Restore the gift of humour! Make us all laugh till our sides split! And *you'll* be laughing all the way to the bank!

Y

YOGA SCHOOL

While no qualifications are strictly necessary to start up a school of this nature, you will certainly need to be advanced in the practice of at least one form of yoga to make your school succeed.

Hatha Yoga is the form of yoga that is most generally taught in Western society. Although this style is aimed at bodily flexibility and glandular health, it is generally perceived as endowing its adherents with mental and spiritual benefits as well.

A yoga school can usually work quite well at home. Many classes around the country are held in a teacher's sitting room or family room, but a separate studio is always preferable. Wherever you hold your classes, the atmosphere should be one of tranquillity, peace and harmony. Flowers and incense can also add to the restful atmosphere.

Remember that even a business as gentle as yoga requires *insurance* for you and your students. It is also wise to register your business.

Business name and ABN registration

http://www.asic.gov.au/for-business/registering-a-business-name/
Note that business names in all states are now registered through the national name registration service known as The Australian Securities and Investments Commission (ASIC).

HOME-BASED BUSINESS IDEAS

SELF-QUESTIONNAIRE

©2020

Please fill in the answers to
this questionnaire and keep
it for your current or future use.
You will be surprised how much you will learn about
yourself and your readiness to go into
your own business!

HOW DO I CHOOSE THE RIGHT BUSINESS FOR *ME*?

It is important to plan before you start out on any journey, and going into your own business is, indeed, a journey! Wisely planned, it will take you from where you are right now to where you want to go.

Just like planning any other trip, you will need to be aware of your goal, the direction you must go to reach it, your preferred method of travel, all the information you will need and what provisions you will require.

Rarely is the going easy in the early stages of starting up a business, particularly in the first year or two. Nor will you necessarily escape a tyrannical boss because, where it's YOUR money and YOUR time at stake, you may find yourself working under the hardest boss of all: YOURSELF!

However, there are huge benefits in running your own business, particularly a home based business. The mature-aged, particularly, can find it a blessing to have some measure of control over their lives at last...that is, if they are neither procrastinators nor workaholics! For an organised, clear-thinking individual with an entrepreneurial creative drive, it can be a wise and exhilarating choice. The knowledge that you are building something solid of your very own for the future with your own two hands is a great feeling.

As the accompanying manual points out, many home-based businesses can be started up with minimum capital outlay, can have almost no overheads, give you flexibility and autonomy...and could offer you more security and job stability for the future than traditional employment! After all, employees can be made redundant at the drop of a hat.

Whether you have been just playing around with the thought of self-employment, or you have firmly made up your mind to take the plunge, it would be well worth your responding to this little self-questionnaire before taking another step. It will help you discover what what your inner motives are for seeking to go out on your own, whether you are ready to do so, what you are hoping to achieve by self-employment...and what you are hoping to avoid!

Please *write* down the answers to the questions. They will help provide you with an invaluable, overall indicator of the likelihood of your success and guide you in assessing your current abilities, strengths, weakness and resources. They will also help you, recognise the most suitable fields of endeavour for YOU...and the goals you should be capable of attaining.

Good luck!

SELF-QUESTIONNAIRE ©2020

1) I am considering self-employment because:

_____
_____
_____
_____
_____
_____
_____

2) Home-based employment particularly interests me because:

_____
_____
_____
_____
_____
_____
_____

3) There were certain things I didn't like about being employed by others such as: (Come on: out with it!)

_____
_____
_____
_____
_____
_____
_____

4) On the other hand, I'm going to miss a few things about it. For example:

_____
_____
_____
_____
_____
_____
_____

5) Things I didn't like about some of the jobs I've had in the past were:

_____

_____

_____

_____

_____

_____

6) In retrospect, I probably could have handled the following work situations a little better:

_____

_____

_____

_____

_____

_____

_____

7) Being in the workplace has taught me that:

_____

_____

_____

_____

_____

_____

8) And I don't want to have to encounter the following type of situation again:

_____

_____

_____

_____

_____

_____

9) The type of businesses I might like to investigate are:

_____

_____

_____

_____

_____

_____

10) They attract me because:

_____

_____

_____

_____

_____

_____

11) The only thing holding me back in tackling any of these would be:

_____

_____

_____

_____

_____

_____

12) I could probably overcome these problems by:

_____

_____

_____

_____

_____

_____

13) Businesses I have considered so far are:

_____

_____

_____

_____

_____

_____

14) These are the fears I have about going into business for myself:

_____

_____

_____

_____

_____

_____

_____

15) There's a good chance I could overcome these negatives by the following:

_____

_____

_____

_____

_____

16) Do I have the necessary skills and experience I would need for any of the businesses I've listed?

_____

_____

_____

_____

_____

_____

_____

17) My educational level is:

_____

_____

_____

_____

_____

18) However, I've also done short courses/ study in the following: (list everything from way back as far as you can remember right up to the present)

_____

_____

_____

_____

_____

_____

_____

19 My favourite hobbies have been:

_____

_____

_____

_____

_____

_____

20) I've also had a fair bit of experience in the following: (list even those you've
engaged in of necessity: e.g. serving on committees, selling through the internet,
typing, driving, cooking, looking after Gran, garage sales, babysitting, training dogs,
fixing cars, home repairs, ironing. If you ever did a tertiary course, what were the
electives? Do you speak another language? Are you computer-literate?):

_____

_____

_____

_____

_____

_____

21) Of the above endeavours, those I enjoyed most were:

_____

_____

_____

_____

_____

_____

22) Those I didn't like were:

_____

_____

_____

_____

_____

_____

23) Why?

_____

_____

_____

_____

_____

_____

24) If it were necessary to further my education at this stage to improve my chances
in business, would I do so?

_____

_____

_____

_____

_____

_____

25) Would I be prepared to go to evening college, do a short course, part-time TAFE or Uni course, an accredited CAE course or take on private tuition? Would I have the resources of time, interest and money?

_____
_____
_____
_____
_____
_____

26) Self confession (Please tick)

1. I'm a slow learner	I'm a fast learner
2. I make things happen	I tend to procrastinate
3. I like to get up early	I like to sleep in late
4. I like face-to-face contact	I hate face-to-face contact
5. Cold calling is OK	I'd rather die than go cold calling!
6. I like using the phone	I hate using the phone
7. I'm computer literate	I'm computer illiterate
8. I can type	I can't type
9. I'm quite creative	Creativity is not my forte
10. I'm darned determined	I'm a bit laid back sometimes
11. I prefer working indoors	I love working outdoors
12. I enjoy working solo	I enjoy working in a group
13. I thrive on pressure	I just can't stand being pressured

_____
_____
_____
_____
_____
_____
_____

27) My medical considerations are:

_____
_____
_____
_____
_____
_____
_____
_____

28) Ideally, what salary do I want to earn per year?
(Put down a preferred salary range.)

_____
_____
_____
_____
_____
_____

29) Would this cover my preferred lifestyle?

_____
_____
_____
_____
_____
_____

(Think of what you propose to do with those earnings. Sure, you'll pay rates,
insurance, the children's education etc. But try to fathom your main lifestyle goals
and dreams. Will you buy property, invest in shares, spend it all till you drop, save it
for the overseas trips or for the kids?)

_____
_____
_____
_____
_____
_____

30) Do I hope to travel in the future?

_____
_____
_____
_____
_____
_____

31) If so, how would I travel? By luxury cruise ship? Economy air? My own private
yacht? Car and caravan? RV?

_____
_____
_____
_____
_____
_____

32) How often would I like to travel? Seasonally? Once a year? Once or twice in a lifetime?

_____
_____
_____
_____
_____
_____

33) What type of car am I aiming for? A Holden? A Porche? RV? A fleet of antique Fords? What is my dream?

_____
_____
_____
_____
_____
_____

34) The way I like to entertain is:
(on a grand scale...or am I the intimate Sunday-barbie type?)

_____
_____
_____
_____
_____
_____

35) I still have the following commitments to my children:

_____
_____
_____
_____
_____

36) On looking over all my answers to the above questions, the most obvious type of businesses that suggest themselves at this stage are:

_____
_____
_____
_____
_____
_____

By considering your financial commitments - both short term and long term when formulating your goals - you will come to a more realistic appreciation of the level of remuneration your new business needs to provide. It is pointless making yourself ill slaving relentlessly, year after year, in an overly demanding and high-risk business if you are actually satisfied with the simple life, have no extravagant plans and no children to support.

On the other hand, if you want a marble-floorerd mansion, a pool and Ferraris for all the family, your business income and risk-taking will need to match those requirements.

The TYPE of business you'd like to be in - food, consulting, clothing manufacturer, newsagency, cruise boat operator etc.- will no doubt offer many possible LEVELS of entry and of operation. By considering your personal and family goals when making your business choices, you will be more likely to achieve balance in life.

For example, let's assume you want a food business. What level of food business would suit you, your family - and your finances? A part-time hot dog van at the beach? A coffee or sandwich shop? A high-class French restaurant? There are scores of possibilities from which to choose but, if you love the simple life, have no aspirations to live like the Great Gatsby and you like going to bed and getting up early, then maybe a sandwich bar or small local cafe would be best for you.

On the other hand, if you're a prospective jetsetter with a massive retrenchment package or considerable savings who longs to live and retire in luxury, a thriving deli or major restaurant may be what you aspire to, regardless of the massive effort - and risk - involved.

Remember, money is worth nothing until you use it. A vault full of dollars and a jar full of cents are of equal value...if you can't do anything with them because worry and overwork have killed you!.

Admittedly money has enormous potential - and that is always a comforting thought, especially in old age. But if you've had to trade your health and happiness for it, what is its REAL value?

So many small business owners realise this too late. Don't let it happen to you!

Work out your lifestyle GOALS first – then find a business to suit them.

Index

www.ingramcontent.com/pod-product-compliance
Lightning Source LLC
Chambersburg PA
CBHW080952050426

42334CB00057B/2600